Villages on Stage

Folklore and Nationalism in the Republic of Moldova

How does folkloric performance contribute to the formation of national identity in a postsocialist state? In the last years of Soviet rule, a folkloric movement developed in the Republic of Moldova. The movement was particularly visible in the organized system of amateur artistic activities, where it spurred the establishment of scores of new folkloric ensembles, outlined rigorous criteria for the performance of "authentic" visions of traditional life, introduced two new categories of folkloric performance, and created new festivals to steadily improve the quality of folkloric performance.

In this book, the author explores the goals, practices, and ideologies of Moldova's new folkloric ensembles in terms of ethnic belonging and exclusion. Although Moldova's political scene is characterized by strong debates about ethnic rights, and the independent state has consistently promoted an image of itself as multiethnic, the author finds that the folklorists and ethnographers involved in new forms of performance are critical of any attempts to depict a "multiethnic culture". Instead, the new forms of performance create the image of Moldova as a "nation of villages", in which members of all ethnic groups should be able to participate equally. Of course, this ideology is also inconsistent, and constructs new hierarchies of cultural belonging through a discourse on authenticity and cultural borrowing.

For the author, the disjunctures between what Moldova's folklorists and ethnographers aspire to create, and what they do create, illustrates both the local dilemmas of postsocialist nation-building, and the shared challenge for ethnographers everywhere to participate authoritatively in public debates about cultural diversity.

Halle Studies in the Anthropology of Eurasia

General Editors:

Chris Hann, Thomas Hauschild, Richard Rottenburg, Burkhard Schnepel

Volume 26

LIT

Jennifer R. Cash

Villages on Stage

Folklore and Nationalism in the Republic of Moldova

LIT

Cover Photo: Folk ensemble from Cahul performing at Independence Day celebrations in Chişinău (2001) (Photo: Jennifer R. Cash).

This work is a revised version of my Ph.D. dissertation, submitted in 2004 to the Department of Anthropology, Indiana University.

Gedruckt auf alterungsbeständigem Werkdruckpapier entsprechend
ANSI Z3948 DIN ISO 9706

Bibliographic information published by the Deutsche Nationalbibliothek
The Deutsche Nationalbibliothek lists this publication in the Deutsche Nationalbibliografie; detailed bibliographic data are available in the Internet at http://dnb.d-nb.de.

ISBN 978-3-643-90218-4

A catalogue record for this book is available from the British Library

Zweigniederlassung Zürich 2011
Klosbachstr. 107
CH-8032 Zürich
Tel. +41 (0) 44-251 75 05
Fax +41 (0) 44-251 75 06
e-Mail: zuerich@lit-verlag.ch
http://www.lit-verlag.ch

LIT VERLAG Dr. W. Hopf
Berlin 2011
Fresnostr. 2
D-48159 Münster
Tel. +49 (0) 2 51-620 320
Fax +49 (0) 2 51-23 19 72
e-Mail: lit@lit-verlag.de
http://www.lit-verlag.de

Distribution:
In Germany: LIT Verlag Fresnostr. 2, D-48159 Münster
Tel. +49 (0) 2 51-620 32 22, Fax +49 (0) 2 51-922 60 99, e-mail: vertrieb@lit-verlag.de

In Austria: Medienlogistik Pichler-ÖBZ, e-mail: mlo@medien-logistik.at

In Switzerland: B + M Buch- und Medienvertrieb, e-mail: order@buch-medien.ch

In the UK: Global Book Marketing, e-mail: mo@centralbooks.com

Contents

	List of Illustrations	vii
	Acknowledgements	ix
	Note on Transliteration	xiii
1	**Introduction: Folklore and National Identity**	**1**
	First Encounters and (Mis)interpretations	3
	Authenticity and the Double Boundaries of Identity	5
	Reencountering Ethnic Diversity	9
	A Critical Ethnography of Folklore	12
	Building the Nation Anew	17
2	**Moldova's National Questions**	**23**
	A Brief History of Moldova: Changing States, Changing Identities	26
	Soviet Nationalities Policies and National Movements	34
	Nation-Building in the New State	37
	Change and Continuity in Ethnic Identity	42
	Ethnic, Civic, and Salient Identities	47
3	**Folkloric Ensembles and the State**	**51**
	Who is a Nationalist?	51
	Identity Personnel in Socialist States	52
	Cultural Policy in Soviet Moldova	54
	Amateur Activity or Folklore? The Postsocialist Organization of Culture	59
	Unofficial Genres: *Folcloric* and *Etno-Folcloric* Ensembles	64
4	**The Folkloric Movement**	**71**
	Folkloric Performance before the Folkloric Movement	72
	The Emergence of the Folkloric Movement	77
	Folkloric Festivals	79
	Judging Authenticity: Festivalul Folcloric 2001	82
	Representations of National Culture	88
	Recognizing Authenticity and Value	89

	National Aesthetics and Traditional Morality	95
	Moral Performance Off the Festival Stage	97
5	**From Village to Stage: Authenticity and Authority**	**105**
	An Ideal Expedition	110
	Repertoire Creation	115
	Methods and Ideology	121
	Village Ethnography and National Identity	125
	Career Choices and Village Origins	127
	Urbanization during the Soviet Period	132
	Social Memory and Identity	133
6	**Inclusion and Exclusion in a Nation of Villages**	**137**
	The Metaphor of the *Horă*	139
	Insider and Outsider Views of Villages	141
	Critique of Ethnicity or Ethnic Exclusion?	143
	Urban or Mixed? The Jewish Example	145
	Lost or Borrowed? The Gagauz Example	149
	Cultural Borrowing and Political Obligations	158
7	**Conclusion: Authenticity, Ethnographic Authority, and Nation-Building**	**163**
	Authenticity and Ethnicity in Moldova's Folkloric Movement	164
	Audience Interest and the State	166
	Multiculturalism, Multiethnicity, and National Culture	169
	Authenticity and Authority	172
	The Ethnography of Ethnographers as Critical Ethnography	174
	Social Responsibilities of Ethnographers, There and Here	181
	Appendix 1: Figure 3.1	187
	Appendix 2: Figure 3.2	188
	Bibliography	189
	Index	205

List of Illustrations

Figures

3.1 Organization of folkloric ensembles and festivals 187
3.2 Official performance categories and genres 188

Maps

1 Historical Moldova and Bessarabia 28
2 Historical Transnistria 30
3 Special administrative regions 38
4 Distribution of ethnic groups 44
5 Villages visited with local ethnographers in summer 2001 109

Plates

1 Rituals of midwifery 83
2 Dressing the bride 84
3 An example of 'kitsch' in costuming 91
4 An example of 'authentic' costuming 93
5 Festival participants learning the traditions of Flower Sunday 94
6 Performance or politics? – Moştenitorii at Gagauz autonomy celebrations 94
7 Fieldwork and repertoire creation 115
8 A longterm informant 116
9 Culture houses as culture brokers 117
10 Dance in the field 118
11 Participant-observation in children's games 119
12 Cazaclia's singing ensemble welcomes visiting ethnographers 120
13 Ethnographers receive an unexpected welcome in Cişmichioi 120
14 Team-based fieldwork between artists and ethnographers 123
15 Documenting carpet designs in Ţîra 124
16 Preparing to dance a *horă* on Independence Day 138
17 A Gagauz version of *Lazarelul* 150
18 Kadînja, kadînească, or Dobrogean dance? 156

(all photographs were taken by the author [2001] unless noted otherwise)

Acknowledgements

This work is based on a dissertation I submitted to the Department of Anthropology at Indiana University, Bloomington, in 2004, and I continue to be grateful to the individuals and institutions I thanked at that time. These are first and foremost the faculty members who guided me through preliminary coursework, field research, and writing up: my advisor, Anya Peterson Royce; committee members, Joelle Bahloul, Maria Bucur, and David Ransel; and Romanian professor, Christina Zarifopol Illias. My initial fieldwork was possible only through the ongoing hospitality, generosity, and patience of Mariana Alecsandri and her family, especially her mother and great-aunt, who provided me with housing, and her daughter Cristina Godovanciuc, who studied to be a professional folk dancer but has pursued a career in public management instead and has a keen sense for changing trends in the way young, urban Moldovans express their relationship to tradition. A number of persons helped me locate valuable initial contacts in Moldova: Beau David Case, William Crowther, Charles King, Eve Nilenders, and Ivan Shidlovsky.

My research into folkloric ensembles was sparked by an invitation from Tatiana Munteanu to participate in the ten-day summer camp she directed in 1999 and by the specialists I met there. The bulk of the research, however, was shaped in critical ways during 2001 by Ion Bălteanu, Eugen Bîzgu, Valeriu Chiper, Iurii Datii and his assistant Diana, Petru Dinjos, Iulian Filip, Afanasi Gargalik, Iulia Gîrlea, Nicolae Gribincea, Tatiana Levandovschi, Olga Luchianeț, Tamara Macovei, Eugen Martin, Vlad Melnic, Elena Munteanu, Gheorghe Obreja, Valentina Oglindă, the Osoianu sisters, Grigore Oxinte, Ana Pagur, Iulia Paladi, Pavel Popa, Igor Solonkov, Elena Spinei, Andrei Tamazlâcaru, Ianoş Țurcanu, and Valeriu Volcov. Many friendships, especially those with Doina Boboc, Ana Bodrug and her family, the Arhip, Macovei, and Movileanu families, Natasha Rusakevich, Ghenadie Şonțu and Olga, Dragoş Țarălungă, and Vlad Us, helped blur the distinction between life and research in important ways. Sabine Cunis, Beth Larson, Kate Sorrels, and their social networks in Moldova also enriched my fieldwork.

Mihai Ursu, director of the National Museum of Ethnography and Natural History in Chişinău, graciously provided me with the necessary institutional affiliation for undertaking this research, in 2001 and subsequently. Varvara Buzilă took up the burden of being my local field advisor as well as a key informant. I especially appreciate the late V. Zelenciuc's welcome, as I made bold to meet members of the ethnography section he headed at the Academy of Sciences. Alexei Rău and his staff at the National Library assured me access to whatever print and human resources they could muster, and I was fortunate to find no shortage of open doors or helping hands at the Academy of Sciences, museums, ministries, and other government and cultural institutions.

My field research on folkloric ensembles effectively came to a close when I left Moldova in 2001, but I have since returned to undertake research on other topics, including cultural policy, hospitality, saints' day festivals, and changing relations between economy and ritual, during the summers of 2005, 2006, and 2008 and for another nine months in 2009–2010. On these return trips, I found increasing support and encouragement from local colleagues: Virgiliu Bîrlădeanu, Ludmila Cojocari, Mariana Harjevschi, Gabriela Popa, Ghenadie Popescu, and Corina Rezneac. My stay in 2009–2010 was spent primarily in the south-eastern village of Răscăieți, where my host family, Ion and Elena Tcacenco, provided a better understanding of the difficulties faced by village-based culture workers during two decades of 'transition' and the place of concerns about the authenticity of folklore within this framework. The story of their relationship to folklore and folklorists-ethnographers deserves to be told as a complement to the present work, and I hope the occasion to do so arrives soon. In the meantime, I thank the Tcacencos and my other contacts in Răscăieți for their generosity and hospitality.

Various portions of the original dissertation were read and critiqued by Kristin Alten, Sebastian Braun, Christina Burke, Kate Costello, Brian Donahoe, Tim Howington, Candice Lowe, Alex Montgomery, Ann Reed, Ronald Royce, and Daniel Saulean. Students in two rounds of a course on folklore and politics at the University of Pittsburgh in 2006 and 2007 helped broaden the comparative scope of the work. Elizabeth Anderson, Marjorie Balzer, Rebecca Chamberlain-Creangă, Hülya Demirdirek, Deema Kaneff, Robert Hayden, Monica Heintz, Yi-tze Lee, Irina Livezeanu, Ruth Mandel, Diana N'Dyae, Charles Stewart, Michael Stewart, and Andrew Strathern have all asked penetrating questions which I have tried to address through revisions. Julie Fairbanks deserves special thanks for reading the penultimate revision, and Agnieszka Pasieka helped me make heads and tails out of my plan for reorganizing sections.

During fieldwork, my contacts in Moldova always expressed concern for my family, and indeed neither research nor writing would have been possible without the ongoing support of my parents, Randall and Suzanne Cash, my sister, Jessica, and my husband, Michael. Geoffrey's arrival made the final push of revisions both possible and necessary. Those who helped keep him distracted also helped me enormously – the workers at SKV Kita, Fanara Almazbekova, and Christel Kautz.

Thanks finally, and especially, to Chris Hann for keeping my feet to the fire after we agreed that it was time to publish. Speedy revisions were possible only because of the excellent conditions for writing and research at the Max Planck Institute for Social Anthropology in Halle. Jutta Turner provided the five maps; Dittmar Schorkowitz checked the accuracy of Map 2. Berit Westwood kept track of all the formatting and other tasks to be completed; and Christian Maslo and Anne Pinnow digitized the illustrations and compiled the index. Jane Kepp admirably completed the task of uncovering the subtle flaws in my logic and writing, along with general copyediting.

Financial and logistical support came from the International Research and Exchanges Board (IREX) in the form of an Independent Advanced Research Opportunities (IARO) Fellowship for nine months of field research in 2001. Two summers of pre-dissertation field research were supported by funding sources at Indiana University: the Mellon Endowment Pre-Dissertation Fellowship from the Russian and East European Institute (1999); the Office of International Programs Pre-Dissertation Fellowship (2000); and Skomp Summer Fieldwork Support through the Department of Anthropology (1999, 2000). In 2001, I also benefited from participating in a summer ethnographic expedition and arts camp organized by and for students from the State University of the Arts in Moldova and funded by the Soros Foundation. Field trips back to Moldova after 2001 were generously supported by the National Endowment for the Humanities (NEH) and the American Councils for International Education (ACTR/ ACCELS), the National Council for Eurasian and East European Research (NCEEER), and the Max Planck Institute for Social Anthropology in Halle. The Department of Anthropology at University College London extended the much valued privilege of library access and membership in an intellectual community through the status of honorary research fellow during 2007–2009.

None of the persons or institutions I have named is responsible for the opinions put forth and conclusions drawn in the following chapters. These are mine alone.

Note on Transliteration

As discussed at length in chapter 2, Moldova's "state language", spoken by the ethnic majority, has long been referred to as the Moldovan language. Contemporary linguistic research, however, concludes that Moldovan and Romanian constitute a single language. I have therefore used standard Romanian spellings throughout. The exception is in the spelling of proper names for people and places. During the Soviet period, Moldovan was written in Cyrillic, and since 1989 the transliteration of proper names from the Cyrillic into the Roman alphabet has produced discrepancies between how proper names are spelled in Moldova and Romania. In some cases, the spelling of my informants' names has also changed over the years, especially as people encounter older spellings in the Romanian identity documents of their parents and grandparents. I have strived, in this publication, to use the most current forms of names in circulation. Place names, also subject to inconsistency, have been spelled according to the current variant found on official maps. Standard English spellings have been used for countries, major cities, and geographic features; where variants in English exist, I have preferred the variant based on Romanian to Russian for all locations in current-day Moldova or Romania (e.g. Chişinău not Kishinev and Moldova not Moldavia). Similarly, in the few cases where a Russian term has an exact Romanian equivalent, I have used the Romanian spelling (e.g. *raion*). All Romanian-language bibliographic entries originally published in Cyrillic have likewise been transliterated with standard Romanian spellings. Particularly problematic spellings are noted throughout the text.

For Michael,
who once asked what nationalism is

Chapter 1
Introduction: Folklore and National Identity

Field notes, 24 July 1999

Shortly after breakfast, the groom arrived at the bride's house, accompanied by family members and close friends. His mother came, but most of the people accompanying him were male. The man and woman who would sponsor the young couple's marriage, the *naşi* (marital godparents), also came to the bride's house. The groom's party entered the house and asked the bride's parents for her. They were met with questions from the bride's parents: how, exactly, was this man going to take care of their daughter? Satisfied with the young man's answers, the bride's mother approached the groom's mother, producing a long strip of white linen which she tied diagonally across the other woman's chest from shoulder to waist. The bride's family then produced a small dish of flour, in which the young couple's rings had been hidden. The bride and groom fished for their rings and, having found them, placed them on each other's fingers.

As the couple pulled their rings out of the flour, shouts erupted from the crowd of onlookers: they wanted the couple to kiss. A robust, dark-haired man in his mid-thirties stepped forward angrily and addressed the participants, almost all of whom had been born and raised in Moldova's capital city, Chişinău. 'It is not our tradition to kiss in public', he said. The crowd was silenced, although a little disgruntled, and the day's wedding preparations continued.

The bride and groom broke a loaf of bread into small pieces and shared it with everyone present. Over the next several hours, members of both families approached friends and acquaintances with bread and wine, inviting them to the wedding to be held later in the day. Invitees toasted the couple, wishing them great happiness and luck, among other things, and accepted the invitation.

> By late afternoon the wedding had officially begun. There was singing and dancing; the bride was stolen in mid-wedding, and the groom was presented with several false brides. The groom refused a boy who had been dressed up as a girl, saying, 'My bride is beautiful like the sun, not like you'. The ethnic Lithuanian guests participated in this ritual as well, presenting a Lithuanian version of bride substitution. The ethnic Gagauz guests taught one of their dances, and everyone tried to catch the rhythm, adding an unfamiliar pulse to their steps and hand movements.
>
> Much later, as the dancing wound down, the bride was seated on the groom's lap, her crown of flowers removed and replaced with a head kerchief. The couple's new godparents tied a blanket around their shoulders, drawing them close to each other. Then the godmother combed the couple's hair and sprayed them with perfume. Guests came forward to tuck money in the bride's kerchief, and their parents cried. Other guests presented the bride with gifts and flowers. Towards evening the wedding ended, and the guests and wedding party returned to their rooms, eagerly anticipating the makeshift disco that would soon follow.

This wedding, the first one I attended in Moldova, was not a real wedding but a day-long enactment of wedding rituals and traditions documented by ethnographers and folklorists working in the Republic of Moldova. The actors and the audience were young people, mostly between the ages of twelve and fifteen, who were attending a ten-day summer camp sponsored by the Council of Europe. Many of them were also regular participants in folkloric ensembles, where they learned what constituted 'authentic' traditions and their proper performance onstage. Their staged performance of a wedding serves well to introduce the activities of amateur folkloric ensembles, the origins of my interest in them, and national identity projects in post-Soviet Moldova.

This mock wedding and its setting also point to the central theme of the chapters to come – namely, the challenges faced by folklorists and ethnographers working in Moldova as they attempt to represent the complexities of local culture and traditions to the citizens of a new state. The challenges are many: to reflect culture and history accurately; to portray tradition in a way that feels real to audiences; and to shape the interpretation of performances in ways that are interesting and meaningful as well as accurate. Moreover, these challenges must be met from within existing institutional and ideological frameworks: the disciplines of folklore and ethnography, the extant folkloric performance ensembles, the nation-state, and a state-run cultural system. Each of these institutions enables and constrains the creative work of folklorists and ethnographers in particular directions. Most important, their work is caught between different institutionalized images of the nation, as both monoethnic and multiethnic, and between the relations to history and power that each image represents. The re-enactments performed by folkloric ensembles are undeniably part of a nation-building project, but what kind of nation do they imagine?

First Encounters and (Mis)interpretations

When I first encountered Moldova's folkloric ensembles in the summer of 1999, at the summer camp where the mock wedding was staged, I intended to study the development of national identity in the context of Moldova as a new postsocialist state, but I had not yet settled on a more specific topic or approach. The Republic of Moldova, formed after the dissolution of the Soviet Union, has a noticeably multiethnic population. Like other postsocialist countries, Moldova has experienced substantial internal and external political pressure to address minority needs by crafting a multiethnic and multicultural nation-state, and successive post-independence governments have all attempted to do so. Yet this endeavour is far from simple – like all identity projects, nation-building can fail. In Moldova, two earlier, separate attempts to craft national identity during the twentieth century had partially failed, leaving complicated layers in people's perceptions of ethnic and national identity and how it might be imagined in a new round of nation-building.

During this first encounter, amateur ensembles, especially those organized for children, appeared to me to be engaged in a program that coincided with the state's official policies. Camp organizers indicated that the ensembles I saw performing had been formed 'recently', which led me to believe they were something new, created for the socialization of children in an independent, post-Soviet, multiethnic Moldova. Because folklore has often been implicated in shaping ethnic and national imaginations, I thought these ensembles would provide an ideal subject through which to study identity in the process of construction. Moreover, the invocation of multiculturalism by the summer camp's organizers suggested that folklorists in postsocialist Moldova might be trying to create a very different kind of nation from that portrayed in studies of folklore and its ties to nineteenth-century romantic nationalism or early twentieth-century political movements. I therefore expected further research on children's folkloric groups to suggest the future of ethnic and national identities in Moldova. As the following chapters reveal, my initial assumptions and understandings were both right and wrong.

At first, for example, I did not realize that the children's groups I saw were primarily performative. From initial discussions with camp participants, I thought of them more as clubs focused on cultural education, and I initially envisioned my research more as a study of the socialization of children into ethnic and national identities through such cultural education programs than as a study of folkloric performance. Studies such as those conducted by Ann Beuf (1977) and Judith Porter (1971) have revealed that children acquire strong attitudes towards ethnic and racial difference from as early as three years of age, even when they have little direct exposure to members of ethnic or racial groups other than their own. Folklore, in particular, has often been intentionally included in school curricula and activities with the aim of cultivating ethnic and national identity. In many cases – such as that of Finland, as documented by William Wilson (1976) – teachers, textbooks, and school administrators explicitly foreground the ideological messages they expect students to gain from engaging with folklore.

Performance ensembles in Moldova, however, reflected a more complex relationship to the use of folklore than the kind of educational programs I initially imagined. Moreover, they were not new but represented the continuation of Soviet amateur artistic activities. Their newness came from a last expansion of these activities in the 1980s, experienced as part of a folkloric movement, and from a new approach within ensembles to tradition and the question of authenticity.

On a second short trip to Moldova in early fall 2000, I learned that children's folkloric ensembles were well organized throughout the country and that ensemble directors and local ethnographers were interested in my research. I then gathered most of the data included in the following chapters from February through November 2001, when I focused on learning about the professional activities and motivations of the adults who organized, directed, and judged children's folkloric ensembles.[1]

In contrast to my initial impression that children's folkloric ensembles supported the state's official orientation towards the creation of a multiethnic and multicultural nation, I found a more complex relationship, both between the ensembles and the state and among the ensembles' own representational goals and multiethnicity. None of the new ensembles explicitly advanced a

---

[1] I also gathered information about my informants' perspectives on children, childhood, and the effects they expected participation in folkloric ensembles to have, but little of that found its way into my dissertation or this book. Although members of the folkloric movement have strong opinions and ideas about childhood socialization, these ideas do not seem to drive their professional activities. Rather, an interest in children or childhood socialization seemed – as is indicated in chapter 5 – almost incidental in the stories people told about their careers and professional activities. Their work with children was given as only one more example of how Soviet policies canalized social opportunities along ethnic lines (cf. Simon 1991).

multicultural or multiethnic vision of Moldova in its performances; many of the values held and professed by ensemble directors were emblematic of romantic nationalism; and all saw themselves as contesting the Soviet state and its emphasis on ethnic relations. Yet the vision that was created through folkloric festivals, when these ensembles performed together, was an ethnically inclusive one of a 'nation of villages'. The criteria of authenticity used when people crafted and judged folkloric repertoires and performances effectively relocated 'real' traditions out of Soviet ethnic stereotypes and into Moldova's villages, regardless of the ethnicity of the villages' inhabitants. In other words, although folkloric ensembles did not support the state's vision of Moldova as a multiethnic nation (or my own initial imaginings), they did propose a vision of Moldova as culturally diverse. As I explain in chapter 6, this diversity is only partial, but the folkloric vision is nevertheless powerful because it draws on people's lived experiences and personal knowledge of villages. Before proceeding with a more theoretical discussion, it is therefore useful to return to an explanation of what the mock wedding I saw reveals about ethnic and national identity in Moldova.

Authenticity and the Double Boundaries of Identity

Like weddings in general, the mock wedding performed at the summer camp provides a ritualized and visual representation of the way collective identities are formed and transformed through the negotiation of the double boundaries that mark off 'insiders' and 'outsiders'. When I viewed the performance, I was surprised at how little the differences between ethnic groups had been dramatized. Indeed, I was surprised that only one wedding had been staged, rather than a separate one for each of the four ethnic groups represented among the camp participants: Moldovan, Bulgarian, Gagauz, and Lithuanian.[2] After all, the stated goals of the camp at which the wedding was performed included the promotion of interethnic understanding among Moldova's youths by bringing them together to demonstrate their traditions and learn each other's. My attention during those ten days – and for a long time afterwards – was focused on what I thought ethnicity should look like.

---

[2] Lithuanians constitute a small ethnic minority in Moldova and rarely appear in public discussions of ethnic relations in the country. Their inclusion in the camp, and the exclusion of members of the large Russian and Ukrainian minorities, requires explanation. The camp organizers solicited minority participants through the government's Department of National Relations, and Lithuanians responded. The readiness of Moldova's small Lithuanian community to send children to participate in a camp focused on the exchange of folklore and cultural traditions reflects the diasporic dimensions of Lithuania's own folkloric movement (see Čiubrinskas 2010). In addition to the four participating ethnic groups, several ethnic Moldovan children from Transnistria participated.

Following Frederik Barth's (1969) argument that ethnic groups are defined by the boundaries enclosing the 'cultural stuff' that is ordinarily taken as representative of identity, I expected to see an emphasis on boundary-making between the groups at the camp. In contrast to previous understandings of ethnic identity, in which the exchange of cultural material between groups could lead to identity loss, Barth argued that a group's identity could actually be constituted and strengthened through contact with others. Members of each ethnic group continually re-create a symbolic boundary between the groups by using diagnostic cultural elements, especially values, to identify their fellow members as well as non-members. Boundary creation has the potential to establish broader social relationships as well, making ethnicity a salient factor in the organization of social life:

> The ethnic boundary canalizes social life – it entails a frequently quite complex organization of behaviour and social relations. The identification of another person as a fellow member of an ethnic group implies a sharing of criteria for evaluation and judgement. It thus entails the assumption that the two are fundamentally 'playing the same game', and this means that there is between them a potential for diversification and expansion of their social relationship to cover eventually all different sectors and domains of activity. On the other hand, a dichotomization of others as strangers, as members of another ethnic group, implies a recognition of limitations on shared understandings, differences in criteria for judgement of value and performance, and a restriction of interaction to sectors of assumed common understandings and mutual interest (Barth 1969: 15).

Interpreting Barth's discussion of ethnic groups in contact too narrowly, I expected only differences between ethnic groups to be emphasized. As he put it, 'ethnic groups only persist as significant units if they imply marked difference in behaviour, i.e. persisting cultural differences' (Barth 1969: 15).

Instead of emphasizing differences in the wedding procedures of Moldova's ethnic groups, this mock wedding incorporated elements familiar to all the camp participants: the groom's family taking the bride from her parental house, the inviting of guests, the preparation of a feast, complete with dancing and music, the presentation of false brides to the groom in mid-wedding, and the unveiling of the bride. Even the composition of the wedding party was familiar to all participants. It included four key actors in addition to the bride and groom: the *naşi* (marital godparents), a married couple who support the new couple and their future family financially and otherwise; the *vornicel*, the groom's closest unmarried friend, who assists the groom in retrieving his bride, usually by speaking on the groom's behalf, and often does much of the formal speaking during the wedding festivities;

and the *vorniceasă* or *druşcă*, the bride's closest unmarried friend. Traditions that were marked as ethnically distinct, such as the Lithuanian bride substitution and the Gagauz dancing, were subsumed into the general ritual structure, which all participants could recognize as a wedding. Cultural similarity incorporated diversity.

My first encounter with ethnographers and folklorists teaching traditions to children left me with a puzzle. If the mock wedding was meant as a pedagogical device for demonstrating Moldova's ethnic diversity, then why did it emphasize the many points of similarity among the participating ethnic groups? The groups all appeared to share the same culture. The answer to this question has two parts. First, it reflects a broader political approach taken by the ethnographers, folklorists, teachers, and other cultural specialists who organized the camp's activities. This approach, which forms the subject matter of the chapters to come, is rooted in an ideology that perceives villages, rather than ethnic groups, as the sources of cultural tradition and diversity in Moldova. From this perspective, I was mistaken to seek diversity at the ethnic level and should instead have looked for regional or inter-village differences. The other, and related, part of the answer is that my perception of similarity was situationally dependent on my role as an outsider. Participants in the mock wedding saw and commented on levels of similarity and difference that I could not see.

Two participants, for example, called my attention to a lack of authenticity in the mock wedding. The first, a fifteen-year-old boy from Chişinău, noted that at 'real' weddings, people were much happier than they were at this wedding. The second, the adult director of the Gagauz folkloric ensemble, called attention to the wedding's composite nature. He pointed my attention to the fact that many variations existed on the traditions that had been presented, as well as a range of traditions that could have been included but were not. In other words, this wedding was not real because it belonged to no one village, group, or region in particular. In both cases the ability to gauge authenticity was rooted in personal experience, and in the second case it was rooted also in the specialized experience of ethnographic fieldwork.

My inability to perceive the particular nature of the mock wedding illustrates what Anya Peterson Royce (1982) referred to as a reference group's 'double boundary'. That is, groups actually have two boundaries under continual negotiation. One defines the group for insiders, and the other defines the same group for outsiders. Although Barth (1969) acknowledged that group members recognize one another, his focus was on how the outer boundaries between groups were created and crossed. Royce (1982: 29) pointed instead to the importance of interactions between insiders in defining a group's boundaries and identity: 'Individuals enclosed by the inner boundary share a common cultural knowledge; hence their interaction may be varied and complex and tolerate a great deal of ambiguity'. At the same time, insiders judge each other more strictly on 'the extent of their cultural knowledge' and 'ability to behave adequately' than do outsiders who ascribe an identity to the group (Royce 1982: 30). The emotional qualities of a wedding, as well as its demand for greater elaboration of ritual elements, reflect some of the criteria used for internal boundary making.

My initial interpretation of the mock wedding as reflecting a shared identity between ethnic groups was not false. Indeed, widespread similarities exist not only in the wedding traditions of Moldova's ethnic groups but also in many other traditions. Camp organizers explicitly called attention to these similarities, and outsiders have documented them. Hülya Demirdirek, a Norwegian-trained social anthropologist who has conducted fieldwork in Moldova's semi-autonomous region of Gagauz Yeri, for example, attributed similarities in weddings, baptisms, and godparenthood among ethnic Gagauz, Ukrainians, Bulgarians, Russians, and others living in Gagauz Yeri to their widely shared belief in Orthodox Christianity (cited in Chinn and Roper 1998: 90). Not only in Gagauz Yeri but throughout the whole of Moldova, 98 per cent of the population identifies as Orthodox Christian. High rates of intermarriage throughout the country, along with increasing mobility and migration, mean that most citizens have substantial practical knowledge of many similarities and differences among themselves.

The general similarities among wedding rituals as they are practised within Moldova's borders enable citizens, as insiders, to engage in highly nuanced discussions about their commonalities and differences along regional and ethnic lines. They can discuss the authenticity and desirability of composite weddings like the mock wedding I observed. Although composite weddings foreground similarities in the attempt to unify participants, they do so at the expense of generating appropriate emotive responses, because they really belong to no one.

The connection between perceived authenticity, emotional response, and the representation of ethnic and national identity that is inherent in insider responses to the mock wedding is instructive for understanding the broader context in which folkloric ensembles in the Republic of Moldova operate. Specifically, Moldova's official image as a multiethnic nation is crafted primarily in response to outsider perspectives on cultural diversity and must respond to international discourses on multiculturalism. Yet as responses to the mock wedding reveal, the creation of a composite vision of national identity runs the risk of being rejected by those expected to identify with it.

Reencountering Ethnic Diversity

Moldova, like the other postsocialist states of eastern Europe and the former Soviet Union, experienced substantial pressure to adopt multiethnic and multicultural policies during the 1990s. In the first two decades of transition from socialism, policy studies and recommendations related to cultural policy, language rights, federalization, local government, and other topics connected to the challenge of governing multiethnic and culturally diverse societies relied increasingly on multicultural theory, without questioning the appropriateness of the theory itself for the local context.

The concept of multiculturalism first appeared in public discourse in English-speaking countries in the early 1980s (Glazer 1997: 9), and it developed into a visibly influential stream in political philosophy by the mid-1990s (Rex 2004: 37). The concept replaced older ones such as cultural pluralism without extended discussion. It appeared to be new, but it carried forward a number of assumptions from previous generations, together with their logical and empirical flaws. As R. D. Grillo (1998) demonstrated, the earlier concept of cultural pluralism had itself been a quickly developed offshoot of the political philosophy of 'pluralism'. The kinds of political diversity initially ascribed to pluralism were unconnected to issues of ethnic, racial, or cultural diversity, but they became associated almost exclusively with these issues during the middle decades of the twentieth century. Instead of acknowledging the mixed record of success and failure in previous political and social experiments in reconciling cultural diversity, the new generation of multicultural political theorists asserted only the possibility and necessity of carrying out such reconciliation. They avoided explicit discussion of culture, in particular, by tracing their concern with the balancing of individual and group rights with respect to citizenship and the state to earlier theories of the political and social rights of 'classes'.

Despite being oriented within a universal political philosophy, theories of multiculturalism reflect the development of pressing social issues related to ethnic, religious, racial, and sexual minorities in Canada, Australia, the United Kingdom, and the United States. In these countries, public discourse on multiculturalism in education, social life, and the arts has been particularly strong (Roach 2005). The concept of culture enables these four types of minorities to be treated together, and protagonists argue that it also makes it possible to tailor the theories to local situations where other minority groups with lifestyle-related demands and grievances appear as more central social and political actors.

The concept of culture, however, generates additional theoretical and practical problems. How, for example, is it possible to create a universal political culture that will serve as an acceptable umbrella for many distinct cultures, each demanding recognition (Taylor 1994)? As an anthropologist, Thomas Hylland Eriksen (2001) noted a more fundamental contradiction inherent in multiculturalism, which is that it requires diversity to be maintained and replicated in a predictable and controlled manner in established cultural groups. Despite claiming to value the radical transformation of politics and society to reflect multiple cultures, multiculturalist theories do not in fact anticipate the continual transformation of cultures.

In practice, the term *multiculturalism* has generally been used as a code for a renewed approach to long-standing social issues – race, for example, in the United States, and religion in western Europe (Ali 2002). The effect is that instead of creating a more comprehensive approach to cultural differences, multicultural theories may simply 'rest on a series of confusions that mask rather than reveal the underlined social realities' (Ali 2002: 478). In the context of the Republic of Moldova, as elsewhere in eastern Europe, multiculturalism has been introduced primarily as a new way of addressing ethnic relations and – as elsewhere – has a large chance of confusing and masking local social realities.

The ideas of key multiculturalists such as Will Kymlicka and Bhiku Parekh especially influenced policy reforms occurring throughout postsocialist eastern Europe and the former Soviet Union. Their work oriented initiatives such as the Council of Europe's Cultural Policy Review Program (Council of Europe 2001), work undertaken by the Canadian Centre for Foreign Policy Development (Opalski 1998), and a host of Soros Foundation programs (e.g. Bíró and Kovács 2001; Tishkov and Filippova 2002; Daftary and Grin 2003). The emphasis on identity, creativity, participation, and diversity embedded in multicultural perspectives is indeed appealing, and even scholars with the strongest critical gazes, including me, have difficulty disavowing the value and desirability of these principles (Eriksen 2001; McGuigan 2004: 100).

Yet the application of multiculturalism to postsocialist states has created as many problems as it has resolved (Hayden 2007), and it threatens to become an unwelcome export from the West (Schwarz 1995). Despite the rhetoric of valuing the specific history and nature of each multicultural society, including local definitions of and perspectives on culture (e.g. Parekh 2000: 9), actual application tends to ignore precisely the most local dimensions of intercultural exchange. This may well result in what Gerald Creed (2011), studying Bulgarian folk traditions of mumming, referred to as 'missed alternatives' – models and visions for supporting social and cultural diversity that derive from local practice. I suggest that folklorists in Moldova have already been engaged in such interpretative work, and I urge a closer look at the way villages may productively shift discourses about the nation.

In the rush to promote 'new' solutions, initiatives focused on multiculturalism forget the existence and effects of previous efforts to institutionalize cultural pluralism by reconciling the demands of ethnic majorities and minorities, promoting cultural diversity, and integrating culture with politics and economics. At the very least, it is necessary to acknowledge that cultural policy formed a key component of development programs in the framework of postcolonial nationalisms and Cold War international diplomacy, and that contemporary forms of cultural policy carry forward some of the assumptions of those previous eras about the malleability of culture for political and economic goals (Geertz 1963; Engerman et al. 2003; Cash 2008).

Reconciling ethnic and other forms of diversity is a perennial issue for modern states, and new states inherit the legacies of previous policies. For example, in the former Soviet Union, nationalities policy and cultural policy covered much of the same conceptual territory now addressed under multiculturalism (Zvorykin 1970; Simon 1991). Both types of policies left lasting effects on the ways local populations define culture and ethnicity, perceive ethnic rights and relations, conceptualize and value diversity, and relate to the state as an arbiter in these matters.[3] In addition, Soviet policies interacted with previous state-building policies and practices and with locally existing conceptions, definitions, and practices. In the Republic of Moldova, the forms of multiculturalism now promoted by international and European organizations thus meet the legacy of several layers of previous state and nation-building policies, as well as local definitions of culture and diversity that have persisted despite historical change and definitions that have emerged in response to it. Thus, even as multiculturalism becomes a taken-for-granted orientation in the societies that initially generated it and fades from overt political debate, it leaves a strong mark elsewhere. The tension between locally articulated models for reconciling diversity and the multiculturalist orientations of the state in Moldova point to more widely shared problems. As Verena Stolcke (1995) pointed out, the value of cultural difference in ethnic terms is now so thoroughly assumed by western Europeans that it even underwrites exclusionary attitudes and policies towards immigrant communities.

A critical ethnography of folkloric ensembles in Moldova thus has the possibility of reopening important questions about how relations between cultural unity and diversity, culture and politics, and ethnic groups and the nation, can be imagined.

---

[3] Vytis Čiubrinskas (2010), for example, demonstrated how experiences with Soviet multiculturalism had already affected the development of multiculturalism in the West as émigré populations from the former Soviet Union formed ethnic communities in diaspora, responding to the political frameworks of both their 'home' and 'host' countries.

A Critical Ethnography of Folklore

Folklore, in its guises as academic discipline, subject matter, and performance genre, has been implicated in nation-building and nationalist movements since the eighteenth century. During the twentieth century, states of all political orientations used folklore, among other media, to build images of the nation for both internal consumption and externally oriented diplomacy (Dorson 1966). Folklore, as is especially visible in folkloric performance, identifies the content of national identity, asserts dominant values, constructs relations with other nations, and defines boundaries for including social groups in the nation and excluding them from it. Yet these same capacities for articulating visions of national identity in the state's interest have also historically made folklore a tool for political protest and contestation. As John Roberts (1999: 123) summarized, the challenge for folklore's development as a scholarly discipline is to acknowledge its fundamental history of political entanglements; folklore has been used both to empower the disfranchised and to disfranchise them further. Since its inception, the discipline of folklore studies has consolidated its authority through discourses about morality, righteousness, and authenticity (Zipes 1988: 21). Moreover, folklore's promise to provide access to 'authentic' traditions has a perennial appeal for those in search of alternative individual and collective identities. Regina Bendix's account (1997: 12) of her entry into folklore, for example, could well describe the appeal of folklore for many: 'At twenty, I began to study folklore out of an emotional attachment to what I perceived as authentic dances and music of the Balkans – a motivation and personal involvement that has led many into studying folklore. Participating in a folk dance group and listening to exotic music seemed to put me in touch with layers of myself that had been dormant'.

Folklore is most often associated with underwriting ethno-nationalism through the elaboration of visions of an ethnically pure nation. Yet folklore does not necessarily generate or support ideologies of ethnic exclusion or chauvinism. Folklore can also promote cultural pluralism. Both exclusionary and pluralistic approaches 'self-consciously tap into evidence of cultural difference from groups living in proximity to one another' (Abrahams 1993: 8). The perception of authenticity is achieved through what Robert Cantwell (1993) described as 'ethnomimesis' – a continual process of representing the collective self and then imitating the representation. Culturally plural visions of the nation can therefore be perceived and experienced as equally authentic if a plurality of traditions becomes the central focus in folkloric representational strategies. The important question, then, is not, Why does folklore promote ethno-nationalism? Rather, one must ask, Under what conditions does folklore promote ethno-nationalism, and when does it promote pluralism? These questions are particularly well suited for Moldova, where folklore has been used for both purposes.

No accurate count exists of the number of folkloric ensembles in Moldova, but they form the majority of the country's nearly fifteen hundred amateur performance ensembles. The general organization of ensembles was inherited from the Soviet period, and at least formally the ensembles remain vehicles for performing official state ideology. During the 1980s, however, a folkloric movement (*mişcarea folclorică*) developed in tandem with Moldova's growing nationalist movement, an occurrence that resembled political developments elsewhere in the Soviet Union (e.g. Carpenter 1996; Levin 1996; Čiubrinskas 2000; Kenney 2002). Like their counterparts in the other Soviet republics, Moldova's folk ensembles turned their attention, during the last decade of Soviet rule, to producing more 'authentic' folkloric performance styles (Smidchens 1996; Doi 2002; Olson 2004). Moldova's folkloric movement involved a collaboration between performers and professional folklorists and ethnographers, along with a host of cultural specialists, that elevated the criterion of authenticity in the evaluation of folkloric performances and created new types of folkloric ensembles and a system of festivals for cultivating the development of authentic folkloric performances.

The authentic vision of the nation promoted through these new folk performances highlighted the role of villages as the sources of both cultural production and cultural diversity. In invoking the village, the 'most classic trope of bourgeois and Romantic nationalisms' (Abrahams 1993: 24), Moldova's folkloric movement contested Soviet authority by producing alternative images of Moldovan national identity. By insisting that performers replicate the traditional costumes, dances, songs, and rituals of specific villages, the folkloric movement combated stereotyped images of 'Moldovans', that had developed during the Soviet period. The recharacterization of Moldovans as villagers provided new models for social organization (Kenney 2002), and at times it conformed closely to political protests in which protesters arrived in Chişinău identifying themselves collectively by their home village. On those occasions, when village men, some of whom wore the traditional tall, lamb's wool hat called a *căciulă* on their heads, marched in the central square, urbanites felt 'as if the very earth were moving'. But the centrality of the village in folkloric performance has not merely been a tool for promoting Moldovan ethno-nationalism vis-à-vis Soviet imperialism, as might be expected. It also suggests new ways for imagining cultural unity and diversity – ways that are neither those of Soviet ideology nor those of internationally circulated multicultural theorists.

The focus of the following chapters is thus on how Moldova's new folkloric ensembles contribute to the construction of post-Soviet national identity. I ask, in particular, how the new 'authentic' folklore envisions relations between the country's ethnic groups and how this vision informs state-building activities. Although both nationalism and folklore studies in eastern Europe have long been considered derivative from western European, and specifically German, traditions, the dilemmas faced by contemporary folklorists and ethnographers in Moldova during the 'third-wave of demotic ethnic nationalisms' (Smith 1991: 38) actually reflect the shared challenge ethnographers everywhere now face in participating in public debates about cultural diversity.

My choice to critically examine folkloric performance as a site for the production of national identity is not, in itself, unusual. In recent decades, studies of the role of folklore in the construction of nationalism have expanded as folklorists have critically engaged with the history of their discipline. Since the publication of Eric Hobsbawm and Terence Ranger's *The Invention of Tradition* (1983), anthropologists and historians, too, have devoted attention to folklore's connections with the production of national identity (Herzfeld 2003: 307). As a result, both national schools of folklore and folkloric performances in Europe have been well studied, and I could have approached my own work along one of the previously established paths, as an ethnographically informed history of Moldova's folkloric movement or of individual folklorists, performers, or ensembles. To do so would have produced a case study suitable for immediate comparison with similar studies of Greece (Herzfeld 1982), Slavonia (Croatia) (Dubinskas 1983), Portugal (Holton 2005), Russia (Olson 2004), Bosnia (Maners 1995), and the Baltic states (Smidchens 1996).

I have not, however, pursued such a historical approach. Documents, archives, and other historical sources in Moldova are generally difficult to locate (cf. King 2000), and I was told on more than one occasion that statistics and publications from the later Soviet period had been thrown out during office reorganizations, and so long-range comparative data could not be reconstructed. Similarly, in 2001, few of the people involved in folkloric ensembles in Moldova had time for the lengthy conversations needed to reconstruct the movement's history or their own involvement in it. They were busy rushing to the multiple jobs they held to make ends meet in that financially difficult year. Moldova suffered heavily from the 1998 Russian financial crisis, and economic growth was slow to resume. In 2001, people were unsettled by the decollectivization of collective farms and the privatization of other collective and state property, which peaked during the 1998–2000 National Land Program (Gorton and White 2003: 308, 314). Urban intellectuals felt these changes acutely in disruptions of electricity, running water, and central heating and in demands for assistance from rural relatives faced with additional hardships. Among my informants, almost everyone had at least two jobs, and as many as five was not impossible. Consequently, interviews were snatched between rehearsals, in transit to concerts, at post-festival meals, and – in the rare moments when longer discussions were possible – between the constant interruptions of incoming phone calls. The frantic pace at which my informants worked and lived in 2001 had an obvious effect on the kinds of data I could gather, but it also shifted my attention to a different set of questions, focused more precisely on what people were doing as they organized, led, and judged folkloric performances, and what meaning their activities had for them. As a consequence of the primacy of the "ethnographic present" in my research, my analysis foregrounds the open-ended, circumstantial, contradictory, highly emotional, and unfinished nature of national ideologies and the identities they seek to reflect and (re)create. Rogers Brubaker (1999) has used the term "nationalizing" to draw attention to the ongoing evolution of national identities through public discourse and state policies. Critical ethnography of folklore in its synchronous dimension, thus also opens a comparative discussion about the political role and aspirations of ethnography in a continually nationalizing world.

During my research I lived in Chişinău, Moldova's capital city, where I had access to and conducted interviews with staff in the national organizations responsible for organizing, tracking, and educating folkloric ensembles. These included the state-level Ministry of Culture and Ministry of Education, the Chişinău municipal Department of Culture and Department of Education, the National Palace of Creativity for Children and Adolescents (formerly the Pioneer Palace), the National Centre for Folk Arts, and the Department of National Relations. Since 2001 the names of several of these institutions have changed, some of them more than once, but I use the names as they were in 2001.

In addition, from my urban base I met a large network of persons involved in the folkloric community, not only ensemble directors but also artists, dancers, academics, instrument makers, and their colleagues and families – all tangentially connected to, and generally supportive of, children's folkloric performance ensembles. I interviewed officials and specialists in key institutions and attended numerous performances and competitions. I observed the rehearsals of four groups in three sections of the city, each with a different profile. One was exclusively a dance-oriented ensemble; another, exclusively musical; and two combined genres in a broad performance repertoire. Two of the ensembles were organized through sector 'creativity centres' (urban counterparts to the former Soviet houses of culture), and the other two were school based. Among the four, I had the most extended contact with the two school-based ensembles, which were located in the Rîşcani sector of the city, where I was staying; this allowed me to document more thoroughly the processes of repertoire creation, teaching, rehearsal, performance, and response to feedback from the competitions in which the ensembles participated. I conducted most of my research using Romanian, following the language preference of my informants, and found that my Russian skills quickly atrophied.

Several people who greatly influenced my understanding of both folkloric ensembles and Moldovan identities appear repeatedly in the following chapters. Varvara Buzilă, an ethnographer employed at the Moldovan Academy of Sciences and the National Museum of Ethnography and Natural History, took me to the camp that originated this project, and I later requested her as the field advisor required by the grant from the International Research and Exchanges Board (IREX) that funded my research in 2001. The directors of three ensembles also figure prominently: Valeriu Chiper (trained as a history teacher, and director of the ensemble Moştenitorii); his friend Afanasi Gargalik (trained as a dancer and choreographer, and director of the Gagauz ensemble Altângic, in the village of Tomai); and Petru Dinjos (trained as a musician and music teacher, and director of a flute ensemble, Buciumaşii).[4] A fourth director of a children's dance ensemble, Pavel Popa, also appears regularly, but he speaks most often in his capacity as a specialist at the National Centre for Folk Arts.

Because the majority of my contacts in Moldova interacted with me in their professional capacities, I have not changed their names. As we met and worked together in 2001 and subsequently, we discussed my intent to use what I learned from them to address the topics of national and ethnic identities in Moldova. This is still a somewhat uncomfortable decision, because the chance of their reported speech being interpreted simply as ethnocentric nationalism is high. For much of Moldova's population, the breakup of the Soviet Union was deeply traumatic, and the "nationalists" who demanded expanded linguistic and cultural recognition during the 1980s are often still blamed for the social, economic and political upheaval that followed independence. Not only is it mistaken to reduce the professional agendas of folklorists and ethnographers to a simple form of ethnocentric nationalism,

[4] The names of folkloric ensembles in Moldova are often highly symbolic. The ensemble Moştenitorii are literally 'The Heirs', and Buicumaşii are 'The Little Horns'. Both names are Romanian. A *bucium* is a long horn instrument, similar to a Swiss alphorn, traditionally played by shepherds and closely associated with images of Romanian culture (Stoica and Petrescu 1997: 106–107). I use the spelling 'Altângic' as recorded in a list of ensembles provided by the National Centre for Folk Arts, but Hülya Demirdirek (personal communication) indicates that this word has no meaning, and the proper spelling of the ensemble's name in Gagauz is Altincik, 'Small Gold'. I have left the spelling as I received it to make future research easier.

as I hope I have successfully argued in the coming chapters, but it is also a source of potential personal pain. On several occasions, the pain of being labelled a nationalist still arises in life stories and memories for some of my informants. They deny this label, claiming instead to have been patriots doing something "for the country". The distinction is subtle but real, and my intent in what follows is to reveal the patriotic vision of their work and lives while prompting further critical examination of its exclusionary dimensions.[5] I therefore take responsibility for any misinterpretations or misunderstandings of what they communicated to me.

During conversations long and short, I repeatedly heard people express pride in their triumph over Soviet power and ideology, though it was a pride still tinged with the pain that had motivated their struggle. This seemed the more important story to tell, and it is the one I have tried to convey: a story about the difficulty of trying to build new institutions and ideologies from within old structures – the state, the nation, and even folklore itself.

Building the Nation Anew

Four core concepts help to link the following chapters: the double boundary of ethnic groups; structural power; cultural intimacy; and salience. The double boundary, as already discussed, refers to the varying criteria of group membership, depending on whether identity is being crafted within a group or between groups. The double boundary is relevant in discussing how folkloric ensembles communicate Moldovan identity amongst themselves and what they communicate to various audiences, depending on the knowledge already possessed by the audience. The double boundary also helps to explain how the folkloric movement succeeds in crafting a vision of cultural unity that incorporates diversity, as well as the fragility and potential contradictions of this vision.

Structural power, as defined by Eric Wolf (1999: 5), is an alternative to the three ways in which, according to him, power is usually understood: as the innate capacity of an individual; as the ability of one individual or group to exercise its will over another; or as the forces that delimit acceptable behaviours in given situations. Structural power, in Wolf's terms, is a fourth modality of power that 'not only operates within settings and domains but also organizes and orchestrates the settings themselves, and that specifies the direction and distribution of energy flows'. The concept of structural power helps us understand how the 'relations that command economy and polity, and those that shape ideation interact to render the world understandable and

[5] Cf. Ronald Suny (1998: 464) for a discussion of the positive and negative values ascribed, respectively, to "patriotism" and "nationalism" in the context of late Soviet Russia.

manageable' (Wolf 1999: 5–6). Nationalism, ethnicity, and the state are each examples of such a fourth modality of power. They are ideas that have become key principles of social organization and governance worldwide and have thus also become essential elements of subjective experience of everyday life. Moreover, they reinforce each other through the ideology of the nation-state; they become more 'real' and more difficult to circumvent, either ideologically or politically, in the construction of any new form of social, political, or cultural organization. Thus, even as Moldova's folkloric movement contests the Soviet state's preoccupation with ethnic relations, the 'new' vision of the nation carries with it a politics of ethnically based inclusion and exclusion, and the continued state organization of folkloric ensembles in Moldova ensures that those ensembles continue to operate within the paradigm of producing 'national' representations of tradition. The state-wide system of folkloric festivals, for example, is responsible for constructing relations of hierarchy between the village, the region, and the nation.

Michael Herzfeld's (2005) concept of cultural intimacy has to do with the slippage of 'private' cultural norms, experiences, values, and behaviours into the 'public' arena of the state. It helps to illustrate why villages are experienced in Moldova as the authentic sources of repertoires and generators of culture and tradition. It also helps to explain why folklore so often underwrites nationalism and how the state and ethnicity continue to draw power. In Moldova, the folkloric movement's success in increasing the number of ensembles devoted to depicting villages onstage draws on cultural intimacy in the context of recent high levels of rural-to-urban migration coupled with institutional discrimination.

While most recent studies of nationalism focus on the successful creation of nations, nation-building efforts also fail, as do states. Both types of failure have occurred more than once in the territory of contemporary Moldova, necessitating a discussion of the salience of the identities proposed by the folkloric movement. Alexander Motyl's (2001) discussion of the relationship between 'life-world' and identity salience provides an entry point. Motyl noted that official identities are embraced by a population – that is, they become salient – only when they resonate with the population's 'life-world'. The reverse is also true: official identities that do not resonate with a 'life-world' will not be embraced. As the life-world changes, so is it possible for identities to lose their resonance. Moldova's history of failed nation-building projects suggests a repeated pattern in which official representations of the nation have lost their salience. And the emergence of new visions of the nation through existing vehicles such as folkloric performances indicates that key social issues and concerns (i.e. the life-world) have changed. In sum, these four concepts emphasize both the compulsion felt by identity specialists to engage in nation-building projects, and the fragility and contingency of national identities.

An overview of Moldova's history, focusing on the difficulties faced by would-be nation-builders (chapter 2), shows that Moldova's political legitimacy is tenacious because its current boundaries descend directly from Soviet political machinations and the German-Soviet Nonaggression Pact (referred to locally as the Molotov-Ribbentrop Pact) during World War II. Moreover, the territories included in contemporary Moldova have divergent political histories and legacies. Previous states – Romania, Russia, and the Soviet Union – all implemented nation-building policies, but these efforts had only partial success, contributing to a layering of political legacies, hierarchies of social, linguistic, and ethnic identity, and persistent contestation of state authority.

The Soviet state used amateur artistic activity, particularly folklore, to cultivate a national identity among ethnic Moldovans, to spread messages about ethnic relations in Moldova, and to encourage international friendship between socialist 'nations' within the Soviet Union and beyond its borders (chapter 3). Organizational gaps in the Soviet culture system, however, particularly at the level of the definition of genres, enabled the emergence of new, self-consciously 'authentic' folkloric ensembles. In the post-Soviet context, the lack of institutional reforms in the organization of culture means that the new ensembles are both legitimated by and vulnerable to state power. Even after nearly twenty years of independence, the legacy of Soviet power is reflected in both institutional and ideological relationships between the state and the arts. Theoretically, the state could once again mobilize amateur performance ensembles to learn, perform, and promote official ideology – in the new context of multiculturalism and multiculturality. Members of the folkloric community therefore continue their work as a critique of state power, even as they themselves work in state institutions.

Relations between institutions, ensemble directors, artisans, and professional ethnographers and folklorists are expressed in Moldova's relatively new system of folkloric festivals and competitions (chapter 4). These relations enable me to talk about a 'folkloric community' committed to promoting authentic folklore, even though its members are drawn from several professions that in other contexts might have conflicting priorities. In addition to the individual directors who lead folkloric ensembles, the folkloric community includes specialists at the National Centre for Folk Arts, functionaries in the ministries and departments of culture and education at both the national and local levels, professional ethnographers and folklorists at museums and the Academy of Sciences, and others. In chapter 4 I also explore the folkloric community's relationship with the public, asking whether general audiences evaluate folkloric performances in terms of authenticity and whether folkloric performances are good vehicles for transmitting messages about Moldova's national identity.

Members of the folkloric community, whatever their direct connection to teaching children to perform folklore onstage, value ethnographic fieldwork. They stress an interdependence between performed folklore and village-based ethnographic collecting. In chapter 5 I describe two ethnographic fieldwork expeditions in which I took part and discuss the transformation of village identity as cultural objects are moved from the field to the stage. The reliance on ethnographic collecting shapes the images of ethnic and national identity that are transmitted by folkloric ensembles in 'authentic' representations of tradition. One of the important outcomes of this process is that the folkloric community asserts that the wealth of traditions shared by or similar among the ethnic groups residing in the villages of Moldova make 'ethnic problems' foreign to the village-dwelling majority of Moldova's citizens. This assertion, which I met time and again, challenged my initial assumption that national identity was first and foremost an expression of ethnic relations within a state.

In chapter 6, therefore, I critically engage my informants' focus on villages as the sites of culture, sources of diversity, and rightful subjects in national representations. I demonstrate that even as the new criteria for authenticity in folkloric ensembles contest Soviet ideology about ethnicity, they nevertheless create hierarchies of cultural purity and social inclusion among the country's ethnic groups. Ethnic groups that have historically predominated in urban areas, depended on commerce or trade for their subsistence, or are perceived as immigrants are less welcome than others on the national stage.

In the concluding chapter, I return to an explicit discussion of my study as an example of critical ethnography. Because one of the effects of the folkloric movement has been to expand the ranks of ethnographers and folklorists to include many ensemble directors, my informants often perceived me as a potential trainee. Many of them expected me to possess greater knowledge of the songs, dances, customs, and traditions collected and performed locally than I did. Others imagined that I might be intending to establish my own ensemble in the United States and was either collecting ideas from their repertoires or studying their methods of instruction and staging. Correspondingly, members of the folkloric community often saw their role as one of teaching me how to be an ethnographer and directed my attention away from the stage and towards villages. As a conclusion, then, I turn away from the subject of identity construction to consider the common dilemmas and responsibilities of ethnographers and folklorists everywhere.

The authority of folklorists, ethnographers, and other cultural specialists is not constant. Our power to articulate national visions that galvanize public opinion and behaviour is linked to changing structures of power, knowledge, and authority throughout society. By the same token, we are also limited by paradigms that are extremely resistant to change. Moldova's identity as a post-Soviet nation-state is only barely and indirectly being discussed by members of its folkloric community, but the effect of their work rests on the balance of change and continuity outlined here.

Chapter 2
Moldova's National Questions

The history of the Republic of Moldova, both recent and more distant, makes the country an intriguing place for research on ethnic and national identity. In the past 250 years alone, the Ottoman and Russian empires, Romania, and the Soviet Union have all governed portions of the territory now encompassed by Moldova's borders. As the boundaries of the state have changed, so, too, has ethnicity, reflecting the ever-changing relationships between social organization, the various states' administrative systems, patterns of immigration and migration, and local systems of power and prestige that correlate with language use, family background, and social origin.

In the modern period, the state has played an important role in ordering ethnic categories and organizing social relations. *Ethnicity* and the related *ethnic, ethnic group,* and *ethnic identity* are fluid terms. In a review of anthropological studies of ethnicity since the 1960s, Marcus Banks (1996) found no standard definition shared by anthropologists working on the topic, let alone by social scientists or the general public. In many respects, *ethnicity* functions as a synonym for *culture,* referencing social groups defined primarily by shared language, history, customs, and place. In this way, an ethnic group is distinguished conceptually from social groups based on other definitional principles, such as class, race, and gender, although they intersect (Williams 1989). Following the work of Frederik Barth (1969), however, anthropologists have increasingly appealed to the concept of ethnicity to explore the processual dimensions of culture, noting that neither modernization, industrialization, urbanization, nor globalization has erased cultural difference or its salience for social organization and action (Cohen 1978).

Although anthropologists and other social scientists have increasingly recognized the processual nature of ethnicity, older assumptions about the objective and fixed nature of ethnic groups are embedded in modern political ideologies and their practical applications in state-building. In particular, states become entangled with ethnicity through the doctrine of nationalism. As Ernest Gellner explained (1983: 1), nationalism – 'a theory of political legitimacy, which requires that ethnic boundaries should not cut across political ones' – has become the dominant theory underlying the establishment and legitimacy of states with industrialized economies. 'In most cases', he wrote, nationalism 'prevails, and above all, it determines the *norm* for the legitimacy of political units in the modern world: most of them must satisfy the imperatives of nationalism, as described' (1983: 49, original italics).

Nationalism enjoys such international legitimacy as a political principle that even states that do not share in the material, social, or historical preconditions of the states that originally promoted nationalism still aspire to organize themselves in the form of 'nations'. This means, at a minimum, that state-building involves processes intended to align ethnic boundaries (including language, history, customs, and religion) with the state's territorial boundaries. Even in the midst of expanding transnational and global phenomena, the nation-state retains its position as the dominant cultural-political form (Malkki 1992: 34), and as national governments lose other powers to non-state actors, they retain strong control over the 'spatializing' effects through which populations and boundaries are brought into congruence (Trouillot 2001: 133).

Nationalism gains its strength as a political ideology largely through its ability to appear natural. As many scholars have demonstrated, definitions of ethnic groups and nations are remarkably similar. Anthony Smith (1991: 40), for example, attempted to distinguish the two by explaining that a nation is '*a named human population sharing an historic territory, common myths and historical memories, a mass, public culture, a common economy and common legal rights and duties for all members*' (original italics). In comparison, he listed six qualities that define an ethnic group, or *ethnie* (Smith 1991: 21):

1. a collective proper name
2. a myth of common ancestry
3. shared historical memories
4. one or more differentiating elements of common culture
5. an association with a specific 'homeland'
6. a sense of solidarity for significant sectors of the population

Clearly, nations and ethnic groups are similar kinds of human groupings. This, as Smith explained, is because nations have been elaborated out of ethnic groups.

Comparing the two definitions, nations seem to possess greater physical and legal reality. Indeed, nations have this appearance because 'a state's ethnic core often shapes the character and boundaries of the nation; for it is very often on the basis of such a core that states coalesce to form nations' (Smith 1991: 39). Smith's perspective on nation formation allows for both the subjective experience of the nation's 'natural' evolution into a nation-state and the objective view that political actors take a variety of policies and practices over both short and long periods of time to create nation-states. In either case, the result is – as Gellner, too, described it – the contemporary international system of nation-states, in which each state appears to have a dominant ethnic profile. In cases of states with multiple ethnic groups, the relations of hierarchy or equality between groups are well established as part of the state's profile. Indeed, Smith noted that the way a state orders relations between ethnic groups is critical to the state's political legitimacy and survival. States that seek to create a 'civic nation' based on interethnic equality are generally more robust than those that strive to create an 'ethnic nation' prioritizing the cultural rights and needs of one or a few ethnic groups over others.

In the Republic of Moldova, the way the new state elaborates its national identity depends on the way it organizes the rights and needs of ethnic groups as they are defined from at least three perspectives. From one perspective, Moldova is a multiethnic country with at least five major linguistically defined ethnic groups – Moldovans/Romanians, Ukrainians, Russians, Bulgarians, and Gagauz – as well as a number of smaller groups, including Roma. This is the classic situation imagined by Smith, in which the problem of nation-building rests in the way each of these groups gains access to state power. From a second perspective, Moldova's national identity depends on the way it defines its largest ethnic group, Moldovans. Ethnic Moldovans share language, traditions, and substantial history with Romanians across the border in Romania. Thus the question arises whether Moldovans constitute a separate ethnic group and nation from Romanians, whether Moldovan ethnicity is better conceptualized as a regional Romanian identity, or whether Moldovans are simply Romanians.[6] The third perspective on Moldova's national identity focuses on the problem of territorial and regional identities within Moldova. This problem is most salient in relationship to the secessionist region of Transnistria (sometimes spelled Transdniestria in English), but territorial and regional identities have also historically blurred into ethnic identities in Moldova, intersecting with both the Moldovan-Romanian question and inter-ethnic relations between the major linguistic groups in the country.

Because so many perspectives exist in Moldova on the way ethnic groups are defined, all the key ethnic, national, and regional names used in this book are contested. I prefer not to refer to ethnic Moldovans as Romanians, because doing so forecloses a serious consideration of the memories,

[6] Most previous scholarship has focused on the second Moldovan-Romanian question.

historical experiences, and value differences that make most ethnic Moldovans feel themselves to be different from ethnic Romanians, even when they acknowledge many similarities. Using the term *Romanian,* however, would have the advantage of drawing attention to the centrality of language in defining ethnic groups and to the fact that no term yet exists that can be applied equally to all citizens of Moldova to reflect their common status as citizens. An ethnic Russian, for example, cannot also officially be considered a 'Moldovan'; he or she can only be considered a 'citizen of Moldova'. To draw renewed attention to the importance of language in defining ethnic identity, I sometimes refer to ethnic Moldovan informants as 'Romanian speakers'.[7] I also always refer to the language spoken by the ethnic majority as "Romanian" to underscore that language and ethnic identity are not necessarily exact correlates.

A Brief History of Moldova: Changing States, Changing Identities

In August 1991 the Republic of Moldova declared its independence from the collapsing Soviet Union. The new state, however, maintained the boundaries of the former Moldovan Soviet Socialist Republic (MSSR), which immediately complicated its political legitimacy and processes of nation-building.

The political legitimacy of the Republic of Moldova is complicated in large part by the fact that it is not easily identifiable with any pre-Soviet state. In this respect, Moldova differs greatly from several of the other post-Soviet states, such as Latvia, Estonia, and Lithuania, which had established national states during the brief period between the two world wars. The post-Soviet governments in those states immediately drew on the traditions of pre-Soviet statehood to establish their legitimacy, portraying the Soviet period as an 'interruption' in their national development (e.g. Muiznieks 1997; Raun 1997; Senn 1997).[8] The medieval principality of Moldova did include much of the territory of the current state, but its history has generally been subsumed under the historiography of the Romanian state. In this

[7] In addition, many English-language sources still refer to 'Moldavia', 'Moldavians', and the 'Moldavian Republic', instead of Moldova, Moldovans, and the Moldovan Republic. The older usage originated in the translation and transliteration into English of Russian and other sources written in the Cyrillic alphabet. I use the latter terms, reflecting the way they are rendered by the local Romanian-speaking majority. Similarly, in the case of the Dneister/Nistru River and Transdniestria/Transnistria, I opt for the latter, Romanian variant. In addition, I use 'Gagauz Yeri' instead of 'Gagauzia'. Both Romanian and Gagauz speakers use the name Gagauzia, but only Gagauz speakers also refer to Gagauz Yeri, and that is the version that appears in official documents.

[8] In contrast, a brief attempt by Moldova's President Mircea Snegur in 1994 to legitimate the new country through parallels to the brief establishment of an independent Bessarabia in 1917–1918 had the opposite effect (King 1994: 355).

context, it is difficult to elaborate a historical narrative that culminates in the formation of the independent post-Soviet Republic of Moldova as a legitimate state. Most attempts ultimately rely on a narrative that foregrounds the illegitimate establishment of the Soviet republic of Moldova in 1940. A more neutral presentation might focus on the history of the territories included in the present state, rather than on a history of the states that contributed the territory.

Within its boundaries, the new state includes two historically distinct regions, Bessarabia and Transnistria. Bessarabia constitutes the bulk of the state's territory. It is bounded on the west by the Prut River, which serves as the international border with Romania, and on the east by the Nistru (Dniester) River. Transnistria is a narrow strip of land bounded, within Moldova, by the east bank of the Nistru and the international border with Ukraine. The ethnic majority in both territories has historically considered itself and its native language 'Moldovan'.

Bessarabia and Transnistria were united under a single government only in 1940, when the Soviet Union gained control of Bessarabia from Romania as part of the agreements outlined in the Molotov-Ribbentrop Pact. Before that time, the two regions' administrative histories and political identities differed significantly. For nearly five hundred years, from the 1300s until 1812, the land between the Prut and the Nistru rivers that is today called Bessarabia formed parts of the principalities of Moldova and Wallachia (Map 1). The name Bessarabia originally referred only to the southernmost portion of the land between the two rivers – that is, the strip of land along the Black Sea coast that ran the length of the Danube delta to the Nistru. This territory was incorporated by the Bassarab dynasty into the principality of Wallachia during the 1400s. The remaining stretch of present-day Bessarabia – the bulk of the modern Republic of Moldova – belonged to the principality of Moldova. Both Moldova and Wallachia became Ottoman vassal states by the early 1500s, although they continued to be ruled by local princes and often fought against the Ottomans.[9]

[9] Both Wallachia and Moldova made agreements with the Ottomans in the 1400s, but Moldova prolonged its independence until the early 1500s by 'forgetting' to pay tribute (van Meurs 1994: 39–40).

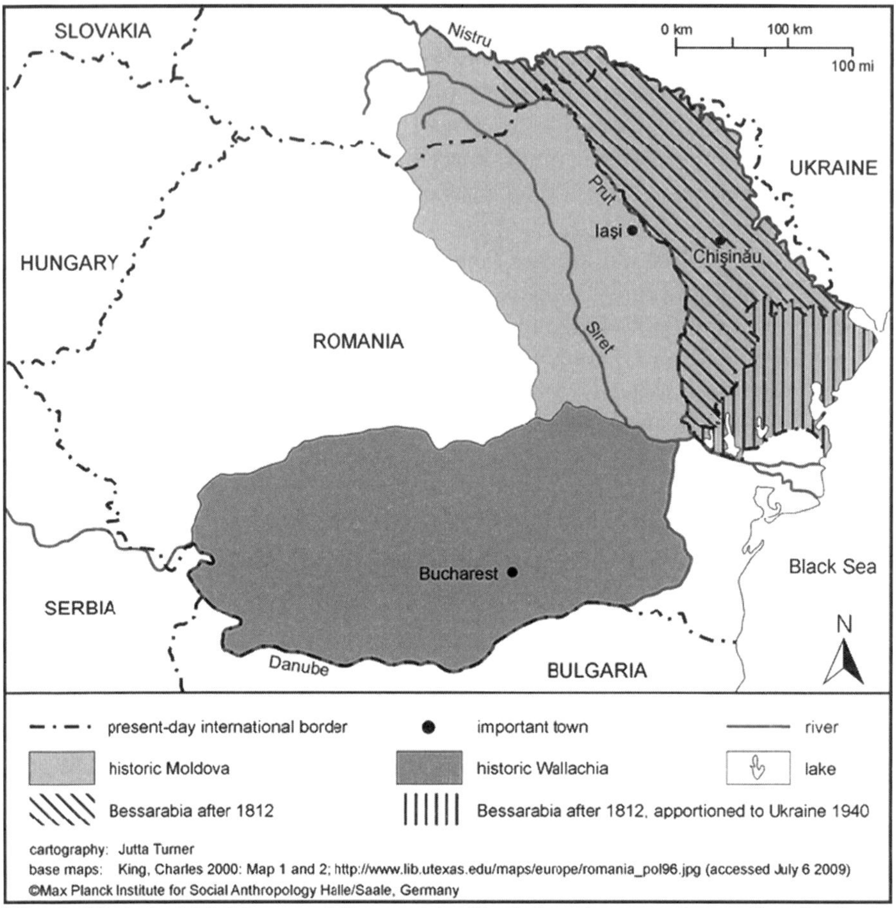

Map 1. Historical Moldova and Bessarabia. Shaded regions are the medieval principalities of Moldova and Wallachia. Bessarabia is shown as it was divided from medieval Moldova and incorporated into the Russian Empire in 1812. Since 1940, the southernmost portion of Bessarabia has belonged to Ukraine. The remainder of Bessarabia corresponds closely to the current boundaries of the Republic of Moldova.

In 1812, under the Treaty of Bucharest, which ended the Russo-Turkish War of 1806–1812, the principality of Moldova was divided between the Russian and Ottoman Empires. The portion east of the Prut River (Bessarabia) came under Russian administration, and the portion west of the river remained an Ottoman vassal until 1859, when it became part of Romania. Russia also won control of the older Bessarabia along the sea coast[10],

[10] This area was returned to the Ottoman Empire after the Crimean War in 1856, but it was again ceded to Russia and was reannexed to the newer Bessarabia after the Russo-Turkish

and it reapplied the name Bessarabia to the full stretch of land between the Prut and the Nistru, northward from the Black Sea to Bukovina. From 1812 through 1917, the redefined Bessarabia held the administrative status of *oblast'* (imperial region) and later *guberniia* (province) within the Russian Empire and maintained substantial, if decreasing, local autonomy.

In contrast to Bessarabia, contemporary Transnistria gained identity only in the twentieth century. During the medieval period, land to the east of the Nistru River was inhabited and controlled by numerous groups (Map 2). More northerly areas east of the river, including Podolia, were long under the control of Poland and Lithuania. Closer to the Black Sea, Crimean Tatars controlled substantial territory during the 1400s; Cossacks dominated significant areas in the 1500s and 1600s; and by the late 1600s both Muscovy and the Ottomans claimed jurisdiction (van Meurs 1994: 39–42).

At the end of the eighteenth century, all of contemporary Transnistria came under Russian control, although in parcels. In 1792 the Ottoman Empire ceded to Russia a territory called Transnistria that stretched from the Nistru to the Bug River (Hamm 1998a: 165).[11] The following year, the second partition of Poland awarded the northern land east of the Nistru to Russia (van Meurs 1994: 45). These territorial gains, however, did not result in the creation of a single administrative region coincident with contemporary Transnistria, because the territories east of the Nistru continued to be administered as integral parts of other political units. During the nineteenth century, today's Transnistria was divided between two *gubernii* located in what is today Ukraine: Kherson, in the south, and Podolia, in the north (Kolstø and Malgin 1998: 106). Contemporary Transnistria began to gain administrative identity only with the establishment of the Moldovan Autonomous Soviet Socialist Republic (MASSR) within Soviet Ukraine in 1924.

In 1940, the MSSR was formally established by combining six counties in Bessarabia with six from the old MASSR (King 2000: 94). By 1991, fifty years of Soviet rule in a common republic had strengthened the economic and political ties between Bessarabia and Transnistria but also sharpened their long-term differences in political identity and created new ones.

War of 1878. It is not part of the current Republic of Moldova, however, because it was apportioned to the Republic of Ukraine in 1940.

[11] English-language geographical sources sometimes refer to this large territory as 'Transnistria', but it has little direct connection to contemporary Transnistria.

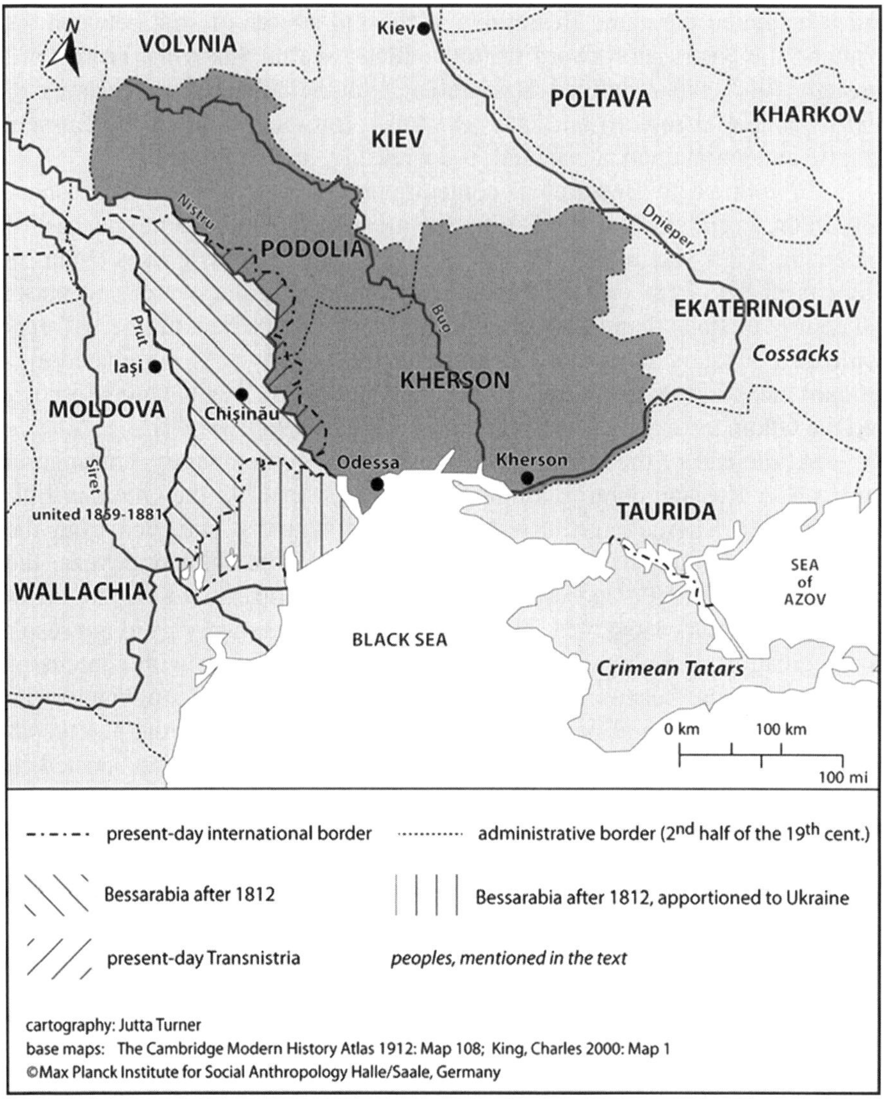

Map 2. Historical Transnistria. The territorial identity of current-day Transnistria, a strip of land east of the Nistru River, was created during the Soviet period. In the late nineteenth century, today's Transnistria belonged to the provinces of Kherson and Podolia. In earlier centuries, Poland, Lithuania, Cossacks, and Crimean Tatars all controlled portions of this territory.

Despite differences in political history, the majority population of both Bessarabia and Transnistria has been referred to historically as Moldovan, reflecting the language spoken by the rulers of the medieval principality. Medieval Moldova's territorial claims rarely extended beyond the Nistru, but during the principality's initial expansion in the fourteenth and fifteenth centuries, many colonists crossed the river, creating Moldovan settlements beyond the east bank. In addition, the frontier conditions that characterized both Bessarabia and Transnistria meant that local inhabitants easily crossed physical and political boundaries, establishing 'Moldovan' villages on both sides of the Nistru well into the nineteenth century (Landis 1974).

As will become clear in the following sections, the relationship between the Moldovan and Romanian peoples, languages, and lands is a source of constant controversy and debate in the current Republic of Moldova. Although the Romanian and Moldovan languages are nearly identical in formal linguistic terms, it is important to stress the historically contingent relationships between the states, nations, ethnic groups, and languages of the two territories. In large part, the majority population of Bessarabia and Transnistria has not traditionally identified itself or its language as Romanian, because the Romanian state, nation, and language appeared only in the last two hundred years, under historical and political conditions that had minimal effect on Bessarabia and even less on Transnistria.[12]

The first Romanian state formed in 1859 through the union of the western portion of medieval Moldova, which had remained an Ottoman vassal after 1812, and Wallachia. Like Moldova, the principality of Wallachia had been an Ottoman vassal since the 1400s. The Treaty of Paris, which ended the Crimean War, stipulated that new princes be elected to govern Wallachia and Moldova as representatives of the Ottoman Empire. Pro-unification parties in each of the principalities ensured that Ion Cuză was elected, making him prince of both. The administrative status and structure of the two principalities changed several times in the following decades as a consequence of power struggles between the European powers, the Ottoman Empire, and local elites. In 1871 the two principalities gained independence, and they finally became the Kingdom of Romania in 1881.

On the linguistic front, literary Romanian was codified throughout the late eighteenth and the nineteenth centuries. At that time two major dialects, Moldovan and Muntenian, were spoken, each of which corresponded roughly to the geography of the unified principalities. Muntenian was chosen as the literary standard for the new Romanian state, and the choice of Bucharest as the capital reinforced the linguistic dominance of Muntenian over the Moldovan dialect. Early language standardization in Romania also emphasized the Romance and Latin character of the language by replacing the

[12] The percentage of Moldovans relative to other ethnic groups in Transnistria is significantly smaller than that in Bessarabia. In the 1990s, for example, two-thirds of Bessarabia's population identified as ethnically Moldovan, but only 40 per cent of Transnistria's population did so.

original Cyrillic orthography (introduced with Orthodox Christianity) with a Roman one, substituting Romance words for Slavonic ones when there were local alternatives, and filling lexical gaps with Italian and French components (Mallinson 1987: 305).

In other words, 'Romanians' appeared well after Bessarabia was incorporated into the Russian Empire. Although some Bessarabian intellectuals knew about the development of Romanian nationalism throughout the nineteenth century, virtually no popular interest in the movement existed, and only a few people shifted to identifying their language or ethnicity as Romanian (Livezeanu 2007). According to some calculations, active nationalists – whether they espoused Romanian or Moldovan nationalism – totalled not more than about one thousand persons before 1917 (Rus 2007: 62). Instead, under Russian rule the Moldovan language became increasingly associated with the peasant status of those who spoke it, while Russian language and culture, associated with urban life and the administrative elites, became increasingly desirable (Livezeanu 1981a: 329–335). An even stronger assigning of greater value to Russian language and culture proceeded in Transnistria, without provision for local autonomy. It therefore should not be surprising that in Bessarabia and Transnistria, the older term *Moldovan,* in reference to both the local population and its language, not only persisted but also retained significant social and symbolic meaning until the Soviet period and beyond. Soviet linguistic and nationalities policies manipulated local Moldovan identity but did not wholly create it.

Contemporary debates over Moldovan identity often address the apparent parallels between the Russification of Moldovans during the Russian imperial period and during the Soviet period. In fact, little intentional manipulation of Moldovan identity appears to have taken place during the imperial period. Bessarabia maintained a number of special administrative privileges, including the mandatory use of Moldovan as a public and administrative language, for more than a decade after its cession to the Russian Empire. The loss of privileges was gradual – for example, Moldovan lost its mandatory status in 1829, but Russian was not mandated as the sole official language until 1854, and Moldovan was not banned in educational establishments until 1867 – and followed general trends in Russian policy (van Meurs 1994: 48; King 2000: 22–23). In general, Russification policies intensified after 1860, eroding the rights of local boyars and curtailing political and cultural autonomy throughout the empire. Yet neither Bessarabia nor Moldovans formed a particular target of Russification.

The ethnic diversity of Bessarabia's population also increased during the period of Russian administration. The Russian government encouraged settlement there from central and western Europe, offering land, tax exemptions, freedom from military service, and other benefits to migrants, who included ethnic Germans, French Swiss, and Czechs (Hamm 1998b: 19). Bulgarians and ethnic Gagauz migrated to Bessarabia during the Russo-Turkish Wars, receiving land and military exemptions. Russian and Ukrainian religious dissenters and runaway serfs also crossed Bessarabia's fluid borders, as did Romanians from west of the Prut River. As a result, foreign visitors in the early twentieth century were particularly struck by the apparent mixture. For example, Emmanuel de Martonne, a French professor assessing Bessarabia's relationship to Romanian rule after World War I, described his inability to match appearances and languages among a group of men from Comrat: 'This man with a broad and beardless face, typical of the Little Russian, calls himself a Gagaoutze. The other styles himself a Bulgarian, but his kindly face with grizzled mustaches, his fur cap, as well as his racy Roumanian speech, remind me of the Oltean type of the Valachian Carpathians. … One of them, who claims to be Russian, calmly admits that his father is Moldovan and his mother Bulgarian' (de Martonne 1919: 10). Other ethnic communities that were highly visible in the early twentieth century, though far less so now, included Jews, Poles, Greeks, and Armenians.

During the first part of the twentieth century, the political histories of Bessarabia and Transnistria diverged even more sharply as Bessarabia became part of Romania and portions of Transnistria gained administrative identity as a Soviet autonomous republic. In the chaos of the Russian Revolution and the onset of World War I, Bessarabia's local government voted first for independence and then for union with Romania. During the inter-war period, Bessarabia was thus subject to the nationalizing projects of the Romanian state. The ethnic majority of Bessarabia had long considered itself and its language Moldovan, but inter-war Romanian policies attempted to persuade the Moldovans that they were actually Romanians by stressing the linguistic identity of the two languages as well as shared history and culture. Meanwhile, the Soviet Union established the Moldovan Autonomous Soviet Socialist Republic within Soviet Ukraine. The autonomous republic had two purposes, one being to provide some local administrative autonomy for the ethnic Moldovan population, recognizing its linguistic and cultural differences from the surrounding ethnic Ukrainians (van Meurs 1994: 78). The other, more strategic purpose was to provide a source of attraction for Bessarabia to (re)join the Soviet Union.

In contrast to Romanian policy, which stressed Moldovan as a regional variant of the Romanian language, Soviet policy emphasized the distinctiveness of the two languages. While Romanian policy in Bessarabia worked to replace Moldovan ethnic identity with a Romanian national identity, Soviet policy in the MASSR worked to elaborate a Moldovan national identity. Bessarabia's population deeply resisted the Romanian nationalizing project, which remained incomplete but nevertheless had lasting effects, especially among intellectuals. After 1940, Soviet policy in the Moldovan Soviet Socialist Republic continued to cultivate the idea that the Moldovan language and nation were distinct from those of neighbouring Romania, with substantial success but without erasing significant differences between the component territories.

Soviet Nationalities Policies and National Movements

Moldova's declaration of independence in 1991 followed several years of development of a national movement. In its early stages, minorities cooperated with ethnic Moldovans in the activities of the Popular Front, but differing agendas soon emerged. By 1991 the movement was dominated by ethnic Moldovans demanding recognition that the Soviet Union had distorted and falsified their national history. In addition to insisting that the Molotov-Ribbentrop Pact had illegitimately severed Bessarabia from Romania – and thus that Soviet rule in Bessarabia was fundamentally illegitimate – the most vocal sector of Moldova's national movement insisted that the majority population and language in Moldova should be called Romanian. The increasingly pro-Romanian orientation of the national movement led to the development of conflicts that I discuss later in this chapter.

The principle of nationality was central to the organization of the Soviet state and to the state's relationship with its citizens. The Soviet Union incorporated both territorial and national principles in its federal structure. In its final form, the union was composed of fifteen national republics, each with the status of soviet socialist republic (SSR). Initially, this form of organization was both a pragmatic response to the demands of powerful republics such as Ukraine and Georgia for national self-representation and an ideological effort to offset the effects of Russian imperialism by supporting the cultural, social, economic, and political 'development' of formerly colonized peoples. Each SSR was conceptualized as the political and territorial unit appropriate for the representation and government of a 'nation'.

The population of the Soviet Union, however, encompassed many smaller ethnic, linguistic, and religious groups, which were classified hierarchically according to size, level of development, and purported level of historical consciousness (Slezkine 1994; Suny 1995). Although the identification and classification of nationalities in the Soviet Union changed over time, by the 1980s common estimates had arrived at the figure of one hundred nationalities (Bremmer 1997: 3). Cultural hierarchy was matched administratively, albeit imperfectly, by the creation of autonomous soviet socialist republics (ASSRs), oblasts, and okrugs. By the early 1980s, fifty-three national groups had been assigned territory (to which they were the 'titular nation'). In addition to the fifteen union republics, twenty autonomous republics, eight autonomous regions (*oblasti*), and ten autonomous areas (*okruga*) had been created (Bremmer 1997: 8). Almost all the administrative units below the level of union republic were located in Russia, but all the republics had minority populations. Each administrative unit had responsibility for supporting the development of its titular group and for producing national socialist cadres. For this reason, early Soviet nationalities policy emphasized the codification of local languages, the establishment of native-language education, and the production of history texts, art, literature, and performing arts specific to each ethnic group.

Through the 1930s, ethnographers, linguists, historians, and other intellectuals actively and sincerely pursued these goals of 'affirmative action' (Martin 2001; Hirsch 2005).[13] This was particularly true in the case of the Moldovan Autonomous Soviet Socialist Republic, established in Soviet Ukraine in 1924, where empirical differences in spoken language and historical experience were elaborated through state-supported research institutions and plans (van Meurs 1994; King 1995). Language received particular attention as linguists in the MASSR codified and promoted a literary form of Moldovan in a sincere attempt to raise ethnic Moldovan consciousness and to validate Moldovans' experience as peasants vis-à-vis both bourgeois Romanians and Russian imperialism. In the 1920s the spoken language in Bessarabia and Transnistria showed signs of diverging from other Romanian dialects in ways that could justify the codification of a separate language (Dyer 1998: 73), which early Soviet linguists pursued. Soviet linguistics was not consistent, however, and by as early as 1938 the codification of Moldovan shifted away from sociolinguistic criteria towards the emphasis of formal linguistic criteria, beginning the process through which literary standard Moldovan would become nearly identical (except for its alphabet) with literary standard Romanian (King 2000: 88).

In later years the implementation of the twin Soviet goals of 'national in form and socialist in content' shifted to a more formal division in which titular languages were used in the arts, humanities, and social services of each republic while the Russian language dominated governance, economics, science, industry, and public life. This shift was due in large part to ideological changes in Moscow, but early efforts to nationalize republican

[13] Ethnographers continued to participate in the 'ethnographic processing' of empirical data to produce and reduce national categories for census and administrative purposes after the 1930s as well. The category 'ethnic Moldovan' appears to have been manipulated rarely, in comparison with other categories (Tishkov 1997: 17).

administrative units – particularly through employment-based language courses – met with a variety of forms of failure (e.g. King 1998). The shift was already occurring when Bessarabia was incorporated into the newly created MSSR in 1940, and residents of Bessarabia never acquired the loyalty to the Soviet project that residents of Transnistria did. By the 1980s, national movements had arisen throughout the Soviet Union in response to a growing perception that non–Russian speakers had become second-class citizens in their own republics, in direct contradiction to official ideological pronouncements. In Moldova, shifts in the linguistic study of Moldovan meant that the distinctions between literary standard Romanian and literary standard Moldovan that had existed in the early 1900s all but disappeared. Indeed, linguists throughout the world deny the existence of a separate Moldovan language (Rogers 1983; Timiras 1983; Dyer 1996). For Moldova's national movement, knowledge of this conclusion from abroad provided additional 'scientific' evidence that the Soviet Union had created Moldovan as an artificial language for purely political purposes.

The pro-Romanian orientation that had developed in Moldova's national movement by 1991 hides the complexity of the national question throughout the Soviet Union just a few years earlier. Ronald Suny (1998: 463–465), for example, identified four distinct types of ethnic problems that emerged in the last years of Soviet rule: tensions between ethnic minorities and titular nationalities at the republic level; resistance of non-Russians to Russian dominance; tensions over the status of ethnic Russians in the non-Russian republics; and the status of other groups living in diasporic conditions outside their 'home' republics. Although the resistance of non-Russians to Russian rule is now remembered as the most spectacular, because it generated the independence of the fifteen union republics, Suny pointed out that greater violence emerged in the tensions between ethnic minorities and titular nationalities. These tensions reflected the struggle of smaller minorities to gain higher status. Whereas all the Soviet Union's national republics contained minority populations, relatively few contained administrative units (autonomous republics, oblasts, or okrugs) for those minorities. In the late 1980s and early 1990s, smaller minorities throughout the Soviet Union demanded greater administrative and cultural recognition, according to the principles of Soviet nationalities policy.

In Moldova, the Gagauz and Bulgarian communities made such demands, as did Transnistria (Socor 1994a). The Gagauz reacted strongly to being legally defined in 1990 as an 'ethnic minority' and briefly even demanded the status of an autonomous republic (ASSR) within Moldova (Thompson 1998: 134; Demirdirek 1999) Under these conditions, mutual support between minorities and the ethnic majority in Moldova's national movement was fragile (Panici 2003: 38–39). Even after independence, the relative absence of tension between majorities and minorities depends on both legal and cultural factors (Demirdirek 1999).

In many cases, the ethnic conflicts of the early 1990s throughout the former Soviet Union reflected a contest between minorities striving to achieve representation according to a Soviet model and majorities who were busy discrediting the whole Soviet project in their efforts to create new nation-states. With the independence of the national republics, ethnic majorities have been able to forget the complexity of the late Soviet national movements. Now, too, ethnic Moldovan intellectuals discount the importance of Soviet definition, organization, and administration of nationality. For ethnic minorities, however, the basic principles of Soviet nationalities policies remain potentially important for advancing claims to territorial autonomy. In the Russian Federation, for example, politics have been marked by the continuity of overt debates about reforming the dual system of territorial and ethnic local government well into the 2000s (Tishkov and Filippova 2002). In Moldova, the legitimacy of Soviet nationalities policy has been more thoroughly discredited, but it remains a potential model for future collective action.

Nation-Building in the New State

Since 1991 the Republic of Moldova has pursued several approaches to nation-building. Nation-building activities in the early 1990s emphasized the ethnic model of the new state that had developed in the rhetoric of the national movement's last stages, but this provoked violent conflicts both in Transnistria and among the Gagauz. The governing Popular Front also gradually lost the support of the ethnic Moldovan majority, partly because of the country's growing economic crisis but also because citizens shifted their support in favour of more ethnically moderate parties (Crowther 1998).

Successive governments since 1994 have continually de-emphasized pan-Romanian rhetoric and increasingly emphasized Moldova's multiethnic character. Much of the language of the 1994 Constitution suggests a 'multiethnic Moldovan *Staatsvolk*' (Neukirch 1999: 52), and in 1995 Moldova outlined a 'foreign policy concept' that further established the country's official commitment to multiethnicity (King 2000: 170). The basis for a territorial approach to nation-building was set, however, as early as 1991, when Moldova extended citizenship to everyone born in the territory or resident in 1990.

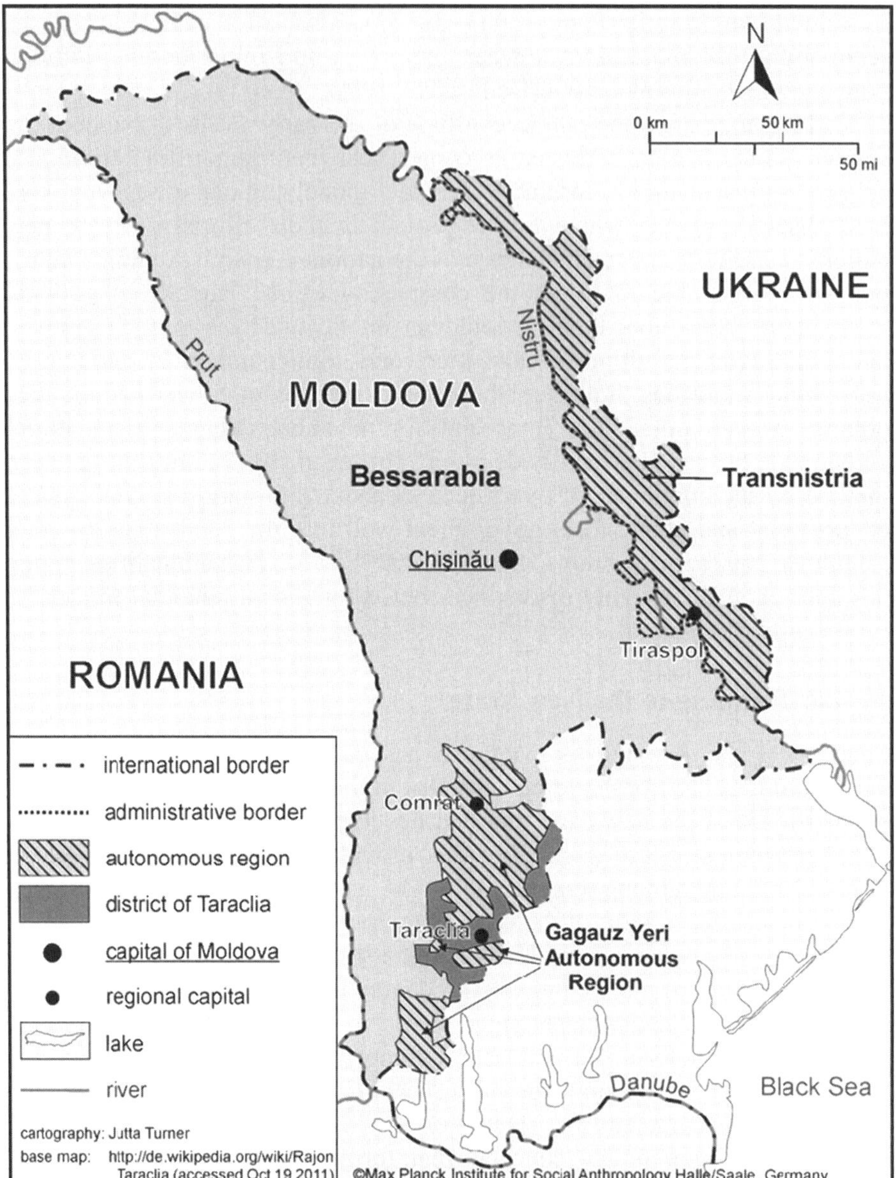

Map 3. Special administrative regions in the Republic of Moldova. In the wake of ethnic and regional tensions in the early 1990s, Moldova formed two special administrative regions, Gagauz Yeri and Taraclia County, to meet the political and cultural demands of its ethnic Gagauz and Bulgarian populations. Transnistria declared its independence from the Republic of Moldova but has no international recognition.

Indeed, Moldova's post-independence government recognizes its population as multiethnic and has created institutions to address ethnic issues. For example, the Department for the Functioning of Languages and National Relations (elsewhere shortened to Department of National Relations) is charged with both protecting the rights of ethnic minorities and promoting the use of Romanian as the state language. The state has also granted ethno-territorial autonomy to the Gagauz, with the formation of a semi-autonomous zone called Gagauz Yeri, and on a smaller scale to Bulgarians, with the creation of Taraclia County, which has an ethnic Bulgarian majority but otherwise has the same administrative status as other counties (Map 3). Gagauz Yeri is not a region of uniform Gagauz settlement but is composed of interspersed Gagauz, Romanian, and Bulgarian villages. This political solution to the tensions of the early 1990s has been touted as setting a precedent in eastern Europe of liberal relations between a state and its ethnic minorities (Socor 1994a, 1994b; Thompson 1998; Benk 1999).

The state has also engaged in an ongoing discussion with Transnistria about the possibilities for creating a 'common state' in which Moldova's government would be further federated along local and ethnic lines. Moldova's continued use of Russian as a major language of inter-state communication and its possible elevation of Russian to the level of a state language can also be cast as examples of respect for ethnic minorities. Thus Moldova's legislative reforms have generally received good reviews from the outside. At the same time, careful reviews of Moldova's constitution, ordinary legislation, and political process reveal that Moldova is less multiethnic than official statements advertise; it is still a 'national state with a titular nation and different national minorities' (Neukirch 1999: 53).

Public opinion surveys might suggest that ethnic Moldovans generally support government initiatives towards multiethnicity. For example, a series of surveys conducted in the 1990s (Crowther 1991, 1997, 1998) suggests that Moldova's Romanian-speaking citizens feel less ethnic chauvinism than do citizens of Romania.[14] Moldova's Romanian speakers also seem to share more political opinions with other ethnic groups in Moldova than they do with Romanians. Similarly, Charles King (2000) argued that 'Romanianism' (which included attempts to unify with Romania) had weakened as a force in Moldova's politics over the previous decade because post-independence politicians had gradually recognized the diverse political interests of

[14] Romania's ethnic composition is also strikingly different from Moldova's. The most recent figures record the population as 89.5 per cent Romanians, 6.6 per cent Hungarians, 2.5 per cent Roma, 0.3 per cent Germans, 0.3 per cent Ukrainians, 0.2 per cent Serbs, Croats, and Russians, and 0.2 per cent Turks. http://www.state.gov/r/pa/ei/bgn/35722.htm (accessed 31 October 2011).

Moldova's citizens. Despite the visibility of the pro-Romanian national movement in the late 1980s and early 1990s, King argued that Moldova's population at large was uninterested in uniting with Romania.

In my own research, I found people to have conflicting opinions about the state's organization of ethnic relations. I found, for example, that both Romanian and Russian speakers in the capital saw the 'republic of republics' as a joke. They saw the semi-autonomous zones of Gagauz Yeri, Taraclia County, and Transnistria as proof of the state's weakness and political ineptitude, not as positive indicators that the state was becoming increasingly stable because it was securing minority rights and promoting inter-ethnic harmony. This attitude reveals the strong appeal of the ethno-nation as a political model. It also reveals a deep mistrust among Moldova's citizenry regarding any interest the state displays in ethnic categories, identities, or relations.

In the years since my initial research, the state's approach to nation-building has continued to develop. On the one hand, little attention has been given to the pre-existing and growing differences between Transnistria and Bessarabia. The conflict with Transnistria remains unresolved. Evidence is mounting that a separate Transnistrian national identity is developing among all ethnic groups in the region (Chamberlain-Creangă 2008; Svet 2009, n.d.), and historical works are being produced to encourage this development (Solonari 2003). Thus, although the initial conflict is now widely regarded as a result of spiralling competition between local and central political elites (Kaufman 1996), actual reintegration of the two territories would necessitate new attention to differences in local political identities between Bessarabia and Transnistria. Indeed, a broader, regional, cross-ethnic identity contributed to the initial conflict as well, because even ethnic Moldovans in Transnistria feared the prospect of unification with Romania and the introduction of Romanian as the sole state language in the early 1990s (Kolstø and Malgin 1998: 104). For the time being, however, political elites and intellectuals in Bessarabia continue to assume that the common identity and interests of ethnic Moldovans on both sides of the Nistru are greater than their differences.

On the other hand, nation-building in Bessarabia has been a central element of national politics. Particularly significant to this process is the nearly decade-long tenure of the Party of Communists of the Republic of Moldova (PCRM) (referred to hereafter as the Communist Party) in the Moldovan parliament. In 2001, parliamentary elections produced a Communist government, which was re-elected in 2005. During its eight-year tenure, the Communist Party pursued a mixed agenda relative to nation-building. From the perspective of Western political analysts, the Communist Party's programs differed little from those proposed by the opposition (in March 2004), and its policies on education, history, and minority languages appeared to continue the general trend of supporting the development of a territorial nation. Yet local protests, as well as analyses of political ritual (Bîrlădeanu forthcoming; Cojocari 2007), suggest that the Communist Party pursued an altogether different strategy in defining the nation, which was to revive the representation and identity of Moldova as a component of the Soviet Union. Although the Communist government's project contained some elements of territorial nation-building, such as efforts to affirm the new state's identity with the medieval principality of Moldova, local scholars insist that it needs to be understood as qualitatively different from previous post-Soviet nation-building projects. This perspective is especially valuable for calling attention, once again, to the parallels between Soviet nationalities policy and more recent theories of multiculturalism. What appears new may in fact reflect continuity.

It is also striking that outside observers tend to view Moldova as experiencing political evolution while inside observers often experience political developments as repeating the past. This is particularly true for cultural specialists, including those most involved in folkloric ensembles, who remain vulnerable to the state dependency of cultural institutions and the politicization of professional appointments (Cash 2009). Political parties, however, also capitalize by reinvoking the political divisions, issues, and sentiments of the late 1980s and early 1990s. The most recent example of this occurred during the contested 2009 parliamentary elections, when four opposition parties succeeded in forming a coalition government. Throughout 2010, the new government attempted, with only partial success, to consolidate its power through a rhetoric that emphasized a return to the 'forgotten' values and agendas of the national movement.

In fact Moldova's political, economic, and social landscape has changed dramatically during the past two decades. Externally, the state has joined numerous international organizations, which influence its internal decision-making. From the perspective of identity questions, the Organization for Security and Cooperation in Europe (OSCE) and the Council of Europe are two of the most important of these organizations; both draw Moldova closer to European norms and values. Moldova has also been increasingly affected by the growth of the European Union (EU). Not only has Moldova signalled its desire to join the union, but since Romania's accession in 2007 it has bordered the EU and been subject to an increasing number of both benefits and restrictions related to neighbourhood policy (Popescu 2006; Skvortova 2006).

Internally, Moldova has lost as much as one-quarter of its population to economically motivated migration since independence (Heintz 2006; Keough 2006).[15] Moldova was deeply affected by the dissolution of Soviet distribution networks, which resulted in the closure of local factories and declining exports throughout the 1990s and 2000s and which left Moldova Europe's poorest country, with a remittance-based economy. With little industry and few natural resources, Moldova relies on agriculture as its primary source of export production, but export-scale farming is not easily achieved. Land reform was completed in 2001 with a highly equitable form of decollectivization, but laws on land sale and rental make it difficult to establish large private agricultural enterprises. Decollectivization has also reduced the productivity of individual growers, stalled the food processing industry, and led to a decline in the social services previously connected to collective farms (Gorton and White 2003; Lerman and Cimpoieş 2006). Outdated processing equipment, international quality standards, and saturated markets also make the export of traditional agricultural products (such as wine) to western Europe difficult. Russia thus remains Moldova's most important trade partner, but this economic dependency often makes Moldova vulnerable to Russian political pressure on sensitive issues, including Moldova's relations with Europe, treatment of Russian-speaking minorities, and relations with Transnistria.

Amidst such striking economic and social changes, it is difficult to believe that ethnic and national identities have not also been changing. Indeed, there is evidence that identities have been shifting. The terrain on which the state carries out nation-building is constantly in motion.

Change and Continuity in Ethnic Identity

The last census conducted in Moldova under Soviet rule revealed a multiethnic population consisting of approximately 65 per cent Moldovan speakers, 14 per cent Ukrainian, 13 per cent Russian, 4 per cent Gagauz, 2 per cent Bulgarian, and 2 per cent other. The 'other' category included Jews, a small but politically sensitive population of Roma (Gypsies) numbering 11,571 persons (King 2000: 176), and representatives of many other ethnic groups found in larger numbers elsewhere in the Soviet Union who migrated to Moldova for work or family reasons. This mixture of ethnic groups, defined

---

[15] Final census data from 2004 indicate a net loss of nearly 400,000 persons to permanent emigration and an additional 273,056 temporarily absent as labour migrants, while unofficial estimates from the same period arrived at figures of 600,000 to 1 million (Rowland 2009: 486). The International Organization for Migration continues to support a figure of some 600,000 (http: //www.iom.md/attachments/008_FAQ per cent20IOM per cent20Moldova.pdf, accessed 16 December 2010).

primarily by language, presents practical problems for the new state, most obviously in the domains of language policy and education. At a more abstract level, the multiethnic nature of the population challenges the state to create a national identity that recognizes and facilitates the political and social inclusion of its diverse citizenry.

The task of social inclusion has been made more difficult by changes in the ethnic balance since independence. The only census conducted since then – in 2004 – revealed a changed ethnic structure: 76 per cent Moldovan, 8 per cent Ukrainian, 6 per cent Russian, 4 per cent Gagauz, 2 per cent Bulgarian, and 1 per cent other (Map 4). In addition, 2 per cent of the population declared itself Romanian. The census was conducted hurriedly, with numerous difficulties, and the published data (http: //www.statistica.md) do not include figures for Transnistria. Yet whatever their shortcomings, the new figures reflect actual population changes. For example, during the late 1980s and early 1990s, large numbers of Russians and other non–ethnic Moldovans left Moldova for Russia and other Soviet republics. Between 1990 and 1994 this out-migration totalled more than 620,000 persons (Skvortsova 2002: 174). Migration into Moldova also increased during this time, as a result of similar processes of people returning 'home' or fleeing real or potential violence elsewhere in the Soviet Union. At the same time, these figures reflect changing social and political attitudes towards ethnic identity. The larger percentage of 'Romanians', for example, reflects the increasing number of persons who consider the linguistic, historical, and cultural differences between Moldovans and Romanians to be insignificant relative to their tremendous similarities. Similarly, the increased percentage of ethnic Moldovans almost certainly reflects the falling prestige of Russian identity under new state policies and social pressures.[16]

The ascription of ethnic identity to individuals was more flexible in Soviet Moldova than it might seem, precisely because language was used as the primary ethnic marker. Ethnic identity was fixed on a person's passport as his or her 'nationality', but other identities could be performed situationally and habitually. People from mixed families, those educated in second languages, and even those who simply preferred to use a second language could all claim multiple ethnic identities. In Soviet Moldova there were many such persons, and their preferred identity was overwhelmingly Russian.

---

[16] Transnistria conducted its own census in 2004, which is even less reliable by international standards than the Moldovan national census. It indicates different trends from those occurring in Bessarabia, with the percentage of ethnic Moldovans falling from 40 to 31.9 and the Ukrainian and Russian shares increasing, respectively, from 25 per cent and 23 per cent to 28.8 per cent and 30.4 per cent (Kolstø and Malgin 1998: 103; Rowland 2009: 488).

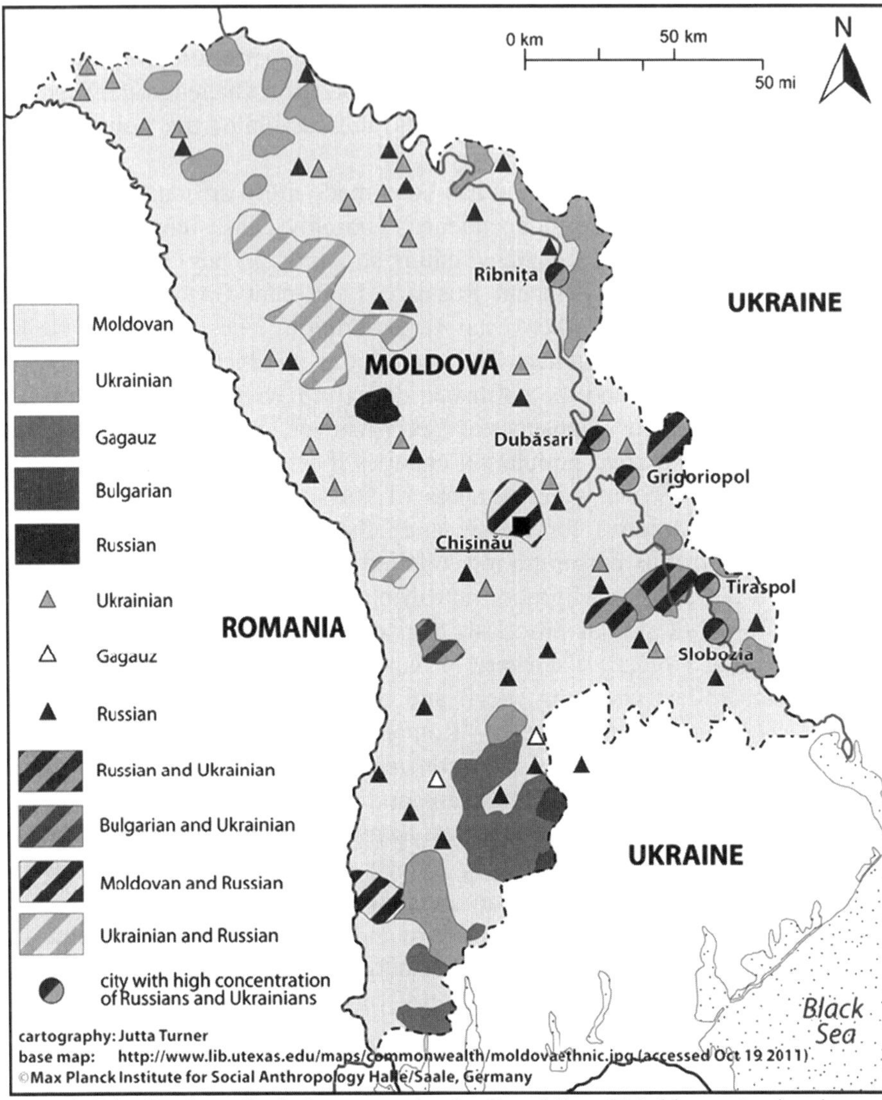

Map 4. Distribution of ethnic groups in the Republic of Moldova. At the time of independence, Moldova's ethnic majority constituted nearly two-thirds of the population and dominated rural areas. Ethnic Russians and Ukrainians predominated in urban and industrialized areas in the north and east of the country. Ethnic Bulgarians and Gagauz were concentrated in rural southern areas.

Between 1959 and 1988 the percentage of ethnically mixed families in the republic increased steadily, from 13.5 per cent to 21 per cent, and more than one-third of urban marriages were mixed by the end of the Soviet Union (Fisher 1980; Skvortsova 2002: 172). These were among the highest rates of intermarriage in the Soviet Union. Moldova had the highest rate for mixed urban families, and only Latvia, Ukraine, and Kazakhstan had higher total numbers of ethnically mixed families (Fisher 1980: 218).

Furthermore, by 1989, 40 per cent of all students studied in Russian-language schools, with the result that nearly 69 per cent of the population claimed Russian as a native or second language (Skvortsova 2002: 170–171). Among ethnic Moldovans in the capital city, 12 per cent claimed Russian as their native language, and only 44 per cent reported fluency in Moldovan (Skvortsova 2002: 171). Soviet policies that prioritized Russian as the language of inter-ethnic communication in the media and education, as well as those that promoted Russian speakers in industry and government, combined with older forms of prestige associated with being Russian and urban to increase the desirability of a Russian identity. By the late 1980s the Russian-speaking population – which briefly attained community consciousness in the early 1990s – included many people whose passports indicated that they were ethnic Moldovans or other non-Russian minorities (Solonar and Bruter 1994: 78). Thus, a number of indicators suggest that Soviet statistics on ethnic identity in Moldova reflect situational choices of identity by many persons, choices that might well have changed with the political and social changes of independence.

Yet the effects of changing statehood on the desirability of certain ethnicities remain unclear as of this writing. From some perspectives, the prestige of Russian identity is clearly declining. Some observers note a splintering within the Russian-speaking community as the non-Russian minorities included in it find value in reclaiming other ethnic identities. This was the case particularly for Germans, Jews, and Bulgarians in the immediate post-independence years (Solonar and Bruter 1994: 80–81). Even ethnic Russians differ in their relationships to Moldova and Russia as 'home' countries. As many as one-half of the ethnic Russians living in Moldova were born there, and up to one-third had ancestors living there before 1940 (Solonar and Bruter 1994: 76; Skvortsova 2002: 170). Migration to Russia was heavy in the early 1990s, but among the ethnic Russians who remained, many clearly think of Moldova as home. Indeed, nearly 40 per cent of Russians and Ukrainians resident in Moldova who were surveyed in 1991 had no intention of leaving, and another 31 per cent were undecided (Solonar and Bruner 1994: 86).

Language and educational reform during the early 1990s also had immediate effects on individual and family decisions concerning children's education. Between 1989 and 1993, for example, an additional 23,000 students joined Moldovan-language primary and secondary schools, while the number of students enrolled in Russian-language schools declined by 28,000

(Chinn and Kaiser 1996: 169). Enrolment in post-secondary (Romanian) courses also shifted to larger percentages of students studying in Moldovan than in Russian.[17] By 2007 the imbalance between ethnic identity and primary language of education that characterized the end of the Soviet period had shifted definitively. New statistics that year indicated that 79.6 per cent of primary and secondary schoolchildren studied in Moldovan, 20.2 per cent in Russian, and 0.2 per cent in other languages (Ciscel 2010: 22). These shifts represent both the increasingly positive reception of Moldovan and Romanian among all ethnic groups and new forms of state-organized restrictions on educational choice. Higher enrolments in Moldovan-language schools also reflect state-mandated closures and openings of schools and classes, as well as the reduction of Russian-language teaching cadres.

From other perspectives, Russian identity retains a large degree of desirability. Data from 1998, for example, reveal that although Russian identity was not the default identity for persons from mixed families at that time, it was still frequently chosen. The study found that among 25 persons from Russian-Moldovan families, 14 preferred a Russian identity for themselves, as did 6 out of 13 persons from Ukrainian-Russian families (Kolstø 2002: 37). Although these data represent a small sample, the figures, when compared with those from other former Soviet republics, such as Estonia, strongly suggest that Russian identity retained greater prestige than the titular identity in Moldova as late as 1998 (Kolstø 2002: 34). More recently, sociolinguistic guise tests carried out with university students have demonstrated that Russian continues to be perceived as a prestigious language in Moldova, even as Romanian also gains prestige. Significantly, recorded voices that are identified as speaking "Moldovan" in these tests, are perceived as less intelligent and self-assured than either Russians or Romanians, duplicating the lesser prestige of Moldovan ethnic and linguistic identity from the Soviet period (Ciscel 2007: 102).

What is clear is that changing statehood has not fixed ethnic identities, and individuals' relationships to ethnicity remain flexible, multiple, and situational. A 1998 survey of twelve hundred persons indicated that situational declaration of identities continued, although not equally in all ethnic groups. Ethnic Gagauz, Bulgarians, Germans, and Jews reported the same ethnic identity that was listed on their Soviet passports. Among ethnic Moldovans, Romanians, Russians, and Ukrainians, participants claimed a different identity from that listed on their passport at rates of approximately 1 to 5 per cent (Kolstø 2002: 33). Ethnic Moldovans were the most likely to report another ethnic identity. Some 6 per cent of respondents reported

---

[17] Although the language of instruction is Romanian, schools are usually identified as "Moldovan-language" schools.

multiple identities when given the option. When surveys combine questions about ethnic identity with questions about native, second, and preferred languages, they reveal further combinations for shifting self-ascription (see Kolstø 2002: 34–36). Similarly, sociolinguistic studies carried out in the early 2000s indicate that even combining factors, including self-ascribed ethnicity, language, family background, and social and political opinions, does not produce a matrix of identity categories that comfortably fit survey samples (Ciscel 2007: 87). Rather, people regularly reposition themselves socially, through the positions they take on 'ethnic' questions.

Ethnic, Civic, and Salient Identities

But what is the national identity of Moldova's population? The literature on nationalism generally acknowledges two kinds of national identity and nationalism: civic and ethnic. In the first, membership in a state is based on citizenship; in the second, only some citizens belong to the nation, and access to national identity is restricted by linguistic or cultural criteria. In fact the two types of nation occur on a continuum and can change over time. Anthony Smith, for example, wrote:

> There is, of course, a close relationship, perhaps even a dialectical one, between attempts to create a civic and territorial national identity and movements aiming to separate from that 'territorial nation' one or other ethnic community or category and fashion it into a new 'ethnic nation'. The more the leadership of the new states strive to create integrated nations out of a polyethnic mosaic, the greater the chances of ethnic dissent and even attempted secession wherever colonialism and nationalism have roused a returning intelligentsia to rediscover their ethnic past and its cultural heritage (Smith 1991: 134).

In Smith's view, ethnic dissent is particularly likely to emerge as postcolonial states attempt to consolidate a civic identity, because under colonialism social and state power is usually distributed disproportionately along ethnic lines. Thus 'ethnic competition for political power in the new states [is] sharpened' (Smith 1991: 133). Because the representation and exclusion of ethnic groups at the level of state power are both real and symbolic, Smith argued that the intelligentsia plays a critical role in determining the state's success or failure as a civic nation-state that grants full political sovereignty to all citizens, regardless of ethnic identity.

The intelligentsia is key to the ongoing process of defining the nation because the activities of its members cross the real and symbolic realms of social life. As Smith put it (1991: 65), the intelligentsia is engaged in a 'twofold strategy of providing 'maps' of the community, its history, its destiny and its place among nations, and of providing 'moralities' for the regenerated community, ones that could inspire present generations to emulate the public virtues deemed to express the national character'. In Moldova, the intelligentsia is faced with answering the ever-present question, Who are the Moldovans? In the past this question has been constructed primarily as a question about the relationship between the ethnic Moldovan majority and the neighbouring Romanians. Since 1991, Moldova's independence has shifted the secondary questions that will provide an answer to the first. Specifically, the intelligentsia must now ask whether the one-quarter to one-third of the population who are not Romanian speakers are also 'Moldovans', and it must provide new 'maps' in the form of representations, images, and narratives to explain its answers.

The strong vein of constructivism in the recent literature on nationalism suggests that intellectuals can create and implement virtually any vision of the nation they choose, by using language, historical narratives, folk traditions, and other cultural artefacts to build a common identity among citizens. As Ernest Gellner put it (1983: 56), the exact elements of culture chosen by nationalists are often arbitrary, and 'any old shred and patch [of culture] would have served as well'. Moldova's history challenges this view. In previous nation-building episodes in Moldova, it has not been so easy to elaborate shreds and patches of culture into national identities that support the state's legitimacy, stability, authority, and prosperity.

Moldova has already been subject to at least two deliberate nation-building projects, both of which ultimately failed. As part of inter-war Romania, Bessarabia experienced policies intended to promote Romanian language and culture and to advance Romanian speakers in local administration and education at the expense of other ethnic groups, especially Jews (Livezeanu 1995). These policies were also intended to replace the Moldovan identity of local Romanian speakers with a Romanian identity, but they failed to do so. Conversely, Soviet policies attempted to build a Moldovan identity among local Romanian speakers that severed their sense of connectedness to Romanians. On balance, the Soviet project had greater success, partly because it built on a real sense of difference from ethnic Romanians. Soviet nationalities policies also created a cadre of national Moldovan intellectuals who were acutely aware of their ethnic identity and embraced the work of elaborating cultural identity. Under broader Soviet conditions, however, this cadre of national intellectuals – among whom enter the people described in the subsequent chapters – was also acutely aware of its limited power and influence vis-à-vis Russian dominance in cultural, social, economic, and political life in Moldova.

Moldova's history of failed nation-building projects therefore invites a consideration of the circumstances under which Gellner's 'any old shred and patch' of culture will not do for the making of a national identity. As Akhil Gupta and James Ferguson (1997) explained, in order for an identity to exist, it must be authenticated and legitimated by the subjects who will adopt it. Yet identity creation is further complicated by the fact that subjects are reconstituted as subjects in the process of adopting or rejecting new identities: 'The subject is not simply affected by changing schemes of categorization and discourses of difference but is actually constituted … by them' (Gupta and Ferguson 1997: 12–13). It is easy to overlook the importance of legitimation and authentication when identity projects succeed in creating groups or communities, but their importance is more difficult to ignore when such projects fail. By considering unsuccessful 'nations', we can better understand 'why certain kinds of identities become salient … but also why some marks of distinction and difference do not form the basis of an identity' (Gupta and Ferguson 1997: 14).

Alexander Motyl (2001) also stressed the importance of understanding what makes some identities more salient than others and certain identity projects more likely to succeed. For Motyl, constructivist accounts of national identity failed to explore the importance of the 'lifeworld' – that is, the 'intersubjectively held knowledge claims that a group – *any* group – presumably takes for granted and that enables its members to communicate with one another' (2001: 62, original italics). Only certain articulations of the nation will 'make sense' within the confines of a particular lifeworld. As a set of 'ontological and epistemological claims' about the world itself, the lifeworld both shapes and constrains the way its members are able to imagine themselves as a community. From the successes and failures of past nation-building projects, it appears that the criteria for authenticity, legitimacy, and saliency that unite Moldova's population have not yet been adequately comprehended by would-be nation-builders. It remains to be seen whether any of the identity projects in process since independence, including that of the 'nation of villages' discussed in the following chapters, is more successful.

Chapter 3
Folkloric Ensembles and the State

The construction of national identity is a complex process with both structural and ideological dimensions. At the very least, the nation must be imagined as both a political and a cultural community; cultural boundaries and content must be located, created, and elaborated in ways that naturalize the state's boundaries; and both citizens and the international community of nation-states should be convinced of the nation's existence. In this triple process, nearly all theorists stress the important work done by 'nationalists', but who are they?

In Moldova, members of folkloric ensembles, and particularly the adults involved in organizing, directing, managing, and judging them, fill the role of nationalist by almost any definition. Chapters 4 and 5 analyze their activities more closely. This chapter, in contrast, outlines how the very existence of folkloric ensembles and their activities is structurally conditioned by the state. Individuals working with folkloric ensembles are not free to create and convey any ideology of their choosing. They are directly enabled and constrained to produce representations of Moldova as a nation, through the state's control of the cultural institutions where they work, its definition and valuation of 'culture', and its definition of performance genres. The 'newness' and consistency of the images and messages conveyed by folkloric ensembles is thus the reflection of an ongoing engagement between the state and culture producers about the role of culture in shaping and reflecting national identity.

Who is a Nationalist?

Theories of nationalism almost always identify nationalists with intellectuals, because the intellectual is 'an individual endowed with a faculty for representing, embodying, [and] articulating a message, a view, an attitude, philosophy or opinion to, as well as for, a public' (Said 1994: 9). Nationalists are thus those intellectuals who articulate visions of the nation for and to a public. Teachers and folklorists are almost always included in lists of likely nationalist-intellectuals, yet as Ronald Suny and Michael Kennedy (2001) emphasized, the identification of particular professions with intellectual functions, and especially with nationalism, varies by place and time. It is therefore necessary to distinguish the social context in which members of particular professions become nationalists.

Anya Peterson Royce and Robert Kemper (n.d.) made a similar, and stronger, point by abandoning the term *intellectual* in favour of *identity personnel.* Like Suny and Kennedy (2001: 5), who pointed out that anyone can temporarily fill the role of intellectual by articulating and transmitting ideas, Royce and Kemper noted that all individuals interact with others through social roles and are therefore constantly perceiving, defining, enacting, and redefining social identities. What distinguishes some individuals is that they take on explicitly defined and recognized social roles through which they are preoccupied with the deliberate documentation, construction, and communication of collective identities. Royce and Kemper (n.d.: 4–5) referred to these people who have a socially recognized responsibility for defining social groups as 'identity personnel' and defined four general role types among them: cultural stewards, entrepreneurs, conservators, and documenters. The roles are distinguished by the individual's position inside or outside the reference group and by whether his or her activity is directed towards defining the group for members or for outsiders. Together, the activities of identity personnel define the outer boundary of a culturally defined group as well as the more subtle inner boundary (see also Royce 1982: 30). Communities usually designate and authorize practitioners of particular occupations – artists, writers, and scholars, for example – to fill these four roles.[18] Persons holding such jobs or social positions are then expected, and expect themselves, to define collective identities.

Identity Personnel in Socialist States

Indeed, the socialist states of eastern Europe and the Soviet Union assigned a special role in the development of socialist society to intellectuals and artists as producers of culture. In Moldova, the term *oameni de cultură* (people of culture, culture workers, or cultural specialists) includes visual and performing artists, academics, and bureaucrats in cultural institutions. The term itself and the common identity and sense of purpose it carries (a theme to which I return in the concluding chapter) reflect the social role established for these

[18] All four roles of identity personnel are manifested in the folkloric community of Moldova. For example, judges at folkloric festivals act as cultural stewards, rewarding 'authentic' performances and correcting others. Ensemble directors act as cultural entrepreneurs when performing representations of local traditions on stage, and they behave as cultural conservators and documenters when they travel to villages to collect repertoire materials.

professions by the Soviet state to raise particular kinds of consciousness and feelings of identity, including national identity.

The relationship between the state and culture was so pronounced under socialism that some writers (e.g. Konrád and Szelényi 1979) have even suggested that the relationship between the two which one expects in capitalist societies was reversed under socialism. Instead of the intellectual's being defined in opposition to the state and living outside state influence and power, as Edward Said (1994) suggested, intellectuals in fact were in charge of the socialist state. Miklós Haraszti (1987) argued that artists, too, were at the 'heart of power' in socialist eastern Europe. Under socialism, 'intellectual activity and the structure of the state were like muscles and bones in an indivisible, organic unity' (Haraszti 1987: 18). Art, he argued, is not necessarily an expression of freedom; it can exist and flourish under authoritarian systems, as is revealed by the activities of 'state artists' in socialist countries, who not only became complicit in their own censorship but also were social planners. *Oameni de cultură* generally, and members of the folkloric community in particular, in Moldova would disagree that they ever controlled the state, although they certainly think culture should be central to the state's concern.

Katherine Verdery (1996) proposed a slightly different model from Haraszti's of the relationship between intellectuals and the socialist state, which comes closer to describing how and why culture producers in Soviet Moldova became thoroughly involved in the production of national identities. Verdery used historians in Romania as her primary example of intellectuals and explained that questions related to national identity proliferated throughout Romanian historiography, to the exclusion of other topics, because the state controlled the production of history. For example, it controlled the number of persons who could be trained as historians, overproducing cadres for the number of available positions. The state then arbitrated production, not only through the straightforward control of publication but also by using scarce positions, research funds, and awards to reward historians who produced especially desirable work, according to the state's taste. In this way, intellectual work was directly constrained by state-level concerns to develop national identity in particular directions.

Although Verdery's model does not account equally well for cultural production in all the socialist states, it is largely applicable to the Soviet state and to the Soviet Republic of Moldova within it. The Soviet state was not a monolithic, unified entity, but it was perceived as a distinct object and source of power because citizens constantly felt its presence through interactions with bureaucrats, institutions, legal codes and policies, as well as myriad forms of public discourse and culture (Gupta 1995; Trouillot 2001).

This perception of the state's agency in independent Moldova is even today built through a combination of institutions, policies, practices, and effects that carry out the work of governance. From this perspective, the formal organization of culture and cultural activities provides the social and political roles for culture generally and for folkloric ensembles in particular.

The Soviet state supported the widespread development of both amateur and professional folkloric ensembles in the Republic of Moldova, as in other republics throughout the union. To some extent, the state's commitment to folkloric activity merely reflected a more general support for cultural development that could be found in other forms, such as the well-developed system of 'culture houses' and libraries. Culture houses were generally charged with achieving 'cultural enlightenment' and promoting 'aesthetic education' among the masses (White 1990), but folkloric activity also contributed to other important political goals. From at least the 1930s, folkloric activity was linked to the development of national art forms and national cadres of intellectuals and to portraying and promoting images of the Soviet nations and the friendly relations between them (Martin 2000: 171). By the 1960s, the intentional use of folklore to encourage friendship among the Soviet peoples was well developed (Zemtsovsky and Kunanbaeva 1997) and drew the attention of foreign scholars following developments in Soviet folkloristics (Dorson 1976: 20). Some of the political goals for culture appear in articulations of Soviet cultural policy, but others were manifested primarily in cultural organization and practice.

Since independence, the Moldovan state has continued to support cultural and folkloric activity with little overt change in organization or practice. Soviet cultural policy, however, has been abandoned, along with official ideology and pronouncements concerning the importance of national art forms and friendship among the Soviet and socialist nations. Yet a new cultural policy has not been fully formulated, even after promptings from the Council of Europe. In the rest of this chapter I explore the de facto relationship between folkloric activity and the Moldovan state as it is manifested in the organization of folkloric activity. I look at the degree to which the state controls folkloric activity and sets political goals or parameters for the meaning and interpretation of folkloric performance. In particular, how does the state control the representation of national identity in folkloric performance? How does it shape the representation of the ethnic majority, ethnic minorities, and relations between them?

Cultural Policy in Soviet Moldova

In the second half of the twentieth century, cultural policy developed in a variety of forms internationally, with the common goal of harnessing 'culture' to achieve other political, economic, and social goals. Between 1960 and 1980, UNESCO encouraged and catalogued, in a book series totalling sixty volumes, the efforts of both socialist and capitalist countries to develop cultural policies (Shevchuk 1982: 73–74). The series supported the elaboration of cultural policy for a variety of political and social goals, and the individual volumes reflect broad interpretations of how policy should be articulated and by whom. For example, even though Belarus and Ukraine were republics of the Soviet Union at the time, they received volumes separate from that devoted to the Soviet Union, indicating that UNESCO supported the elaboration of policy at local and regional levels in addition to the level of the central state. In the new postcolonial states of Asia and Africa, cultural policy was identified as a cornerstone of national development – for harmonizing ethnic relations as well as advancing political and economic development (Marriott 1963). Some writers distinguished aspects of culture that promoted development from those that did not, advocating for a 'comprehensive policy on cultural revival' to cultivate only the most desirable aspects of culture (Ejofor 1984: 64).

Specialists in the domain of culture encouraged comparison among countries in order to develop policies that best matched a state's identity, even if the result was a decentralized approach in which the state exercised minimal control over or gave minimal financial support to culture. In the United States, for example, Frederick Dorian (1964) used comparisons with the policies of nine western European countries to argue that the United States, too, needed a clear cultural policy that would promote the development of democracy.[19] Since the 1960s, attention to cultural policy worldwide has only increased, with the establishment of university training programs, academic journals, and other research and monitoring organizations (Netzer 1978; Miller and Yudice 2002: 29). Yet since the 1990s, the scope of acceptable political goals and ideologies towards which a state should direct culture has narrowed substantially, to explicitly foreground democracy and diversity (de Cuellar et al. 1997). Thus, as the Republic of Moldova officially formulates new visions of the purpose of culture, including folkloric activity, it faces the constraints of internationally accepted standards and ideologies.

Even before the concept of cultural policy gained widespread currency in the post-war period, the Soviet Union supported the development of arts and culture for ideological reasons (e.g. Mally 1990, 2000; Fitzpatrick

[19] Folklore, however, rarely received high priority in the United States (Dorson 1976; Shay 2002: 40; Bulger 2003). For purposes of international diplomacy, for example, modern art and performance were prioritized (Cockcroft 1974), except when delegations considered it necessary to demonstrate American mastery of classic European styles (Prevots 1998).

1992). By the 1970s, official Soviet cultural policy held that cultural activity should have an educational function, and exposure to culture was expected to produce persons capable of and willing to build a Communist society (Zvorykin 1970). Moreover, Soviet cultural policy held that economic and political goals could be more easily reached if citizens were adequately educated and entertained. It was important to raise the population's 'cultural standard' because that improvement 'determines, in large measure, the progress made in technology, in the organization of production and in the social activity of the workers, the development of the principle of democratic self-government and the transition to a communist type of society' (Zvorykin 1970: 48).

In the Moldovan Soviet Socialist Republic, as elsewhere in the union, the positive benefits ascribed to culture supported the institutionalization and expansion of a wide variety of cultural activities. 'Culture' included the performing and plastic arts, literature, libraries, museums, and cinema. Most cultural activities in these categories were organized and overseen, at least indirectly, by the MSSR's Ministry of Culture, although that ministry responded in turn to indications from the Soviet Ministry of Culture.

The Soviet state thus deliberately encouraged the expansion of cultural activity in each of its republics. By the late 1980s even the most remote villages in Moldova each boasted a culture house, which served as the central point of cultural activity. Culture houses contained lending libraries for children and adults, village museums, and auditoriums for special performances, including themed holiday revues and festival events. They hosted children's, adults', and mixed performing groups and held handicraft workshops and film screenings. In 2002, the Moldovan Ministry of Culture reported the continued existence of 1,245 culture houses, 1,333 libraries, and 49 museums, but it also noted severe structural problems in more than 60 per cent of the buildings and a general decline in activity. By 2005, 22 of the culture houses had ceased operating (Tcacenco 2009: 133–134).

Throughout the Soviet period, statistics maintained by the Moldovan Ministry of Culture in Chişinău tracked the extent and expansion of cultural activity in the republic in order to document the population's increasing access to and participation in culture.[20] Between 1979 and 1986, the number of amateur associations in the whole USSR doubled, under orders from political authorities (White 1990: 85). Yet the type of culture in which people participated was relatively unimportant for officials at the republic level, and statistical categories did not keep pace with local-level changes

[20] The collecting of such data continues. Statistics from 2005 show that 65,329 cultural activities took place in Moldova that year, with audiences totalling 8.8 million persons (Tcacenco 2009: 136).

during the late Soviet period. As a result, in 2001 officials could not provide me with accurate calculations of folkloric activity as distinct from other cultural forms, although they themselves knew which performance genres were most widespread.

Although cultural activity was generally valued, folkloric ensembles served additional purposes for the Soviet state. In contrast to classical music and dance, for example, folk ensembles required significantly less equipment and were thus easier and less expensive to sustain in villages and rural regions. Folk ensembles were widely cultivated throughout the Soviet Union by the early 1930s. By 1934 folklore was widely promoted among the general population and considered 'very valuable'. In addition to the establishment of folklore clubs at farms and factories, folkloric materials were collected by 'teachers, agronomists, workers of machine-trade stations, and members of the collective farms' and published in local magazines and newspapers. In the 1930s folklore was also taught 'as a special subject in pedagogical institutions and universities' (Oinas 1961: 81). Folklore ensembles were similarly established in the Moldavian Autonomous Soviet Socialist Republic. News of their performances was spread through local newspapers and magazines such as *Krasnaya Bessarabia, Sovetskaya Moldavia, Molodoj Moldovei, Komsomolskaya Pravda,* and *Trud* from 1936 onwards.[21]

Folkloric forms were also explicitly encouraged for the purpose of building national art forms (Doi 2002). Amateur ensembles provided leisure activities but also groomed talented youths to perform professionally, whether in folk or European genres. Meeting a 'professional' standard was, indeed, one of the goals of amateur ensembles (Zemtsovsky and Kunanbaeva 1997: 11–12). In my interviews with local ensemble directors in Moldova, they now reverse the value hierarchy implied by official Soviet policy, asserting that traditional forms of music and dance are not 'simpler' but foundational. The musician Petru Dinjos, for example, explained that young

---

[21] Although Soviet policy makers explicitly articulated some rationale for encouraging folkloric performance, they also responded to existing legacies of folkloric performance. At the end of the nineteenth and beginning of the twentieth centuries, folklore was already being collected in Bessarabia (e.g. Madan 1897; Arbore 1899, 1906). Folklore collection continued throughout inter-war Romanian rule, and published collections from this time are housed in Moldova's national library (e.g. Buzdugan 1922, 1928; Teodorescu-Kirileanu 1922; Codreancu and Ştefănescu 1931; Madan 1932). Foreigners also conducted fieldwork in Bessarabia – for example, the Austrian scholar of Romance languages Matthias Friedwagner, who published his work for Romanian audiences in both Romanian and German (Friedwagner 1927, 1931). Folk ensembles, as well as the collection and replication of folklore and costumes, had already been encouraged under inter-war Romanian rule in Bessarabia (Livezeanu 1995: 102–119). Some dance circles formed prior to Soviet rule were especially powerful, such as the one in Giurguleşti, which taught dances to the newly formed state ensemble Joc in 1949 (Curbet 2005: 13).

children should learn to play traditional wooden recorders, flutes, and clay ocarinas before standard wind and reed instruments. Pavel Popa, a specialist at the National Centre for Folk Arts, explained that Moldovan children begin dancing in traditional concerts as early as six or seven years old but do not start ballet lessons until fifth grade. For both men, local performance forms were appropriate for the early stages of children's physical and artistic development.

Moreover, the cultivation of folk ensembles during the Soviet period facilitated cultural diplomacy, not only internationally but also through the internal Soviet system of festivals, travelling concerts, and command performances for inter-republic tourism and delegations. Certainly opportunities to travel abroad were among the reasons former performers gave me for having danced and sung in ensembles throughout their teenage years.

Folkloric activity in independent Moldova continues without an explicit political justification, because the country has not yet adopted a new cultural policy. In 1999 Moldova's Ministry of Culture joined the Council of Europe's Cultural Policy Review Program. After two years of work, the review committee published a preliminary set of recommendations for Moldova in October 2001 (Council of Europe 2001).[22] The reviewing has continued with additional projects led by the European Cultural Foundation and the German Marshall Fund of the United States, but implementation of key recommendations has been slow (Ohana 2008a, 2008b: 16–17). Since at least 2004, specialists in cultural policy at the Soros Foundation and the Centre for Cultural Policies (Centrul de Politici Culturale) in Chişinău have been promoting the establishment of a fund for culture to provide some grant money for special initiatives, in addition to the Ministry of Culture's annual budget. In December 2009, cultural specialists finally voted in favour of petitioning the government to establish such a fund. A comprehensive policy, however, has yet to be articulated.

---

[22] The review takes a strong multiculturalist perspective and specifically equates multiethnicity with multiculturalism, urging the Moldovan Ministry of Culture to promote the 'multinational' and 'multi-lingual composition of the Moldovan population … as a self evident cultural strength' (Council of Europe 2001: 37). This review is only one example of many in which international organizations have encouraged multiculturalism at the state level in Moldova. I have written elsewhere (Cash 2007) about the subtle but significant differences in the ways local culture producers, including members of the folkloric community, define culture and perceive their roles relative to the state. The review does note, accurately, that the cultural contributions of Moldova's ethnic groups could be more thoroughly supported by more active collaboration between the Ministry of Culture and the Department of National Relations. This department provides organizational support and advice for ethnically defined NGOs. Few of these NGOs foreground cultural heritage activities or classes, but the department organizes two festivals annually that highlight minority cultures and folklores.

Amateur Activity or Folklore? The Postsocialist Organization of Culture

The organization of culture and folkloric activity in the Republic of Moldova thus continues to resemble strongly that of the Soviet period, but without an overtly articulated policy or ideology that outlines the role of culture or its relationship to the state. Organizational categories and definitions of genres, however, shape folkloric activities even without an explicit policy.

One of the most important features of any folkloric ensemble in Moldova, for example, is its status as either a professional or an amateur formation.[23] Professional folkloric activity is highly visible and a source of local pride. There are four well-known professional ensembles performing folk music that were established during the Soviet period – Fluieraş, Bucurie, Mioriţa, and Noroc – as well as Joc, the state ensemble of folk music and dance (Zelenciuc and Guboglo 1979: 37).[24] In the Soviet period, Joc travelled extensively in the Soviet Union and abroad to represent the Republic of Moldova. A sixth professional folk dance company was recently established in the city of Comrat, the capital of the semi-autonomous Gagauz region, with a core of former Joc dancers. Numerous professional individual vocalists also specialize in *muzică populară*, one of the types of recognized folklore. These singers have loyal fans and are greeted with great enthusiasm when they perform.

Professional individuals and ensembles give concerts for paying publics, free public concerts, and private concerts. Their talents are particularly visible around major holidays. The month of March sees a large number of folkloric performances in celebration of the holiday Mărţişor.[25] Folkloric

[23] Donna Buchannan's (2006) ethnography of folkloric performance in socialist Bulgaria described a fuller range of professional folklore than I do here, but there are many parallels, especially because Bulgaria's official organization of culture followed the Soviet model.

[24] These ensembles all have Romanian names. The first two translate, respectively, as 'little flute' and 'happiness', and the fourth, as 'luck'. The third name is essentially untranslatable. *Mioriţa* refers to the faithful sheep in a Romanian ballad who warns her master that two other shepherds intend to kill him. Thus forewarned, the shepherd does not attempt to save his own life but instructs the *mioriţa* to tell his mother that he has settled in a new and wonderful country. Each of the names carries a strong connotation of Romanian culture, illustrating that 'national' culture in the Soviet period was associated primarily with the titular nationality. They also reveal that firm distinctions between Romanian and Moldovan culture and identity were not achieved during the Soviet period, even at a symbolic level. The name Joc means 'dance'.

[25] The name of the holiday is a diminutive of 'March' in Romanian and also refers to a small decoration made of red and white thread. The decoration is traditionally given at the beginning of March and then worn until it falls off or until the end of the month, when it is ritually disposed of. The tradition is practiced throughout the Balkans, especially in Macedonia and

performances may also be incorporated into the celebration of state holidays and into local celebrations and commemorations, with both professional and amateurs performing. The tenth anniversary of territorial autonomy in Gagauz Yeri, for example, was marked by an afternoon of folkloric performances, and patron saint's day celebrations (*hram*) in villages and cities often feature folkloric performances. In addition, professional musicians often perform in restaurants, at weddings, and at other family celebrations, enhancing the sensation that folklore is omnipresent in Moldova.

In the rest of this chapter and the following ones, however, I concentrate on the activities of amateur ensembles, and most specifically on those organized for children and adolescents, for two reasons. First, the folkloric movement in Moldova and the new types of ensembles it promoted were propagated most thoroughly through amateur ensembles. Thus, it is the amateur ensembles that most clearly reflect new visions of the nation, coinciding with the national movement of the late Soviet period and the establishment of Moldova as a new state. Second, all amateur artistic activities are still meant to have a pedagogical and socializing effect on participants. Anne White (1990: 75) concluded at the time of independence that most ensembles were 'too busy preparing for concerts' to fulfil this function, but I argue that the teaching and training undertaken by these ensembles occur precisely during the ongoing preparation for judged performances. Members of the folkloric community strongly believe that they are preparing future professional performers who will fulfil the role, not only of entertainer, but of *purtător de cultură* (a carrier and transmitter of traditional culture and values). In practice, members of folkloric ensembles do not learn 'about' folklore (as I had initially imagined they might); they learn 'folklore' in the form of songs, dance, and a variety of rituals.

The organization and operation of amateur folklore ensembles in the Republic of Moldova reflect significant continuity with the Soviet organization of culture and leisure. Unlike the decentralized clubs and dancing circles likely to be encountered in non-socialist Europe or the United States (e.g. MacKinnon 1994; Bröcker 1996; Shay 2002: 19), amateur folkloric performance groups in the Soviet Union were organized deliberately and overseen by the state through houses of culture, Pioneer houses, local schools, and factories and economic enterprises. Each of these institutions was subordinate to a republic-level institution such as the Ministry of Culture, Ministry of Education, or trade union. Simultaneously, they were subordinate to local government. Although people working directly with ensembles could and did initiate new activities – as the Komsomol activists studied by Alexei

---

Bulgaria, but was elaborated by local culture workers during the Soviet period as a specifically Moldovan tradition and holiday (Cojocari 2011).

Yurchak (2006) did – the state ultimately set and monitored the basic scope, purposes, and range of activities undertaken by a folkloric ensemble. Moreover, because each republican ministry reported to a Soviet-level ministry, many of the choreographic materials, training methods, and ideological orientations used by local ensemble directors ultimately originated in Moscow or were perceived to have done so.

Although several organizations facilitated amateur performances, the Ministry of Culture in each republic held primary responsibility for organizing cultural activities throughout the republic. The ministry's central administration was divided into separate sectors for the plastic and performing arts, museums, publishing, and libraries. Republican institutions such as the national library; major museums, theatres, and performance halls; the centre for folk arts; music and art schools; and artistic unions also fell under the direct administration of the Ministry of Culture. In Moldova, as in the other republics, cultural activities and trainings in villages and towns were in principle overseen and administered through *raion*-level directorates of culture in coordination with the ministry. In practice, the structural independence of local directorates of culture from the ministry, like the independence of the local administrative units to which they were directly subordinated, was heavily curtailed.

The formal organization of culture has changed little since Moldova gained independence. Changes have included (1) the severing of subordinate ties to the Soviet Ministry of Culture in Moscow; (2) a severe reduction of funds in all domains of cultural activity, especially in villages; (3) the moderate appearance of non-state financial resources (e.g. grants, international projects, individual and corporate sponsorship); (4) the limited appearance of non-governmental organizations (NGOs) and cultural foundations to represent the interests of particular cultural sectors; and (5) an increased independence from state support for some cultural agents, especially individual artists and performers (see also Ohana 2008b: 17–23). Each of these changes is significant for folkloric ensembles, yet the overwhelming structural continuities generate important constraints on and motivations for contemporary folkloric activity.

Most significantly, the majority of children's ensembles in Moldova are still organized through the Ministry of Education and the Ministry of Culture. The Ministry of Education is responsible for schools, the system of former Pioneer houses, now called creativity centres (*centre de creație*), and the former Pioneer Palace, now called the National Palace of Creativity for Children and Adolescents or simply the 'National Palace' (fig. 3.1).[26] Local

---

[26] In 2001, organizational charts like that shown in the appendix were not readily available for Moldova, and I compiled the chart myself. Such charts are now increasingly prominent on

departments of education are responsible for the local creativity centres. This means that in Chişinău, the municipal Department of Education is responsible for five creativity centres while the national Ministry of Education is responsible for the National Palace.[27] The National Palace runs activities much like those offered in the city's five local creativity centres but is administered separately. There are forty creativity centres throughout the country, one for each of the local Soviet administrative units (*raione*). When the country was redistricted into larger *judeţe* (a term taken from Romania's administrative system), in 1998, local administrations received additional creativity centres, but the return to a structure of thirty-two *raione* in 2003 largely reversed this situation.

The Ministry of Culture organizes children's ensembles through its art schools and culture houses. Local administrations have directorates of culture, which are directly responsible for the culture houses as well as local libraries. The local directorates of culture are overseen by both the Ministry of Culture and the local administration. Whether organized within the system administered by the Ministry of Culture or the system administered by the Ministry of Education, individual folkloric ensembles have similar relationships to state and local governments. The major difference is that the Ministry of Education's National Palace, which sponsors folkloric groups, has no direct equivalent in the Ministry of Culture. The National Centre for Folk Arts (Centru Naţional de Creaţie Populară) primarily sustains adult activities and does not sponsor ensembles. It has organizational connections to children's ensembles only through adults who work with children, and in this capacity the centre offers seminars and workshops, functioning as a general source of expertise on folk arts in Moldova.

The end products of all these institutional links are the ensembles, festivals, competitions, and seminars that proliferate in independent Moldova. The seminars provide staff at local culture house and creativity centres with ongoing training, the results of scholarly research in folklore and ethnography, assistance in choreography, and expert advice.

As during the Soviet period, the formal relationship between local and national governments in Moldova continues to affect the organization of culture, education, and ethnic organizations. Local and national governments are still organized as parallel structures, so that each *raion* has organs analo-

---

government websites, but the Ministry of Culture still lists only its departments and subordinate institutions, without a corresponding graphic representation of hierarchy, parallels, and coordination. See www.mc.gov.md/structura and /instit_subord (last accessed 23 June 2011).

[27] There are five centres with activities related to the plastic and performing arts. In addition, Chişinău's municipal Department of Education operates four centres for the technical arts (technical modelling, drafting, design), two for natural and ecological activities, and one for touristic activities (hiking, camping, orienteering).

gous to those of the national government. Instead of a ministry of culture, each *raion* has a directorate of culture; instead of a ministry of education, it has a directorate of education; and so on. Although state-level ministry officials say this arrangement gives local directorates of culture autonomy for cultural programming, in practice local government and administrative organs often find themselves still supervised by the national government. Even local culture houses, schools, and their employees can easily be affected by the ideological orientation of the majority party in power at the state level.

At both national and local levels, amateur folkloric ensembles are organized under a number of different titles. This makes it difficult to identify, classify, count, or control their activities, even as they are felt to be a ubiquitous presence among the performing arts. Three types of folkloric ensembles are generally recognized today – *folcloric, etno-folcloric*, and *popular* – each distinguished by the perceived authenticity of its repertoire. *Folcloric* and *etno-folcloric* ensembles perform folk songs, dances, and ritual sequences that its members have collected either from their home villages (in the case of *etno-folcloric* ensembles) or from a limited number of identifiable villages (in the case of *folcloric* ensembles). *Popular* ensembles have no such restrictions on the authenticity or origins of their repertoires. Like its Russian equivalent *narodnyi*, the Romanian term *popular* can be translated with regard to the arts as either 'national' or 'amateur'. In certain genre categories, most notably theatre, the term can therefore refer to either folkloric or amateur activities.[28] In addition to theatrical groups, which may or may not perform folkloric materials, there are also many ensembles with folk-inspired repertoires among bands (*fanfar* or *taraf*) and choirs.

The distinctions among the three types of ensembles are new and are not reflected in the organizational structure of amateur activities, which continues to follow Soviet principles for classifying the performing arts. The Soviet classification system privileged a primary distinction in the performing arts between dance, music, and theatre and then subdivided those catego-

[28] Writing about amateur theatre in the first decades of the Soviet Union, Lynn Mally (2000) recounted the debate over the Russian adjective to be used as the descriptor for non-professional theatre. *Narodnyi* became increasingly used after the 1930s, but it raised a debate over how 'national' the repertoire of an amateur theatre should be. Was national theatre to stick to a national language (i.e. not Russian), to folkloric motifs, to works written by 'national' playwrights, or to some other criterion? Mally's research focused on amateur theatre in Russia, not in the national republics. Nevertheless, the three categories of ensembles in Moldova suggest the presence of a similar debate there. A contact at the Ministry of Education explained that a drama group described as doing *teatru popular* might be doing ordinary drama (as amateurs, therefore *popular*), or it might be doing folk theatre (i.e. traditional forms of oratory and dramatic events linked to specific holidays).

ries according to generally accepted European classifications, with a few specific distinctions.

Unofficial Genres: *Folcloric* and *Etno-Folcloric* Ensembles

Describing the classification of genres within the performing arts illustrates key aspects of the relationship between folklore and the state. Vilmos Voight (1976: 491–493) pointed out that genres 'develop according to social and artistic standards', and typological hierarchies are likely to reflect these. Certainly, the typology still in use by the Moldovan Ministry of Culture both undervalues and continues to support folkloric forms. In Moldova as elsewhere, genre categories are not ordinarily questioned, and whether applied to folklore studies or the arts, they are assumed to be primarily 'classificatory categories for the organization of cultural objects' (Bauman 1992: 57). Yet genres are, more accurately, 'elements of social practice ... both grounded in and constitutive of social relations, implicating a range of conceptions of speaker and audience and defining a range of possible meanings' (Bauman 1992: 58; see also Kallberg 1996: 4, 8–9). In this case, the 'range of possible meanings' reflects the Soviet state's concerns with modernity and mass entertainment and leisure as counterparts to its concern for cultivating national identities. In turn, the continuity of the Soviet classification system, and the lack of modifications to it reflecting new ideas about the importance of authenticity in folkloric performance, hints at the many ambiguities in the status and role of the folkloric movement.

Calculations of the extent of folkloric activity in Moldova are thus only estimates, but by any account it is the most widespread genre of amateur cultural activity. The Ministry of Culture, for example, provided data drawn from eleven counties and the city of Chişinău on children's 'artistic formations' for the year 2000 (table 3.1). These figures reflect 1,479 performance groups, with a total participation of some twenty thousand children. Although the officials with whom I spoke could not distinguish precise numbers of participants per category of group, they agreed that the five most frequently represented categories were *folcloric* and *etno-folcloric* formations, *fanfare* (marching or brass bands), *popular* music orchestras, *popular* dance groups, and choirs. Among these five, only choirs were not usually considered folkloric groups.[29] The remaining ensemble types were folkloric

[29] The folkloric quality of choirs raises an interesting discussion. Choirs are generally considered non-folkloric, for two reasons. First, Andrei Tamazlâcaru, a leader in the Moldovan folklore movement, maintains that choirs were not organized in villages before the Soviet period, so they are not traditional from a village-based perspective. Second, choirs do not necessarily sing folkloric pieces. They may sing religious or world music pieces, for example. When they do sing folklore, the pieces are usually composed. Thus, even choirs with folkloric

theatre, *popular* theatre, youth theatre, puppet theatre, ballroom dancing, and 'light' (pop-rock) music ensembles (fig. 3.2). The director of the National Centre for Folk Arts provided another estimate of amateur ensemble participation, calculating that each of Moldova's eleven counties had at least three hundred ensembles. This figure, which included adults' and children's ensembles of all genres, meant that more than 3,300 performance groups and perhaps as many as 44,600 persons were active in a country with a population of some 4 million people.[30]

Table 3.1. Children's Artistic Formations in Moldova, 2000.

County	Number of Groups	Number of Participants
Taraclia	58	866
Bălți	274	3,715
Edineți	210	2,835
Soroca	136	1,457
Chișinău	101	2,116
Ungheni	102	1,184
Orhei	173	2,281
Lăpușna	165	2,072
Tighina	75	668
Cahul	65	816
Găgăuz Yeri	53	859
City of Chișinău	67	1,140
Total	1,479	20,009

Source: Figures compiled by V. Melnic, Ministry of Culture, June 2001.

repertoires stand a good chance of being 'inauthentic'. Nevertheless, some individual choirs are respected for their authentic performances of folklore. In this respect, the folkloric quality of Moldova's choirs is distinct from those of Latvia, where choral singing dates to the late sixteenth century, and song festivals began in 1873 (Carpenter 1996: 97). Members of Moldova's folkloric movement acknowledge inspiration from the resurgence of song festivals in the Baltics and thus are especially careful to mark the local authenticity of choral singing. They do not generally acknowledge any inspiration from the Russian folkloric movement, despite its claims to have preceded other national movements (Levin 1996).

[30] Iulia Paladi, director of the National Centre for Folk Arts, personal communication, 19 March 2001. I multiplied the number of ensembles calculated by Paladi by the average number of participants indicated in the Ministry of Culture figures in table 3.1 (i.e. 13.5 persons per ensemble), to arrive at a likely maximum. Adult ensembles generally have fewer participants than children's groups, and neither set of figures accounts for the possibility of the double-counting of persons who participate in more than one ensemble.

As these data indicate, many varieties of folklore are being taught to and performed by children in Moldova, but the varieties are not rigorously defined or tracked by the state. Rather, the state tracks the number of performing groups, the geographical-administrative distribution of performing groups, and the approximate number of performers. In some cases, ensembles recorded in the statistics may only be 'potential' groups that do not rehearse or perform regularly, but can be called into existence on important occasions (cf. Habeck 2011: 9). Even with the inadequacy of statistics, it is clear that since the 1980s, the number of *folcloric* and *etno-folcloric* formations has grown. Yet neither category is officially recognized in the state's classificatory scheme, meaning that all such ensembles are officially counted as other types.

Folcloric and *etno-folcloric* ensembles are distinguished in opposition to *popular* ensembles. Superficially, a *popular* group is characterized by a lively presentation of music and dance, with few dramatic sequences. *Folcloric* and *etno-folcloric* performances are more likely to include longer dramatic sequences, and many have slow-paced music and singing, although their dances are still fast and strongly accentuated. Insiders, however – meaning those who organize, direct, and judge folkloric activities – identify *popular* groups by their repertoires, which are composed, stylized, and designed especially for stage performance. *Popular* repertoires are often ethnically mixed; during the Soviet period such mixed repertoires facilitated performances demonstrating the international friendship of Soviet people. Today, specialists may respect *popular* ensembles for the artistry of their performances but insist that their repertoires are not 'real' folklore. In contrast, *folcloric* and *etno-folcloric* groups try to incorporate more accurate interpretations of music, dance, and dramatic ritual or traditional materials from villages in Moldova.[31] Specialists differ in their use of the three terms, sometimes treating *folcloric* and *etno-folcloric* as synonyms. The distinctions given to me by Pavel Popa in March 2001 were as follows:

1. *Etnografic* or *etno-folcloric*. These ensembles are based in villages, use material from the village in which they are based, and reproduce traditional materials without much adaptation for the stage. These are like museums, simply preserving the material.
2. *Folcloric*. Ensembles of this type are occupied with propagating traditional materials on stage.
3. *Popular*. Popular ensembles are found in large villages or cities. They take material from villages and present it on stage. These are

[31] Some groups also include music and dance taken from villages in Romania and Bukovina (Ukraine).

> the most dangerous form of ensemble because their renditions of traditions can be bad. Their repertoires are built from expeditions to villages. In this sense, the programs of these works are 'copies' and may be bad, if the original was bad, or if the copying process is bad.

These definitions focus on two related themes: the closeness of a performing group to the source of its repertoire, and the degree of stylization involved in stage performance. By this definition, none of the groups based in the capital city at the time of my fieldwork should have been considered *etno-folcloric* groups, because none performed a repertoire drawn from the city's own communities. Yet several ensembles claimed exactly this status. In the absence of official definitions or regulations, the distinctions between the three types are frequently blurred in practice and are subjects of ongoing negotiations over folkloric authenticity, as I describe in subsequent chapters. Here, I return to the organizational relationship between children's folkloric ensembles and the state.

As the foregoing description and accompanying diagrams demonstrate, folkloric performance is organized and sustained at a number of points in Moldovan society, primarily by the state. Folkloric genres abound in amateur activities, but the state supports them primarily as performative, not ideological, experiences. The state lacks definitions and other criteria with which to control folklore, except as a generalized performance genre. Instead, the development of repertoires, criteria for performance, and structure of relationships between performers and audience depend on the working relationships established between ensemble directors and the 'experts' in the national organizations. New *folcloric* and *etno-folcloric* ensembles also deliberately cross generic boundaries as they seek to (re)produce traditional, village-based performance styles. For all these reasons, local specialists argue that the folkloric movement of the 1980s effectively de-ideologized folklore, even though the structural relationship between the state and the performing artists has changed little.

Folkloric performance remains vulnerable to organizational changes within the state (Cash 2009), but the creation of new types of performances and of venues such as festivals in which to develop them allows folklorists and performers to articulate visions of national identity and belonging that are not overdetermined by the state. Some aspects of the relationship between the state, intellectuals, and cultural production described by Katherine Verdery (1991) as typical of socialist states are still applicable for understanding post-Soviet Moldova, but many are not. The institutions (including ensembles) and individuals responsible for culture, education, and the development of ethnic relations in Moldova are all officially subordinated to the state, but the state cannot constrain intellectuals to produce a national ideology according to its own needs and interests. The state no longer has exclusive control over education, the press, or employment; it no longer provides full, or adequate, financial support for many of the institutions over which it has administrative control. The Moldovan state lacks the material incentives to ensure that society complies with its preferred ideologies, and indeed, the new state has no clearly or consistently articulated ideology in the form of a cultural policy. Rather, individuals within the state organizational structures that support folkloric performances see themselves as having participated in a series of victories over the Soviet state during the past twenty years and have an ambivalent relationship with the current state.

In 2005 the National Centre for Folk Arts proposed a new government regulation on the activity of amateur artistic formations, which was approved in October 2006. The regulation introduced the category *formație folclorică* (folkloric formation), which would 'research, evaluate, and promote authentic folklore, customs, and popular traditions' and whose members would wear 'national costume corresponding to the folkloric hearth (i.e. home)'. In addition, the regulation defined three categories of *popular* ensembles – music and dance, dance, and orchestral (*taraf*) music. The classification scheme did not explicitly distinguish levels of authenticity to which the three *popular* forms should adhere, but all three were required to 'promote', or propagate, traditions. The new categories still do not fully reflect the range of distinctions that members of the folkloric community apply to performance ensembles. For example, the regulation defines no separate category of *etno-folcloric* ensemble. Certain ambiguities also remain, such as exactly how 'the folkloric hearth' is to be interpreted. Although judges at folkloric festivals will almost certainly insist that a formation's 'home' is its host village, the law itself is unclear.

Nevertheless, the intent of the new classification scheme is clear. It was written with the purpose of encouraging an increased commitment to authenticity, rather than enshrining an existing hierarchy. Indeed, the four types of ensembles just mentioned – the folkloric formations and the three kinds of *popular* ensembles – appear first in the scheme, followed by various forms of theatre, choir, dance, music, and circus, all of which receive fairly normative descriptions. The regulation also outlines the criteria that ensembles must meet, every three years, in order to achieve the new status of 'model', which entitles them to additional salaries for professional accompanists. The model status already existed (and many folkloric ensembles held it at the time of my research), but the new regulation awards it on the basis of adherence to principles of authenticity, rather than on the basis of virtuoso performance.

What the regulation shows clearly is a shift in the way amateur artistic activity is organized and valued in Moldova. The general definition for all types of amateur activities states that an amateur ensemble is 'a group of persons with developed artistic qualities and aptitudes, constituted within a state institution with the goal of researching, valorizing, and promoting a type of artistic creation'.[32] The group has the responsibility to develop talent and systematically perform for the public, but nothing is said about *why* these are its goals. Although the state is meant to organize, supervise, and finance these activities, no indication is given of the value they hold for the state or why the state perceives them as worthy of subsidy. The law appears to have had little effect on the actual activities of folkloric ensembles, although through its promise that folkloric ensembles might be awarded 'model' status, it gives ensembles an incentive to enhance the authenticity of their repertoires, and festival juries greater power to insist on authenticity.

In the following chapter, I further describe the vision of ethnic and national identity that folkloric ensembles hope to communicate to their audiences. This message, in its briefest form, relocates the source of Moldova's national identity – its culture and traditions – away from ethnic groups and into villages. Self-consciously 'authentic' folkloric ensembles therefore suggest a new focal point for identity politics among Moldova's citizens. Yet a number of factors inhibit even the most authentic ensembles from effectively communicating such a singular message. Consequently, I also begin to trace the source and limits of the authority claimed by folkloric ensembles to mediate the relationship between their audiences and the state by teaching audiences about 'authentic' forms of culture and tradition.

---

[32] Interestingly, the final version of the law stresses the relationship between an artistic formation and the state more than the draft proposed by the National Centre for Folk Arts did. The original version defined an amateur formation as 'a group of persons organized on the principal of voluntary association with the goal of researching and promoting an artistic domain'.

Chapter 4
The Folkloric Movement

Though classified as an art form in Moldova, folkloric performance is dedicated entirely to representing the traditional lives and customs of Moldova's people. *Folcloric* and *etno-folcloric* ensembles create an image of Moldova as a nation of villages through their onstage performances and the backstage discourse of authenticity that underwrites the image. The image is created especially during folkloric festivals, which function triply as spectacles for local audiences, training grounds for young performers, and competitions for opportunities to perform on national and international stages. Participation in folkloric festivals is also a prerequisite for the desired 'model' status discussed briefly in chapter 3, which brings extra financial support from the state.

Representation of village traditions by folkloric ensembles can be both visual and textual. Visual dimensions of representation include 'choreography, costuming, and other elements of production', and textual dimensions include 'company biographies, histories, mission statements, program notes, and publicity releases' (Shay 2002: 22). Moreover, the textual dimensions of representation that appear in the deliberations, decisions, and comments of juries function as a kind of 'mission statement' in action, which in turn directly affects who and what is represented visually in televised gala concerts. As Anthony Shay (2002: 7) noted in his study of several countries, performances by national folk dance ensembles 'often create and perpetuate devastatingly accurate portraits of national prejudices, class strife, and ethnic and religious tensions, expressing a reality often avoided in the verbal discourse of strident nationalism and chauvinism'.

Even where official state ideology and self-representation minimize social divisions and antagonisms, these tend to resurface in the artistic renderings of folkloric performances, because real choices have to be made about whose daily lives and customs are to be represented and how the relations between represented groups are to be structured and depicted. Although the 'folk' depicted onstage need not be conceptualized as a 'nation', they usually are, and the relations depicted are most often those between ethnic groups, nations, and states.

Folkloric Performance before the Folkloric Movement

The folkloric movement (*mişcarea folclorică*) that introduced *folcloric* and *etno-folcloric* ensembles in Moldova in the 1980s developed as a reaction against the composed music and dance, ostentatious costumes, and stylized performances of *popular* groups during the Soviet period. Today, *popular* repertoires may still contain pieces based on ethnographic material that has been substantially rearranged and highly stylized, and even pieces that have been composed without an original tradition as their model. Although supporters of the folkloric movement recognize that rearrangement and stylization often enhance stage presentations of folklore, they object to the deliberate academic composition of what is presented as folklore. As the subsequent two chapters illustrate, the critique adopted by the folkloric movement, now exemplified by new ensembles and embedded in the judging at folkloric festivals, conveys many social truths about village life but overlooks key ways in which ethnicity intersects with social relations in villages and with broader patterns of rural-urban interrelations. As Michael Herzfeld (2005) acknowledged, many sincere struggles against the state are advanced precisely through the implication of local idioms but require some forgetting of other aspects of local experience. Such is certainly the case with the Moldovan folkloric movement's critique of Soviet power.

For the folkloric movement of the late twentieth century, the problems with the composed and stylized folklore of *popular* groups were twofold. First, it inaccurately represented local tradition. Second, local tradition was subordinated to the goal of developing and promoting Soviet ideology, especially as it related to international friendship. Both aspects of the critique hinged on the use of ethnicity as a focal point in folkloric performances and repertoires. *Popular* groups could and did perform the folklore of multiple ethnic groups. In some cases they performed folklore from the Soviet 'nations', and in others, the folklore of other socialist countries. In the worst cases, according to my informants, *popular* groups simply performed 'folklore' for which no one could identify an ethnic origin. Today, ensemble directors and other specialists refer to these unidentifiable dances and pieces of music as *ţigăneşte* (Gypsy).[33]

---

[33] The term means 'Gypsy' but is used pejoratively, rather than as an accurate ethnonym. Whether Gypsies as Roma have distinctive forms of dance and music is another debate in the folkloric community that parallels the debates about Jewish culture, described in chapter 6.

For the folkloric movement, ethnicity was a political rather than a cultural concept, which, when introduced to the arts, led to three related and problematic practices in performing 'national' dance, music, and traditions: the mixing and alteration of once ethnographically accurate folklore; its subsequent unrecognizability as the cultural property of any ethnic group; and its connection to the aims of the Soviet ideology of international friendship. Movement members built their critique against ethnicity by arguing that villages, rather than ethnic groups, were the repositories of authentic traditions. Moreover, they argued, the overt depiction of ethnic relations through and as tradition misrepresented real social relations in villages, which depended on principles such as kinship and neighbourhood. From a village perspective, ethnicity was a political principle that mattered to the state but not to 'ordinary' people.

The kinds of performances that members of the folkloric movement objected to are suggested by manuals produced mostly by Moldova's Ministry of Culture but occasionally in Moscow for amateur ensembles. In 2001, ministry officials, ensemble directors, and other specialists generally reported having discarded the old manuals at the beginning of the 1990s. The national library, however, still housed several volumes published in the 1960s, as well as a few from earlier and later decades. These manuals confirm much of what members of the folkloric movement decried. For example, a 1971 volume that reflects collecting from as early as 1945 presents a series of ballet warm-up exercises, followed by the musical scores for several pieces of popular music and then movements for popular dances (Mardar 1971). The approach taken in the collection encourages the mixing and matching of movements with music, as well as the infusing of balletic movements into folkloric dance, which would have led to both stylized performances and pieces of unidentifiable origin. At the same time, the volume contains nearly fifty musical scores, annotated with the name of the village where each score was collected and the date of collection. An ensemble director with a background in folklore, ethnomusicology, or ethnochoreology who used the manual could almost certainly have matched the music adequately with movements drawn from specific folkloric dancing traditions, so the use of the manual would not necessarily have produced 'inauthentic' performances.

A 1957 volume shows a similar mix of attention to ethnographic detail, but with some important oversights. This volume provides no attributions for the included music, although it does give detailed instructions on body positions and movements for the dances, as well as a variety of costumes to match (Oshurko 1957). Moreover, this volume, entitled *National Dances of Moldova,* includes pieces representing the Gagauz people and

Bulgarians, although it provides no additional notes for body movements and postures specific to either group. It leaves readers either to draw on their personal knowledge of ethnically specific kinetic styles or to blend the styles.

As these two examples indicate, manuals published prior to the appearance of the folkloric movement included much that members of the movement would have approved. Yet the discourse surrounding folkloric performance attributed to it additional ideological meanings. A 1953 article in *Sovetskaya Moldova* (Soviet Moldova), for example, heralded the role played by amateur ensembles in both the collection and preservation of folklore and the creation of new dances, but it was the new dances that were described at length: 'Amateur ensembles compose new dances, dedicated to the light and joy of the new nation's life, work, socialist competition, and the fight for peace. In the dusk of a summer day, on the banks of the river, the kolkhoz youths gathered to learn the new dance 'Happiness', composed by the dancing collective from the village club in New Hanaseni, Leova raion'.

The article goes on to congratulate other ensembles besides the club from New Hanaseni for having composed dances based on the themes of camaraderie, friendship, and the battle for peace. The names of the ensembles reflect Soviet values: Friendship, Victory, Youth, Work, Competition, and Harvest Celebration. Like the professional ensembles mentioned in chapter 3, some well-known amateur ensembles carried names that reflected Moldovan traditions or fairytale figures, such as Mioriţa, the title of a ballad; Marţişor, the name of a March tradition; Liana, a woman's name but also the fictional character Liana Ileana Cosînzeana; and Ciocîrlia, the skylark, a bird that is often mentioned in folk songs because of its distinctive trilling and its migratory tendencies (Koroleva 1989: 30). Yet it is clear from the article that the dominant discourse surrounding amateur performance emphasized the achievement of progressive, modern, Soviet goals, values, and ideals through folkloric performance, rather than the conservation, preservation, or unchanging continuity of tradition, even though these functions are also acknowledged.

The ideological emphasis on Soviet values continued to appear in Moldovan folkloric performances throughout the decades of Soviet rule. As an illustration of the immediate context for the emergence of the folkloric movement, my consultant Pavel Popa provided me with a manual published in the late 1980s (Ministry of Culture 1988). The volume demonstrates the pervasiveness of messages of international friendship and stereotyped national identities that characterized children's performances at the time, even as it reveals elements of change. The volume, whose translated title is *The Stage of the Amateur Performer*, contains short plays, choral compositions, music for brass instruments, and folkloric dances. Many of the choral compositions are obviously meant to invoke patriotism for the Soviet Union and one's home republic, with titles such as 'Lenin', 'Pride of the Republic', and 'In the Brotherly Family'. The plays demonstrate more clearly how Soviet ideology was combined with folklore. The speaking parts and inclusion of characters whose ethnic identities are explicitly stated assist in this function.

For example, one play, titled *May You Grow Big* (*Să creşti mare!*), is intended to focus attention on the significance of birthdays in children's lives. The piece, which combines oratory with short, folkloric song and dance sequences, won second place in a 1984 republic-level competition. The three main characters are literary personages: Guguța, a bumbling Moldovan peasant created by the writer Spiridon Vangheli; Ivanushka, the hero of many Russian fairytales; and Doina-Doiniță, a beloved personage who teaches Moldovan children to sing and dance. The three eventually engage the audience in celebrating the birthday of an honoured child, but the action begins promptly with references to Moldova's place in the rapidly modernizing Soviet Union. The three characters form a train and move across the stage, reciting the following lines, which rhyme in the original:

> Guguța: Our train goes only forward.
> Ivanushka: We can take with us any well-behaved child.
> Doina-Doiniță: Attention! Attention! Citizen-travellers! Look through the window and tell me, what you see?
> Ivanushka: I see my beautiful country,
> Like a luminous bread,
> With flowering orchards,
> With fields full of grain,
> With woods and plains,
> With the calm voice of the skylark,
> And with peace in every house,
> My country is the most beautiful!
> Guguța (while unrolling a map of the USSR):
> Like a leaf on the grapevine,
> My golden Moldova,
> Very rich, very beautiful,
> And with much sun [i.e. bread] on the table!
> For all of her sisters [i.e. Soviet republics],
> We have many colours,
> And now all together,
> In a prism, are gathered,
> This is an exceptional homeland,
> Field of flowers, in the morning!

In addition to its obvious overtures of friendship towards Moldova's 'sister republics', this short interchange includes the most important stereotypes associated with Moldova – those that depict it as a warm, 'flowering' republic, known for its orchards and vineyards – and it pays homage to Soviet rule for bringing both food and peace to 'every home'. The text also conveys a sense of local geography, drawing the borders of Moldova in the shape of a grape leaf and marking the importance of the country's central and southern zones by calling attention to the woods (*codru*) and plains. These motifs were repeated constantly in children's performances held in kindergartens, schools, and culture houses on regular occasions throughout the year, meaning that children and adults alike absorbed the symbolic geography of Moldova as a peaceful, happy, food-producing member of the Soviet Union.

Another piece in the 1988 volume, 'The Leaf Reddened on the Grape Vine: A Description of the Celebration of the Viticulturalist', reiterates these themes in a more didactic fashion. The introductory text, which the ensemble's director presumably read to the children, indicates that Soviet Moldova is also called a 'sanatorium with grapes' (Ministry of Culture 1988: 95). Again Moldova is pictured as a warm, inviting place, where – in this case – one's health can be restored while one enjoys the pleasures of life. This perspective is clearly that of an outsider, however, and the international focus is also clear in characters including a Kazakh and a 'Turk'. As in the first piece, Moldova's identity is crafted in relation to these outsiders, not to the locals who live there.

Although Popa offered me this manual as an example of the kinds of folkloric activities that the folkloric movement opposed, it also reflected the complexities of the movement's efforts at reform. Three of the short plays in the book, including 'May You Grow Big', had been written by Tudor Colac (1987), who in 2001 was still a respected folklorist specializing in children's folklore. Andrei Tamazlâcaru, while he was a professor in the folklore department at the State Institute for the Arts in the 1980s, had contributed the verses and musical arrangement for the choral composition 'Green Leaves of Jasmine'.[34] Thus the manual reflected both the way participants in the folkloric movement had previously contributed to the promotion of less authentic folklore at some points in their careers and the way they gradually began to introduce more authentic works into the existing system of amateur cultural activities.

---

[34] From 1964 to 1999, the primary institution for post-secondary education in the performing and visual arts in Moldova was the State Institute for the Arts in Chişinău. From 1999 to 2002 it was called the University of the Arts, and today it is called the Academy of Music, Theatre, and the Plastic Arts.

In some cases they also provided ironic readings and performances of the less authentic pieces. Although it is difficult to reconstruct how the performances were originally received, audiences would have been prepared for ironic commentaries on key symbols of Soviet ideology. Many writers in the late 1980s, including those who specialized in children's literature, were well known for their ironic uses of motifs such as hospitality, bread, and brotherhood (Solonar and Bruter 1994: 88–89 n. 39).[35] Colac's text, in particular, holds significant potential for ironic readings and performances. For example, it is Ivanushka, the Russian character, who says, 'We can take with us any well-behaved child', and it is he who begins the Sovietized description of Moldova by calling it 'my country'. Thus, in performance this character could create distance between the Soviet (i.e. Russian) ideology he espouses and the symbols that local people could claim as truly Moldovan. Several of the symbols used in the text, such as the leaf on the grapevine (a reference to wine) and the 'sun' (a round loaf of white wheat bread) on the table, are deeply implicated in local traditions and ritual practices. During performance, Soviet ideology was transmitted but also ironized and ignored; the Soviet Russian claims Moldova as 'his' country, but the audience is meant to see him as a fool because all the symbols indicate 'their' country. By encouraging the audience to remove the Soviet overlay, these symbols became rich vehicles for transmitting what audiences recognized as more 'authentic' visions of national identity. Pieces like this are no longer performed by folkloric ensembles, but similar scripts are still performed in school plays and recitals, without the explicit references or comparisons to other peoples and republics of the Soviet Union.

The Emergence of the Folkloric Movement

Michael Herzfeld (2005), as part of what he meant by 'cultural intimacy', described the intimacy that exists between institutionalized forms of power and those who contest it. In the same vein, Moldova's folkloric movement emerged out of state-organized cultural institutions and education even as it participated in them. This becomes abundantly clear in the way participants recall the origins of the folkloric movement and in their collective professional biographies.

To the degree that the movement had a leader, most of my informants acknowledged the guiding influence of Andrei Tamazlâcaru, who, when he

---

[35] Vladimir Solonar and Vladimir Bruter specifically mentioned the writings of Petr Kerare and Grigore Vieru as examples of the kinds of literature that fuelled national sentiment among ethnic Moldovans and precipitated antagonism between ethnic Moldovans and other minorities during the late 1980s. Vieru was also a well-known children's writer whose poems were often set to music as folklore.

was a professor in the folklore department at the State Art Institute in Chişinău, had organized the ensemble Tălăncuţa, initially as an extracurricular student club.[36] The ensemble set the standard for authentic performance, with its emphasis on direct collection of repertoire materials through fieldwork, careful reproduction onstage, and costumes that accurately copied materials, styles, and decorative motifs worn before the Second World War. Key members of the ensemble joined as university students between approximately 1980 and 1984, and as they graduated, each of them created at least one additional etno-folcloric ensemble for children or adolescents in the kindergartens, schools, culture houses, and Pioneer houses that employed them. Eighteen of the early members remained in the ensemble in 2001. Others, who took jobs outside the capital city (many returning to their home villages), maintained ties to both the ensemble and Tamazlâcaru.

Movement members who had not participated in Tălăncuţa also emphasized the importance of ethnographic field expeditions in their university educations. Many of the movement's participants were performers who had double-trained as ethnographers or folklorists. As university students they undertook summer practicums in which they were sent to villages to record and collect information about local traditions, arts, and material culture. Materials from these expeditions were not put directly onstage but were archived for later use by trained composers and choreographers. Because these performers had collected folkloric material themselves, they recognized the changes composers introduced in their music and dance compositions.

In addition, as I describe in chapter 5, many movement members and their initial audiences in the 1980s were first-generation rural-to-urban migrants with direct experience of village life, dancing, music, customs, and traditions. The folkloric movement reacted against the systematized 'invention of tradition' (Hobsbawm and Ranger 1983) reflected in *popular* performances, and its members insisted that performed folklore should be as similar as possible to the materials they themselves knew or had collected from villagers. The state's organization of culture, described in chapter 3, anticipated that post-secondary training would produce directors for *popular* ensembles. Yet among university teachers and leading figures in folkloric performance, the combination of artistic training with ethnographic fieldwork was meant to yield culture workers who could 'distinguish peas from wheat' (Curbet 1989). These efforts evidently succeeded; new ensemble directors trained and encouraged by the likes of Andrei Tamazlâcaru used

[36] Tamazlâcaru took Tălăncuţa with him when he left the university to work at the Musicians' Union in the early 1990s, and the group became a 'state ensemble' with all the associated benefits of funding and disadvantages of having to put on command performances.

the weight of professionalism that came from their education to shift the way folklore was perceived and performed.

In the past thirty years, the folkloric movement in Moldova has succeeded in redefining folkloric performance in several ways. First, members of the movement have established *folcloric* and *etno-folcloric* ensembles as distinguishable types. Second, they have established exclusively folkloric festivals and competitions designed to increase the level of authenticity of local groups' repertoires and performance styles. Third, they have forged and strengthened working relations between ensemble directors, performers, dance and music experts, professional ethnographers and folklorists, folk artists, and other specialists to create what I experienced and refer to as a professional folkloric community. Fourth, the criterion of authenticity may be assisting in a redefinition of the social place and role of folkloric performers. Festivals, which I turn to next, reveal particularly well the composite changes engendered by the folkloric movement.

Folkloric Festivals

Folkloric festivals function as one of the primary mechanisms for developing ensembles with authentic repertoires and performance styles and thus creating a new image of the nation of Moldova. As of 2001, some twenty folkloric festivals, most of them for children and youths, were being held in Moldova annually or biannually. Only one, called Maria Drăgan, was exclusively for adults; others, such as the country-wide festival La Vatra Horelor, was technically for adults but often included youth ensembles with teenage participants, as it did in 2001.[37] More than half the festivals began after 1989, and many of them opened during the financially difficult years of 1994–1999. A disproportionate number were held in the capital, but six were deliberately organized as 'republican' events, with participants recruited from throughout the country.[38] Festivals first held in 1989 or earlier were organized through national institutions; examples include the folksong festival Tamara Ciobanu, organized through the Musicians' Union; the

---

[37] La Vatra Horelor means literally 'at the hora's hearth', which suggests that the festival's role involves identifying the geographical centre and 'home' of a particular kind of dance, the *horă*, which Romania and Romanians also claim as their national dance. Like ensemble names, festival names reveal the widespread equation of Moldovan and Romanian identities. While these ethnically symbolic names undermine specialists' attempts to deemphasize ethnicity as a meaningful component of authentic folkloric performances, other festivals provide the symbolic grounds for building images of national identity that are ethnically inclusive. For example, several festivals are organized around religious holidays and themes.

[38] A list of the festivals, including details of organization, sponsorship, and content, appears in a previous publication (Cash 2004: 71–72). The designation of many state-level events as 'republican' rather than 'national' reflects unchanged Soviet terminology.

country-wide Folkloric Festival (Festivalul Folcloric), run through the National Palace of Creativity for Children and Adolescents; and La Vatra Horelor, organized through the National Centre for Folk Arts. Newer festivals have been initiated by individuals and organizations at multiple points in the systems of culture and education outlined in the previous chapter, including county- or *raion*-level departments of culture, local departments of education (e.g. the city of Chişinău), and even individual ensemble directors. These locally organized events may be considered international if they bring in participants from nearby countries such as Romania, Bulgaria, and Ukraine.

In many cases, festivals require cooperation between more than one institution. Thus, the National Palace's Folkloric Festival relies on local departments of education to organize and judge preliminary competitions in each county. Duminica la Florii (Flower Sunday), the one festival organized by an individual ensemble director, is a more vivid example of collaboration across the structural schema. The official program for Duminica la Florii bears the names of Moldova's Ministries of Culture and Education and the City of Chişinău (the administration itself, not the Department of Culture). Each of these organizations contributes financial support. The festival itself, however, is staged in three villages in Cahul County. Thus the organizer relies on organizational support from the county Department of Culture and from the staffs of three village culture houses. The organizer also enlists the help of villagers in one village (his birth village) to house and feed participants. Private citizens donate food, labour (cooking the large meals), money, and other assistance. For example, the owner of a local restaurant provides the celebratory banquet for ensemble directors, jury members, and special guests.

Moldova's folkloric festivals reflect the expanding professional activities of the folkloric movement and substantial support for folkloric activities from throughout the administrative structure. The growth in the number of folkloric performances in Moldova is also part of a general trend throughout the former Soviet Union. For example, Anatolii Khargin (1995: 89) observed that some sixty or seventy festivals were being held annually in Russian territories, regions, and republics in the early 1990s, versus fewer than five before 1989. Clearly, festival expansion marks new interests and concerns related to cultural activity, but *whose* interests are increasing is difficult to discern. Participants at a conference organized by the International Conference on the Organization of Folkloric Festivals (CIOFF) in the early 1990s concluded that post-Soviet festivals operated very differently from those with which CIOFF was more familiar. Russian folkloric festivals in the early

1990s were distinguished by disproportionate budgets, an over-emphasis on gala performances, and a dearth of audiences (Khargin 1995).

Folkloric festivals in Moldova share in these characteristics. They are still organized primarily as spectacles, as they were in the Soviet period, imagining a passive audience that will be entertained and educated by successive performances. Often, however, the festivals draw no local audiences. In 2001 audiences often consisted primarily of other performing groups, and juries sometimes complained that local officials and culture workers had failed to 'gather people' as they did for other public meetings. The lack of a sizeable or stable public audience does not necessarily mean that interest in folkloric performance is non-existent at the village level. Festival organizers certainly rely on substantial local assistance and support, which indicate interest of a certain type. Festival participation always encompasses many goals and meanings, especially those related to identity (Guss 2000), and in this case it is the non-participation of a public that calls attention to the specific meaning and function of folkloric festivals. Despite their shared emphasis on spectacle, neither Moldova's nor Russia's folkloric festivals are instruments of political control and ideologization like the Song to Romania festival described by Anca Giurchescu (1987), nor are they the joyful expressions of mutual enthusiasm for folklore among participants, organizers, and audiences that festivals are commonly imagined to be.

Folklorists ordinarily distinguish festivals by their public nature, participatory ethos, complex structure, and multiple voices, scenes, and assumed purposes (Stoeltje 1992: 261). Events that call themselves festivals, however, are usually 'contemporary modern constructions, employing festival characteristics but serving the commercial, ideological, or political purposes of self-interested authorities or entrepreneurs' (Stoeltje 1992: 261–262). It is by examining the participants, not just the audience members or consumers, that the community to which the festival belongs becomes visible (Stoeltje 1992: 266). In Moldova, festivals sharpen the criteria of authenticity that are applied to folkloric performances, which both creates the boundaries of a folkloric community and consolidates the vision of Moldova as a nation.

Folkloric festivals are important events in Moldova because they are all competitions. As such, they provide the opportunity for juries and competitors to gauge a director's success in collecting materials, teaching children, and mounting traditions on stage. The sole reward an ensemble can expect to receive for participating in a festival is verbal praise and advice from the jury. Some festivals award 'places', in that winning groups are sent to higher levels of the competition and may eventually perform in a gala concert. In principle, ensembles receive some monetary reward for participating and winning, but this is neither standardized nor publicized. Ensemble directors hope to have transportation costs covered and food provided, but even this is never guaranteed. Over the long term, good performances may pay off for ensembles that achieve 'model' status and become eligible for additional state funds or state-funded staff positions and for those that receive offers or permission to travel abroad as national representatives.

In the short term, the lack of compensation reflects the pedagogical orientation of the festivals. At the end of a competition session, most festival juries comment orally on the performance of each ensemble and offer recommendations. Participants, ensemble directors, and audience members have the opportunity to hear the juries' comments and learn what constitutes a good, authentic performance of folklore. The comments also communicate hierarchy among the ensembles, establishing relations of leadership and emulation.

Judging Authenticity: Festivalul Folcloric 2001

The 2001 edition of the Festivalul Folcloric (Folkloric Festival), sponsored by the National Palace, provides an excellent illustration of the way the new criteria for representing tradition onstage are interpreted, applied, and developed. This festival is one of the longest-running folkloric festivals in the Republic of Moldova. It began in 1989, when the National Palace was still officially the Pioneer Palace and before Moldova achieved independence. The Folkloric Festival was also instituted before the other two folkloric festivals sponsored by the National Palace, for Christmas and New Year's Day and for Easter. I discuss this festival because, among all the festivals I attended, its jury gave the greatest amount of criticism and advice to participating ensembles. In 2001 I sat with the jury during its deliberations and travelled to the festival locations with its members. I also heard ensemble directors contest the jury's comments, something they rarely did at other festivals. They did not argue with the jury in the festival hall, and I witnessed only one director directly confront the jury, but as I met with ensemble directors in the months following the festival, several continued to discuss the judges' decisions. One director in particular – not the one who confronted the jury during the festival – was still arguing about the jury's decision with friends and colleagues six months after the competition. His ensemble participated in at least six separate competitions in 2001, but none of the others attracted his attention in the same way.

Because it is a country-wide competition, the National Palace's Folkloric Festival occurs in three stages. First, county administrations organize competitions, and the three or four winning groups in each county are then sent to zonal competitions. Moldova is conceptually organized into three or four ethnographic zones: northern, central, southern, and sometimes Transnistria. The National Palace's festival recognizes three zones; participants from Transnistria must compete in the northern, central, or southern zone. Winners from each of the zones proceed to a gala concert in the capital. No jury members attend the gala concert, which is unjudged but is filmed for television. In 2001 I accompanied the jury to the northern and central competitions. I was unable to attend the southern competition because of lack of transportation, but I attended the gala concert, where I witnessed the outcome of the jury's decisions for all zones.

Plate 1. An early performance of a new mini-show in Moştenitorii's repertoire, demonstrating rituals associated with midwives.

According to the festival's rules, competing groups were required only to present a 'mini-show' incorporating several folkloric genres. Additional criteria emerged during the jury's deliberations. The jury was composed of the director of the National Palace and three experts he had chosen – a musicologist, a choreographer, and an ethnographer. All four jury members lived and worked in Chişinău at the time and came as representatives of national-level organizations, not as regional specialists. Jury members were chosen for their ability to gauge authenticity in music, dance, ritual, and material artefacts, but their levels of regional expertise varied, which allowed ensemble directors to critique their pronouncements. While some ensembles presented loosely organized concerts of music and dance, winning groups organized their mini-shows around a ritual such as a wedding or a set of rituals such as the spring rituals, and they incorporated songs, dances, instrumental pieces, and dramatic scenes around the central theme. Winners also documented the fact that their repertoires had been collected from village informants. The informal rules observed by the winning groups, but not by all ensembles, reflected the jury's preference for a particular definition of authentic folklore and its proper staging, a definition that had been developing for several years.

Plate 2. A performance of "dressing the bride" before her wedding, part of a longer performance of wedding traditions.

The jury's decisions were relatively simple in the northern district. Their biggest concern was the number of groups they should accept for the gala performance – that is, whether they needed to have representatives from each county or whether their choice should be based entirely on overall quality. In the central zone competition, however, the jury wrestled with their criteria, eliminating three groups from Chişinău that were otherwise known to be fine folkloric ensembles, for reasons that I discuss next.

In all folkloric competitions, the preference is that a performing group or individual use a repertoire collected from his own village or from a group of nearby villages. At the very least, the repertoire should come from the performers' own ethnographic zone. This requirement poses a problem for groups based in cities, particularly those in the capital, because folklorists and ethnographers see Chişinău and other cities as having no traditions of their own. Geographically, Chişinău is in the centre of the country, which imposes other difficulties, because the central ethnographic region as a whole is known for having few traditions. Some people say the lack of traditions results from the city's influence on the surrounding villages. Some say that traditional ballads are extant, but not dances. In any case, when competition rules specify that multiple performance genres must be included, villages located in the centre of the country are at a disadvantage because they have access to fewer locally specific genres.

At the central zone competition, all three groups from Chişinău were disqualified for failing to represent the centre. In fact the jury wanted strongly to disqualify only one of the three groups but eliminated all three for the sake of consistency. As consolation, they decided to invite the other two groups to the gala as 'special guests', but they waited to alert the directors until after they had finished judging the southern zone competition. Thus, on the day of the central zone competition, all three groups publicly received dismissive criticisms.

The one group that the jury really wanted to disqualify performed a mini-show of a wedding. It included multiple genres: two dramatized traditions (the dressing of the bride and the forgiveness of the bride and groom by her parents), oratory, song, and dance. The group's general repertoire was built almost exclusively on elements the director had collected in or near his native village, and this performance was no different. By common interpretation, this ensemble was almost ideal as an *etno-folcloric* group. Its one substantive weakness was that the children were from Chişinău, in the centre of the country, whereas the repertoire was from the south. Jury members questioned whether they should include this ensemble in the gala, considering that a group actually located in the southern zone might better perform the same or similar traditions.

The zonal requirement was prominent in the jury's backstage discussion, but jury members downplayed it when publicly explaining the group's disqualification. Instead, they noted faulty interpretations of tradition. First, the jury's dance expert declared that one of the dances was 'scenic' – that is, composed for stage performance and never performed as a real village dance

– and a second, although sharing a name with an authentic dance, was not in fact that dance. Thus the group had failed to present authentic folkloric dances. The ethnographer on the jury contested the group's rendition of pre-wedding rituals. When dressing the bride, the group sang a song that in other parts of the country was associated with the unveiling of the bride at the very end of a wedding.

The director of this ensemble, although he did not contest the jury's decision that day, discussed his group's elimination for months afterwards. He argued not only that had he presented the bride's dressing as it was done in his village but that another ethnographer, researching a neighbouring village, had documented and even published the same ritual-song combination. The ensemble director believed the jury's decision had been based not on the actual merit of his group's performance but on personal disputes between him and members of the jury. Personal relations certainly play a role in jury decisions, and they influenced the judging on this occasion as well, but not explicitly. Instead, jury members presented their opinions, even during the closed deliberations, with appeal to shared criteria of authenticity. Even personal relations of affinity or antagonism between ensemble directors, jury members, and other specialists in the domains of ethnography, folklore, and performance are expressed publicly through the common language of authenticity and tradition. Consequently, as juries choose winners and losers in these competitions, regardless of the personal dimensions of their decisions, they build an increasingly complex and nuanced standard for 'authentic' folklore – a standard that lends greater legitimacy and authority to ensembles that aspire to achieve authenticity than to those that do not. In this way, juries help to refine the membership and identity of the folkloric community.

A similar dispute over the jury's decision arose at the northern zone competition. In this case the jury criticized an ensemble for singing a 'corrupted' piece – that is, a piece in which two songs had been incorporated into one. During the post-festival dinner, the criticized director protested that the piece had been sung as she had collected it in the village, appealing to the greater authority of the village than to the 'expert' from the city. Indeed, none of the experts had conducted fieldwork in the woman's home village, and one member of the jury proposed to come do fieldwork there and prove the local woman wrong. In the end, the argument halted only when the same jury member noted that if you asked a village teenager for a traditional costume today, he would bring you a pair of jeans. Thus, although 'experts' fill the role of judges, their authority is second to local knowledge and practice. When the local ethnographer refused to concede authority to the city ethnographer, the only way for the city ethnographer to regain her authority was to concede that although authoritative traditions do come from villages, villagers themselves are not necessarily authorities on tradition. The ensemble director acquiesced at this point, shifting the conversation to address the increasing unruliness of village youths since the end of Soviet rule. This, at least, was an opinion everyone seemed to share.

In Moldova's folkloric community, individuals build the authority to pronounce on the authenticity of folklore and the merits of ensembles and performances through ethnographic experience. Organizers of folkloric festivals and competitions acknowledge this by selecting jury members on the basis of the expertise candidates have gained by participating in multiple ethnographic expeditions. As in the National Palace's Folkloric Festival, dancers and musicians who serve on juries base their judgements on repertoires they themselves have learned and, specifically, repertoires they have collected. When professional ethnographers are chosen for juries, a balance must be struck between their institutional affiliation, academic qualifications, and fieldwork experience.[39] The value placed on an expert's personal knowledge, however, limits the authority of jury members. When a jury member pronounces on the accuracy of repertoires collected in villages or areas where he or she has not participated in expeditions, ensemble directors (who have collected their own material) may legitimately challenge the jury's decision.

Thus, another change achieved by the folkloric movement in Moldova is in the definition of a 'folk performer'. Today, those who perform national genres are judged by their colleagues according to their ability to demonstrate intimate knowledge of and contact with village life. Festivals enable members of the folkloric community to identify 'true' folk performers, whether these are individuals or groups, on the basis of the way they infuse stage performance with the experience of village life. Festivals also encourage performers and judges to continuously expand their personal ethnographic knowledge as well as their talent for mounting or perceiving accu-

[39] Because ethnographers and folklorists are academics and not performers, their authority is also determined by the criteria of academia. This complicates jury selection, because publications count heavily in establishing an academic's relative authority, but ethnographic and folkloric publications may not be based on a person's own field research. Ethnographers and folklorists may build their academic credentials on ethnographic data already published, archived at the Academy of Sciences, or otherwise collected and made available by someone other than the ethnographer himself. These practices help to explain why some directors thought I might be compiling folklore from festivals and the performances I attended. Alternatively, ethnographers and folklorists with substantial field experience may have few publications. Determining an individual's professional authority and judging the quality of his research are difficult tasks, moreover, because the organizational structure of academia and academic publishing has changed little since the Soviet period, and people claim that publications can still be easily blocked by their superiors.

rate and compelling representations of this knowledge. Jury members track the changing levels of commitment of ensemble directors, commenting among themselves about whether or not an ensemble's repertoire has changed in the past few months, year, or ten years. Indeed, of the three Chişinău ensembles eliminated during the central zone competition of the 2001 Folkloric Festival, jury members complained that one ensemble (which was later issued a special invitation to the gala) had changed little of its repertoire in recent years. Competitions and festivals therefore also encourage folkloric performers to continually seek out new ways of conveying authenticity.

Representations of National Culture

As the foregoing discussion illustrates, the village holds a more immediate and explicit role in folkloric performance in Moldova than does the nation. This does not mean that participants in the most authentic realms of folklore and folkloric performance are uninterested in representing the nation as a social unit or in defining the qualities of national identity. Indeed, as I discussed my research interests with people early in my fieldwork, I was encouraged to describe my project as a study of the 'promotion of national culture' in children's ensembles. What this naming suggests is that members of the folkloric community do not perceive the *creation* of a national culture to be the central goal of folkloric performances. Rather, they believe national culture already exists, albeit in village-based variations. The problem for folkloric ensembles, then, is how best to 'promote' or 'transmit' this culture across generations and to people in urban areas. In comparison with *popular* groups, *folcloric* and *etno-folcloric* ensembles seem far removed from identity politics and the ongoing contests for state power among Moldova's ethnic groups.

Yet when one asks *which* nation's culture is being promoted and transmitted, 'authentic' folkloric performances in Moldova yield a rich commentary on ethnicity. Most ensembles claiming authenticity have repertoires collected from Moldova's majority Romanian-speaking population, but some have repertoires drawn from minority groups. The gala performance of the National Palace's 2001 Folkloric Festival, for example, included a group with a Bulgarian repertoire. At least one Gagauz group competed in the southern zone competition; it was disqualified, but it regularly participated in other folkloric festivals, including the multi-village Duminica la Florii and the country-wide La Vatra Horelor. Nevertheless, only a few ensembles perform traditions of ethnic minorities, so they are better considered exceptions than indicators that members of the folkloric community would accept a normative definition of Moldova's national culture as inherently multiethnic.

In chapter 6 I discuss further how the criteria of ethnographic authenticity work to exclude the traditions of many of the non-Romanian ethnic groups resident in Moldova from being identified as authentic folklore. The criteria themselves, however, are deliberately non-ethnic, as well as non-ideological and non-political. From the perspective of *folcloric* and *etno-folcloric* ensembles, *popular* groups incorrectly emphasize the social significance of ethnicity by acting as vehicles for the promotion of Soviet ideologies. In contrast, folklore that claims greater authenticity denies interest in ethnicity and claims the village as the source of all real traditions. At first glance, the organization, criteria, and competitions of authentic folkloric ensembles seem to be promoting a vision of the Moldovan nation as a collection of villages with boundaries that coincide with those of the new state.

This view – of a Moldovan nation whose boundaries coincide with the contemporary state – is further supported by criticisms levelled at ensembles that have repertoires or costumes clearly collected in Romania. Two ensemble directors who pointed my attention to pieces of folklore and costumes they had collected in Romania were openly criticized by their colleagues. The colleagues argued that as professionals, they should collect, preserve, and perform traditions from inside Moldova's boundaries. In this case the critics' professional opinions did not fully reflect their personal convictions about the nature of national identity. That is, they supported the view that Romanian-speaking Moldovans were Romanians and agreed that, logically, traditions practised by Romanian speakers in Moldova were Romanian traditions. They disagreed with the practice of using traditions found in Romania as if they were authentic 'Moldovan' traditions when their existence in Moldova had not been empirically verified. This kind of fine distinction, between professional responsibilities to preserve and valorize local traditions and personal convictions that ethnic Moldovans and Romanians constitute a single people, also contributes to the distinction that many members of the folkloric community make between 'patriotism' and 'nationalism'.

Recognizing Authenticity and Value

If we consider *folcloric* and *etno-folcloric* ensembles in opposition to *popular* ensembles, then the existence of two basic types of folkloric performance in Moldova draws attention to the importance of boundaries in the creation of national identity. Both types of ensemble create images of local culture onstage, so they are equally good candidates for representing the nation through performance. The *popular* ensemble emphasizes ethnicity and comments on the country's exported agricultural products while demonstrating the vivacity and modernity of local life through composition, choreography, and brightly coloured costumes. The *folcloric* or *etno-folcloric* ensemble largely overlooks ethnicity, only half-acknowledging its existence by allowing multiple ethnic groups to appear onstage, but it stresses the importance of villages and emphasizes local economic and artistic self-sufficiency. The *folcloric* type of performance claims greater authenticity, but do *folcloric* and *etno-folcloric* ensembles produce a more accurate depiction of Moldova's culture than *popular* ensembles do? Which representation of national identity is more authentic – one that defines the nation's differences from other nations or one that examines the nation's internal diversity?

Self-consciously 'authentic' performances of Moldova's folklore depict the country's internal diversity by representing villages onstage. In accordance with Royce and Kemper's (n.d.) typology of identity personnel, *folcloric* and *etno-folcloric* ensembles performing for local audiences function ideally as cultural stewards; they show a village's traditions to its own inhabitants. The 'best' ensembles, even as they advance through zonal competitions to perform on the national stage, still perform village traditions as if they will be judged by co-villagers. These ensembles have the explicitly pedagogical function of teaching local audiences how to be 'Moldovan' in their everyday lives. Significantly, they encourage Moldovans to identify first and foremost with their home villages.

As cultural stewards, folkloric ensembles select and present diagnostic behaviours and traits of 'Moldovan' villagers, such that a composite picture of Moldovan identity emerges from authentic folkloric performances. Yet as I discuss next, inherent contradictions sometimes exist among criteria for authenticity, and these may interfere with the audience's ability to consistently perceive what members of the folkloric community consider most significant about local life and culture.

For non-specialists, the most visible dimension of the folkloric movement's notion of authentic tradition is costuming. This was the element of folkloric groups that people called on most often in explaining which ensembles were *folcloric*, *etno-folcloric*, or *popular*. The folkloric movement of the 1980s tried to eliminate the costumes worn by *popular* groups, which were described to me as examples of 'kitsch'. These specifically included circle skirts that fell above the knee, bright colours (especially red), and patterns on both shirts and skirts that 'belonged to no one': large abstract carpet motifs, grapes, and sunflowers.[40] These patterns signified Moldova's

[40] In addition to costumes and other textiles, many elements of material culture are dismissed as kitsch. Anything with bright colours is always suspect, but beyond that the qualities of kitsch become difficult to standardize. Large or overly naturalistic designs (e.g. detailed

identity in the Soviet context, because Moldova was known within the union for its production of wine and sunflower oil.

Plate 3. A dancer with a *popular* ensemble preparing for a public performance during Independence Day celebrations. The short circle skirt, ballet shoes, and stylized grape and flower motifs in the embroidery make this costume an example of 'kitsch', although the use of white in the costume is preferred over other, brighter colours.

In general, 'authentic' costumes suggest that traditional life is village life. An authentic costume is sewn from handwoven cloth, and an abundance of wool is visible in the form of stockings, skirts, vests, capes, and hats. Colours are produced from vegetable dyes. Shoes are hand sewn from pigskin. Costuming further distils the image of village life into practices organized around the household economy. It is a way of life denied to city inhabi-

roses), non-traditional materials (e.g. wood overlay, which is considered Ukrainian but not Romanian), plastics (which are new), and, in one case, chewing gum wrappers (which put art in the category of post-modern) were pointed out to me as examples of kitsch.

tants, and a life that downplays evidence of relations between cities and villages. The ideal village denies urban influence, the effects of industrialization, participation in commerce beyond the village, and the existence of ugliness in village life.

Although juries claim that inauthentic costumes can be forgiven for financial reasons, shoes are important. *Opinci*, which are like moccasins worn by both males and females on top of heavy woollen knee socks and attached with leather straps that are wound up the leg to the knee, are considered the most authentic footwear. Yet an entire ensemble wearing *opinci* produces an inaccurate depiction of village life. In a traditional village, *opinci* were the shoes of the poor. Villages did not consist of a single economic stratum, and wealthier villagers wore other kinds of shoes, as is demonstrated in photographs taken in the early decades of the twentieth century. At dances and celebrations in particular, villagers in pre-Soviet times strove not to wear *opinci* at all, but shoes with harder soles, such as boots and high heels.

Hard-soled shoes give the dances what is seen as their distinguishing quality – a noticeably strong rhythm. Indeed, even non-specialists judge the quality of a dance by its 'temperament' (speed, energy), and dances from the different regions of Moldova are distinguished by their relative temperaments. For example, the southern dances are said to have the greatest temperament, whereas northerly dances are slower and more elegant. The belief that soft-soled *opinci* are the most authentic shoes conflicts with the need for hard-soled shoes to give dances strong temperament. In terms of judging, more 'authentic' shoes can translate into less 'authentic' dancing. Under current criteria, however, dancers must simply dance with firmer steps in the softer shoes.

Not only are villages the authentic sources of repertoires, but an ensemble is supposed to represent social diversity within a village. Village-based *etno-folcloric* ensembles are often applauded for including both adult and youth performers. Costumes, too, are expected to be diverse. The ensemble with the highest score at the city festival Duminica la Florii in 2001 appeared in a range of costumes that bordered on the visually chaotic. A jury member who was also the director of one of the city's creativity centres assured me that this approach was definitely authentic and preferable to uniform costuming. In her eyes, the variation in costumes reflected traditional village practices in which girls going to a dance would have each tried to look uniquely beautiful.

Plate 4. The ensemble Ilincuţa, from a village outside Chişinău, received high marks in the city festival Duminica la Florii (Flower Sunday) for the authenticity of its costuming. The jury considered the mix of patterns in the girls' overskirts (*catrințe*) to be an authentic representation of actual village dress.

Many costumes are recently produced, but groups that have collected old clothing from village households are extremely proud of it. Although juries often insist that costumes – because of their expense and the poor economy – should be among the last criteria for assessing the overall quality of folkloric groups, directors are engaged in ranking their colleagues' ensembles through costuming. One director pointed out that another had a southern repertoire but used costumes from the ethnically Romanian region of Bukovina in Ukraine (this was the director of the group disqualified at the central zone competition, mentioned earlier). In fact only a few of the ensemble's costumes were from Bukovina. These should have been the most authentic of the group's costumes, because they were actually collected from villagers, but they were considered the least authentic because they did not match the ensemble's repertoire. The majority of the ensemble's costumes were actually in a southern style that corresponded to its repertoire, but they had been specially manufactured and so did not count as highly as authentic costumes. All ensembles suffer from similar inconsistencies in the degree of authenticity they achieve in costuming, repertoire collection, and performance. Yet rather than constituting absolute weaknesses, these inconsistencies provide tools that ensemble directors manipulate to rise in the elusive but hierarchical ranks of the folkloric community.

Plate 5. Buciumaşii, an ensemble specializing in traditional wind instruments, on Duminica la Florii. The festival schedule included a trip for participants to have willow branches blessed at the local church.

Plate 6. Moştenitorii, ready to join a parade marking Gagauz autonomy.

National Aesthetics and Traditional Morality

By training people to appreciate the aesthetics of authentic traditional handicrafts, members of the folk community hope also to train performers and audiences to value and enact a set of behaviours and moral qualities that they consider specifically Moldovan (cf. Holton 2005: 72). The national qualities become especially clear through criteria of authenticity that are applied to textiles, instruments, and other elements of material culture as props in folkloric performance. These objects are considered 'art', but they are not judged by the usual standards of inventiveness, imagination, and innovation, which stress the artist's extraordinary qualities. Rather, good and authentic material culture testifies to its creator's status as a moral exemplar in the community. The national qualities most often discussed in my presence as being represented in material culture were work, nature, and beauty.

The aesthetic criteria for textiles pertain largely to colour and pattern. Bright colours are to be avoided, as are large, naturalistic patterns, because they are seen as relatively late developments, influenced by the availability of commercial dyes from Germany and the adaptation of Ukrainian folk motifs. If chemical dyes are used, then those that approximate colours from natural dyes are the more highly valued. Thus, a carpet produced even within the last twenty years, if it displays subdued colours and patterns – particularly small, abstract, repeating patterns – is valued more highly by ethnographers than an older carpet that deviates from these criteria. The small, abstract, subdued patterns claimed for 'local tradition' are seen as the manifestation of the artist's heightened awareness of nature, calmness of spirit, patience, and capacity for imagination that remains faithful to traditional values.[41]

The moral qualities claimed as national through such aesthetic judgements of authenticity are also subtly gendered. Most of the material objects included in folkloric presentations are those traditionally made by women: clothing, linens, pillows, carpets. In contrast, ceramic jugs of wine – both ceramics and wine being produced by men – appear occasionally in folkloric performances, but as props, not as central elements in the image of traditional life being portrayed onstage. Juries never comment on the authenticity of a jug used to serve wine to guests in a staged wedding, but an ensemble

[41] Indeed, contemporary weavers report that they are unable to work unless they are in a calm state. The weavers I interviewed were also members of the folkloric community and participated in trainings, craft fairs, and the like organized by state institutions. Their perspective therefore contributed directly to the developing discourse about authenticity, and they were in turn influenced by the perspectives of other community members. At the same time, weavers in other cultural traditions similarly draw attention to the way carpet designs reflect the internal states of those who wove them (e.g. M'Closkey 2008).

may be severely reprimanded for dressing a bride in a white wedding gown instead of traditional clothing.

Similarly, criticism directed at the short skirts worn by girls and women in *popular* ensembles suggests that the skirts are immodest in comparison with traditional female clothing. All specialists in the folkloric community know that the short skirts worn in *popular* ensembles were necessitated by the inclusion of ballet movements for the legs, and they acknowledge that a dancer wearing a long, narrow traditional skirt could not turn her legs out or lift them to any height. Therefore, skirts were shortened to permit folkloric dance to become more balletic. They counter, however, that traditional standards of female beauty emphasized modesty, and dance should reflect these standards with small (but accentuated) steps and narrow skirts. Moral uprightness for both men and women is reflected in a tall body stance; clear, accentuated, downwardly directed steps; minimal movements of the upper torso; and costumes that accentuate the vertical line of the dancer's figure.

The gendering of national qualities is also reflected in the attention ethnographers give to the quality of linens, both on and off stage. Linens are judged by their whiteness, the fineness of their weave, and the intricacy of their small, simple decorations executed in punching, embroidery, or crocheting. The qualities of linens indicate their maker's aesthetic sense and her industry. A contemporary linen maker explained the connection. When she was growing up, she said, a girl's linen work was closely examined. Linens were used on all ritual occasions, especially baptisms, weddings, and funerals, and girls supplied the linens their families used on such occasions. They also made linens, including embroidered pillowcases, for their future household. These were displayed in a girl's parents' *casa mare* (lit. 'big house') – a special room or occasionally a separate house used primarily for receiving guests – so that guests could see the girl's handiwork. A girl who produced good linens was considered to have patience in work, because the whole process, especially the whitening, was physically difficult and time-consuming. Patience in work was important because, as the linen maker told me, 'if you are patient in work, you will be patient in life'.

Folkloric festivals are ideal settings for communicating the aesthetic and social values that the folkloric community sees as belonging to national tradition. Festivals communicate through both visual and textual modes of representation, and the spectacle form further controls and mediates audience reception. Yet the audiences consist primarily of other performers before and after they take the stage. Although this promotes the training of performers in folklore as an artistic genre, especially one marked by a particular vision of tradition and traditional life, it raises the question of receptivity among the general public. Do audience members who are not also performers receive the same messages about authentic tradition that performers receive? How do 'authentic' folkloric ensembles communicate to the wider public?

Moral Performance Off the Festival Stage

The meaning of a performance can be located in its form, content, or context (Royce 1984). In Moldova, the meaning of folkloric performances changes significantly when ensembles perform outside of the festival context.

Beyond the festival circuit, the Moldovan public still makes no strict distinction between more and less authentic versions of folklore. Performances by *folcloric* ensembles drew tears from urban audiences in the 1980s and early 1990s when they performed traditions that reminded audience members of their home villages, but this response was also conditioned by the political context of the times. At the height of the national movement, folkloric ensembles often participated in anti-Soviet rallies, and audiences easily associated authentic folklore with an anti-Soviet political stance. Today, self-consciously authentic ensembles are less particular about the contexts in which they perform, and directors may have their groups perform at political events towards which they personally have no sympathy or even feel antagonistic.

In consequence, audiences often enjoy folkloric performances of varying authenticity indiscriminately. The public has greater exposure to concerts by *popular* ensembles than to those of the more self-consciously authentic folkloric groups. And judging from responses at public and televised concerts, the public clearly still likes the many *popular* groups and their composed pieces. Although many families whom I knew outside of the folkloric community claimed to value authentic folklore, they often had difficulty, when we watched televised competitions together, in distinguishing levels of authenticity among ensembles that were gradually discarding old costumes, repertoires, and staging. Indeed, most audience members could not accurately gauge authenticity, because the ultimate criterion was ethnographic accuracy based on sustained research, which they had not conducted. Moreover, few audience members seriously attempted to engage with questions of authenticity, because viewers usually expected to be entertained, not educated.

Current theories of national identity emphasize the importance of social processes involving representation, consumption, and participation to explain how a sense of common national identity is created among the individual citizens of a state. For example, Benedict Anderson (1991) argued that national identities are fundamentally modern forms of collective identity, initially enabled by print capitalism and other media (including folkloric performances) that allowed spatially dispersed readers or viewers to imagine themselves part of a large linguistic or cultural community. Anderson argued that print capitalism was key to the development of national identities because it increased access through the wide distribution of newspapers and similar publications in vernacular languages. What he did not say was that common identities could only be imagined through reading because readers accepted the publications' claims to represent the social world authoritatively and accurately. The formation of national identity through folklore, as through print capitalism, depends on access to performances, the content of the performances, and the authority that the audience attributes to the performance. For Anderson, consumption or participation implied consent, acceptance, and the adoption of the proposed identity.

Folkloric performances certainly provide audiences with the opportunity to imagine themselves parts of larger communities, including the Republic of Moldova as a bounded, territorially defined nation-state. To argue, however, that the images promoted by these performances correspond to images of collective selfhood, especially nationhood, held by the general population in Moldova requires a deeper analysis of consumption and participation. For Anderson, as for many other theorists, nationalism and national identity are part and parcel of the broad structural changes in politics, economy, and society that originated in western Europe, intensified there in the nineteenth century, and extended throughout the rest of the world during the past two centuries.

Accordingly, most theories of nationalism assume that national identity emerges in the presence of a capitalist economic system and its accompanying consumer behaviours. Anthropologists working on identity and the construction of personhood in eastern Europe, however, argue that the distinctive nature of production and consumption in socialist and postsocialist economies precludes the straightforward application of existing theories of identity to postsocialist contexts (Verdery 1991: 18, 1996: 26; Dunn 1998; Berdahl 1999). Because socialist states planned consumption and controlled the goods, including literary and artistic works, available to the public, neither consumption nor participation can be assumed to transparently reflect choice and, by extension, the expression of identity. Yet as Adele Barker (1999) pointed out, socialist states did not control the meanings or experiences that the public attached to controlled goods. Post-Soviet producers, including folkloric performers, face a similar problem in that they cannot dictate how consumers use their goods.

Controlling the way audiences receive the meaning of a performance is made more difficult in that folkloric performances often take place in contexts that contradict the messages the ensembles most want to transmit. Although folkloric festivals in Moldova do not draw audience members from the general public in significant numbers, folklore is publicly visible on other occasions, such as holiday concerts, political gatherings, and public commemorations. When folkloric ensembles perform outside of competitive festival settings, the authenticity of their repertoires or performances is rarely the central focus. In this context, what meaning do their performances have? Do they still communicate a critique of Soviet ideology and offer a new vision in its place? Is it important for ensemble directors to do so?

To approach this question, one might ask how organizers choose to include a folkloric group in a public spectacle and why ensemble directors accept performance invitations. In other words, the meaning of a folkloric performance could be controlled by the context of performance. In some cases this does happen. For example, in 2001 I watched the ensemble Moştenitorii perform at a commemoration of the death of Ştefan cel Mare, or Stephen the Great (1435–1504), who unified the medieval principality of Moldova. Since the late 1980s, if not earlier, he has become a symbol of the Romanianness of Moldovans and the legitimacy of an independent Moldovan state.[42] A commemoration of Ştefan cel Mare's death is therefore a commemoration of the Romanianness of the Moldovan people, their desire for independence, and the legitimacy of a Moldovan state. The director of Moştenitorii shared these values and performed with the other adults in his ensemble as an act of personal commemoration.

Yet at a certain level, event organizers and ensemble directors do not issue or accept invitations to perform with the intention of signifying special relationships between performed folklore and audience. For example, the group Moldoviţa performed for the Communist Party's celebration of Lenin's birthday in 2001. This group was technically a *popular* dance group, but because of the expertise of its director, Pavel Popa, who worked at the National Centre for Folk Arts, it was considered an authentic ensemble. Judging from Popa's position as an authority on folklore and his involvement in encouraging the performance of authentic folklore, one would not expect his ensemble to have performed for the Communist Party. For many citizens, especially urban intellectuals, the party's electoral victory in 2001 was threatening. It signalled a return to Soviet-era ideology and practice

[42] Ştefan cel Mare figures prominently in the capital's symbolic landscape. The major road in downtown Chişinău was renamed Boulevard Ştefan cel Mare at the end of the Soviet period, and a monument to Ştefan cel Mare stands prominently in the middle of a small paved square at one corner of the central park, with the House of Government to its right. The figure gazes towards the cathedral, bell tower, and arc of triumph, which are located diagonally across from it.

regarding ethnic and national relations; the denial that Moldovans were culturally, historically, or linguistically Romanian; and the establishment of Russian as the acceptable language for public use. More immediately for my informants, including Popa, the Soviet period referenced the institutionalized practice of stylizing and hybridizing folklore. Several ensemble directors I knew kept a close eye on the way Communist-organized public events incorporated folklore.

The strong opposition to Communism among members of the folkloric community, along with the role they assign to authentic folklore, suggests that ensemble directors would scrutinize the ideological circumstances of performance opportunities before accepting or declining invitations. Indeed, some do[43], but clearly not even professional opposition to Communist ideology or the politicization of art prevents 'authentic' folkloric ensembles from occasionally performing at political events they do not support. The reason Moldovița performed at the Lenin's birthday event in 2001 was simply that it was paid to do so.

Economic factors influence a director's choice to perform, but so do personal relations. An ensemble may perform at an event because a director's official superior or someone on whom he relies for other favours and support requests or commands his participation. Bonds of friendship and kinship may also motivate a director to accept an invitation. For example, in August 2001 Valeriu Chiper took his ensemble, Moştenitorii, to perform at the folkloric festival that accompanied the celebration of Gagauz Yeri's quasi-independence from Moldova because the invitation came through two friends – Afanasi Gargalik, the director of the Gagauz ensemble Altângic, and a member of Gagauz Yeri's local Department of Culture. Gargalik did not actually expect Moştenitorii to come; he knew Chiper did not support the formation of Gagauz Yeri as an autonomous region within the Republic of Moldova and expected him to demonstrate his political stance by refusing the invitation. In this case, however, Chiper publicly recognized the demands of friendship as being more important than individual political convictions.

Moştenitorii also performed in 2001 at a celebration of Doctor's Day organized by the administration of one of Chişinău's districts. Doctor's Day is a holiday carried over from the Soviet period, but like Women's Day, it is considered basically innocuous. Chiper's wife did work in the medical profession, but the immediate reason for his ensemble's performing was again that an acquaintance in the local administration had asked. On other occasions, ensemble directors may be told by their superiors to show up for a

[43] For example, Petru Dinjos, the director of the ensemble Buciumaşii, reported refusing a well-paid offer to participate in the summer camp described in the introduction because its director was 'not serious' about folklore.

performance. The appearance of a folkloric ensemble at a public or semi-public celebration does not, then, necessarily represent transparent support for the occasion being celebrated or the sharing of political values by ensemble directors and those who invite them. The participation of children certainly cannot be taken as evidence of their or their parents' agreement with or support of the celebration.

When directors decide whether or not to perform in contexts that promote political values other than their own, they experience their choice as limited. Although individual choices are always limited, ensemble directors often experience their limitations as a continuation of the political complicity associated with the Soviet period. They expect both their performers and their audiences to assume the possibility that performance is compulsory and thus to separate the context of performance from its meaning.

Though not unique to Communist or socialist societies, political complicity has been experienced and described as a factor deeply limiting social agency in eastern Europe. Gail Kligman (1998: 14), for example, wrote that 'the social dynamics of everyday life were structured by the socialist system itself and contributed importantly to the longevity of the regime. Duplicity and complicity were the hegemonic mechanisms through which social relations came to be organized and by which the organization of socialist society was perpetuated, yet ultimately destroyed'. As Vladimir Tismaneanu (1998: 114) put it, 'the vast majority of the people who lived under communism were participants in the systemic self-reproduction: some were active supporters of the status quo, others were just 'cogs in the wheel', adjusting themselves to the existing constraints and trying to secure for themselves and their families minimal forms of decent survival'.

As illustrated in chapter 3, most financial and institutional support for folkloric ensembles in Moldova still originates with the government and, by extension, the political parties that control it.

'Authentic' folkloric ensembles are not alone in their dependence on organizations they explicitly oppose. Most of Moldova's population relies (or has until very recently relied) on state-owned industry and social services, regardless of personal political convictions. Ensemble directors, party members, and the general public all know, as Tismaneanu wrote (1998: 114), that not 'everybody [is] equally responsible for the system's actions'. Ensemble directors count on this shared knowledge and decide when their groups will perform according to a complex moral calculus in which the profitability of an opportunity sometimes wins out. And, as Popa further explained his decision, perhaps the children of the Communist Party members who were in the audience would appreciate the performance and be drawn closer to folklore and authentic traditions.

The history of an individual director's decisions forms part of the collected knowledge by which specialist members of the folkloric community determine others' commitment to the aims of the folkloric movement. Non-specialist audiences do not have full access to this information. Without additional information, spectators cannot know that Moştenitorii's director supports Romanian identity and Moldovan sovereignty but does not support Gagauz autonomy within Moldova. They cannot distinguish folklore that is performed as a gesture of friendship from folklore performed as a sign of political support.[44] Spectators may be knowledgeable enough about the conditions under which performances are organized to resist interpreting the messages of folkloric performances in direct relation to the ideology of performance organizers. In this way, Moldova's local audiences are more sophisticated consumers of folklore than outsiders. They do receive the vision of a moral nation of villages that folkloric ensembles promote, but they also receive much more information, including a clear message about the impossibility of recovering or reinstating truly moral behaviour.

To some degree, folkloric performances everywhere are marked by the plurality of meanings and goals held by organizers, performers, and audiences. Lynn Maners (1995), for example, urged students of folkloric dance and ensembles to consider folkloric forms as 'commodities' with 'social lives'. Like Arjun Appadurai (1986), from whom he borrowed the concept of social lives, Maners argued that folkloric forms, like other commodities, have 'careers'. Correspondingly, a folkloric form's meaning or power to unite performers and audiences (producers and consumers) socially, artistically, or ideologically changes during different phases of its career, and moments in which performers and audiences agree on the meaning and value of folkloric performances may actually be atypical rather than normative.

David Guss (2000) made a more extensive argument for the value of acknowledging multiple aims and reactions to a single event. He noted that participants, sponsors, and audiences at folkloric festivals might have different ideas about why they are involved in the same event. Each may see the festival as an opportunity to create, reaffirm, or instill identity based on tradition, but the identities may be very different and even antithetical to one another. Instead of approaching festive forms as 'mere instruments of social control' (Guss 2000: 12), Guss argued that folkloric festivals are sites at

[44] In 2001 I did not collect audience responses through questionnaires or other systematic methods. Then and during subsequent research, however, I found that the only audience members willing to talk at any length about the meaning of a performance were already 'insiders' of some degree – for example, the parent of a participating child, a teacher who was a director's colleague, or another cultural specialist.

which new social orders emerge by creatively recycling the concepts of authenticity, tradition, and the division between 'high' and 'popular' arts – all of which have been previously associated with folklore.

The plurality of meanings that participants and spectators assign to folkloric performance is, however, limited. As I have tried to illustrate in this chapter, the very organization of folkloric performance in Moldova shapes and constrains the audience's access to its intended meaning. The continuity of the Soviet organization of arts and culture means that audiences approach folkloric performances as entertainment and suspend their critical engagement with the production of national identity, unless they have otherwise been introduced to the goals of the folkloric movement and its criteria for authenticity. Only spectators who have been initiated into the discussion of authenticity can distinguish performances as more or less representative of 'authentic' traditions and distinguish among the kinds of images of national identity that are produced through folkloric performance.

In other words, the expression and production of identities through folkloric performance operates along a double boundary that marks the relationship between performers and audience. The multiplicity of meanings ascribed to performances can generate the new social orders suggested by Guss, including the ephemeral moments of collective national imagining identified by Maners. Multiple meanings, however, also mark multiple boundaries of social groups based on shared knowledge and values. Among Moldova's general population, even the folklore performed by *popular* ensembles is generally assumed to be an authoritative representation of tradition, and so it too, still has the power to shape the way in which national identity is imagined.

In the following chapter, I examine how folklore's historical association with authenticity and authority in Moldova is both useful and limiting to members of the folkloric community in their efforts to promote a national culture and local aesthetic and value systems while opposing overtly political ideologies.

Chapter 5
From Village to Stage: Authenticity and Authority

On a hot summer morning in July 2005, I bounced along in the back seat of a car that was part of a groom's party speeding toward his bride's village. There were five of us in the car: a good friend of the groom's, who drove, the videographer, the groom's younger brother, me, and Doina Boboc, the young woman who had invited me. Doina is a professional *cobză* player whose various jobs have included working as an accompanist for the ensemble Moştenitorii.[45] She was insistent that I attend this wedding from start to finish because it would be 'traditional'. That she, the bride's cousin, had already departed from tradition by joining the groom's party was a minor detail that could be overlooked.

It was a jolly ride. Balloons and paper ribbons streamed out as we raced the other cars in the convoy. The videographer leaned out the window with his camera to capture the passing scenery. Spirits were high, and the groom's younger brother, who was sharing the back seat with Doina and me, was full of questions about the United States. The other men in the car began to tell stories they had heard about both the wonders and the horrors of life there, and as the catalog of differences between the two countries mounted, Doina chimed in with a pun summarizing all that was being said: 'You are the United States of America, but we are the united villages of Moldova' (*Voi sunteţi statele unite ale Americii, dar noi suntem satele unite ale Moldovei*). Her pun turned on the nearness of the Romanian words for state (*stat*) and village (*sat*) and playfully called attention to the centrality of the village, as an empirical reality and a source of political meaning, in Moldovan life.

Doina's pun applies nicely to the folkloric community's representation of Moldova as a 'nation of villages' to explain social and political experiences offstage and well beyond the festival circuit. In the following chapter I return to the political and social possibilities embodied in this vision, in

[45] The *cobză* is a traditional stringed instrument, similar to a guitar, found also in Ukraine, Russia, and Poland. It has a highly convex resonator box and is usually plucked to provide accompaniment for other instruments.

terms of inclusion and exclusion. Here I focus on the meaningfulness of the village for members of the folkloric community. What is it that makes the village the source of 'authentic' traditions? How does it gain salience and authority as a means of collective identity for performers and audiences? The answers, I argue, are linked both to ethnography and to patterns of rural-urban migration coupled with structural discrimination.

The commitment to village-based research in local traditions of ethnography throughout eastern Europe is a point of both convergence and divergence with Western anthropology (Hofer 1968; Maday 1968; Cole 1977; Halpern and Kideckel 1983). The ethnographers I worked with in Moldova considered villages the sources of authentic tradition in part because scholarship defined them as such. At present it is difficult to identify a distinct and indigenous 'Moldovan' style of ethnographic or folkloric scholarship, largely because political changes have continually limited and shifted access to foreign scholarship and promoted certain kinds of research over others. Yet these politically related developments also constitute the specificity of local scholarship. What Anna Kutrzeba-Pojnarowa (1982: 3–4) wrote about the effects of political history on the development of ethnography in Poland could also be said of Moldova: the diversity of topics addressed by ethnography 'arose in consequence of the contact between Polish and worldwide scholarship, many times established and just as often interrupted'. Contemporary folklorists and ethnographers in Moldova draw on ideas and scholarship created over the past century and longer in pre-revolutionary Russian, Soviet, pre-socialist and socialist Romanian, French, German, and other national schools of folkloric and ethnographic research. Local treatment of the village, theoretically and methodologically, draws on and gains legitimacy from the attention given to village life by each of these schools. Yet the members of the folkloric community maintain that the village's authority onstage is more immediately connected to life experience than to theoretical abstraction. In the rest of this chapter I explore that experience and the way the village gains salience and authority as a locus for collective identity.

First, I consider how the village functions as the methodological centre of folkloric activity. Following the general procedure of many schools of folklore and ethnography, members of Moldova's folkloric community collect and label village traditions. As I discovered by accompanying ensemble directors on a collecting expedition, even folklorists who diligently record life history data from their informants ultimately make decisions, as they transfer field materials onto the stage, that reduce the personal dimensions of folklore. As folklorists prepare collected materials for performances, they present ever more abstract visions of local social and cultural life. I demonstrate how even the most 'authentic' folklore being performed in Moldova transforms songs, dances, and other traditions with complex origins into the creations and property of individualized villages. I then also investigate the extent to which the very methods used by members of the folkloric community contribute to 'nationalized' visions of culture through these village-focused performances.

Second, I consider how my informants' personal and professional lives intersected in the image of the village promoted by folkloric performance. In this respect I am engaged in the sort of critical ethnography described by Michael Herzfeld in his preface to *Anthropology through the Looking-Glass* (1987). Herzfeld wrote that 'an anthropology that makes an ethnographic problem of itself offers pragmatic insight into the social worlds that it examines and to which it belongs. Above all, it permits access to the *rhetoric* of social life, not to some spurious gloss on reality … but as the accessible dimension of social reality itself' (1987: x, original italics).

In my case, investigating why members of the folkloric community pursue the representation of the village yields a better understanding of how they individually and collectively experience and respond to the broader demographic, sociological, and political dimensions of urbanization. From this perspective, my informants represent the lives and sentiments of a broad segment of Moldova's population. At the same time, members of the folkloric community occupy a unique social position in that their professional activities provide an outlet designed specifically to produce and distribute rhetoric, images, representations, narratives, and other commentaries on shared social experience. My final intent in this chapter is therefore to investigate the factors in the individual lives of ethnographers and folklorists in Moldova that lead them to focus their energies on researching and representing villages, above and beyond other social groups, in their professional activities.

By experience and training, ethnographers in Moldova find the village's authenticity self-evident. The number of villages in which an ethnographer has conducted research adds to his or her prestige and authority. This is generally known among non-specialists, and people with some knowledge of ethnography were always asking which villages I had visited. When I arrived in Moldova in February 2001, my village trips on two previous occasions had been few: I had visited only Sadova, Hîrjauca, Trebujeni, and the historic fortresses at Orhei Vechi and Soroca. So far, my informants thought, I had seen little, and they were concerned that I needed more trips to villages. By November 2001 the list of the villages I had visited was significantly longer. Besides the ones already named, I could count Cucoara, Anenii Noi, Cîşliţa-Prut, Tomai, Cazaclia, Slobozia Mare, Văleni, Brînza,

Giurgiuleşti, Cişmichioi, Stolniceni, Ţîra, Ghindeşti, Cenuşa, Clîmăuţi, and Ciopleni, as well as the city of Comrat. Even though many trips were limited to visiting culture houses and their immediate surroundings, other ethnographers now considered me to have seen something of the country.

Everyone who urged me to go to villages, especially the ethnographers, wanted me to see the country in a literal sense. They asked me which American state it most resembled, wondering about Texas and California. Not having been to either of those states at the time, I suggested Kentucky or West Virginia, because of the greens of the grass-covered hills. They pointed out the black dirt. The 'blue' houses of the villages also made an impression on me, as did the ubiquity of green and blue paint on fences, even in the capital, where windows and public stairs might also be painted in these shades. I kept asking about these colours – why blue? why green? The houses, it turned out, were 'white', because their bluish colour came from whitewash.[46] And although the blues and greens that I kept remarking on in fences and windows rarely drew return comments, my remarks on the greenery of plants were well appreciated.

Moldova has rich, fertile soil, suitable for growing many kinds of plants, and people enjoyed telling me about the country's agricultural abundance. Marking a general decline in environmental health, they also told me that Moldova had more trees and cleaner water in the past. I was supposed to see all these things in my travels out of the capital. In addition to orienting me to the particularities of Moldova's countryside, people expected that my trips to villages would teach me what I needed to know as an ethnographer. From my initial perspective, however, these trips – often brief and limited to watching performances, eating meals, and visiting with a few people in a single home or culture house – provided little opportunity to learn about villages themselves. Over time I began to ask, rhetorically, why these trips were so important to local ethnographers. What did they see that I could not? And how could they 'see' anything in such brief visits? One set of answers to these questions, which I offer in this chapter, comes from focusing on the importance of villages and village-based fieldwork for establishing authenticity and authority in folkloric performance. In chapter 6 and the conclusion I address other aspects of ethnographic seeing.

Between February and November 2001 I eagerly participated in two ethnographic field expeditions. The first was organized at my request by Valeriu Chiper. The second was a summer school organized by students at the University of the Arts in Chişinău and funded by the Soros Foundation.

---

[46] I have not been the only visitor struck by the aesthetics of pale blue and lavender houses. Anne Applebaum (1994: 268) also noted them as particular to both sides of the Romanian-Moldovan border.

These expeditions gave me the opportunity to learn more about the individual experiences and motivations underlying the folkloric community's existence, organization, and activities. In this chapter I concentrate on describing the first expedition, because it was organized to demonstrate the process by which Chiper built his ensemble's repertoire.

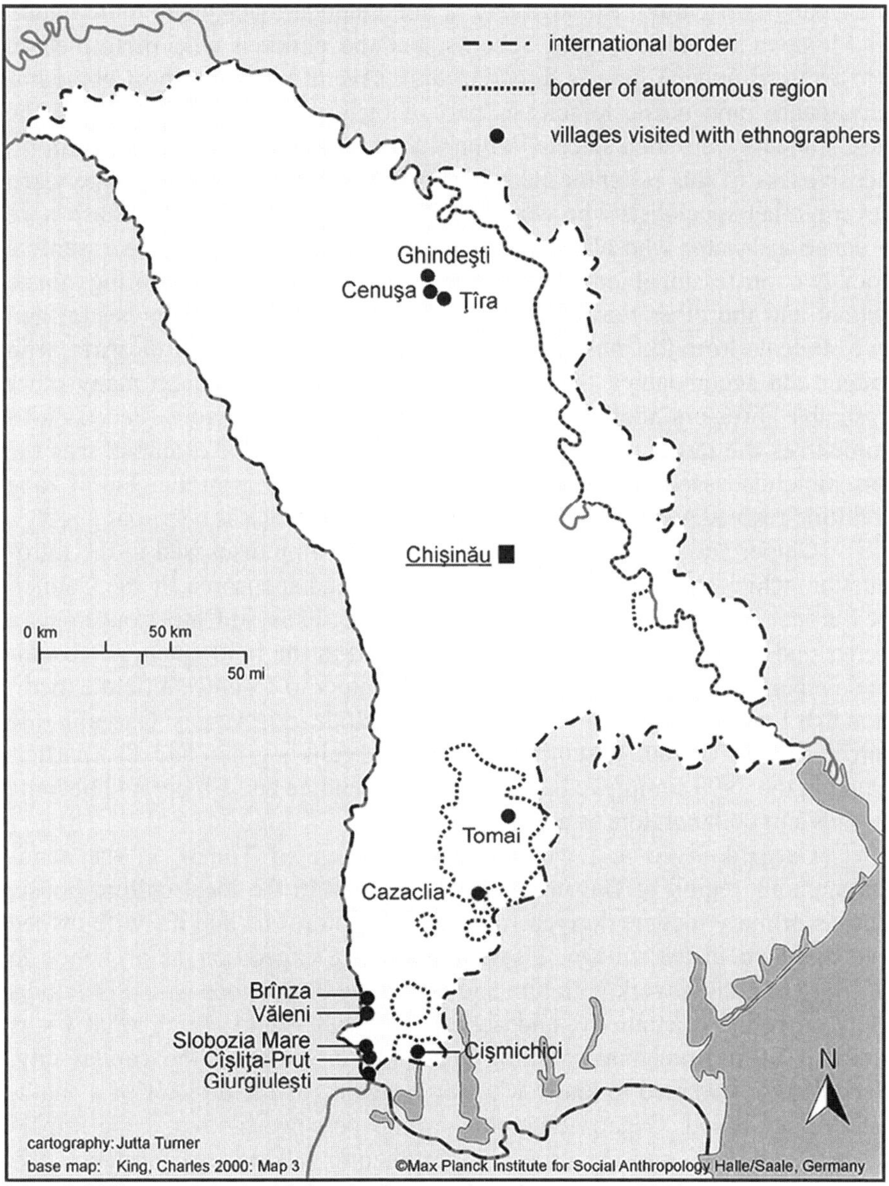

Map 5. Villages visited with local ethnographers in summer 2001.

An Ideal Expedition

In 2001, Valeriu Chiper was the director of Moştenitorii, a children's ensemble based at school number 11 in Chişinău. As an ensemble director, Chiper was unique for at least two reasons: his pedagogical specialty was history, not performance, and he taught ethnography to students as part of their daily curriculum. Ethnography is not a standard academic topic taught in Moldova's state-supported schools, but the children who performed in Moştenitorii under Chiper's direction took several years worth of ethnography, dance, and music lessons as part of their specialized focus. Only the best students were then selected to participate in the ensemble. The comprehensiveness of this program meant that Chiper also selected and supervised several other specialists who worked with and under him. In 2001 these were a dance instructor who also worked with the state *popular* dance ensemble Joc; two professional musicians, one employed at a neighbouring music school and the other the director of Fluieraş, a professional orchestra; and two students from the music conservatory at the University of the Arts, who taught and accompanied the ensemble on the *cobză*. Although many other ensemble directors admired the breadth of Chiper's activities, he was also sometimes the target of strong criticism. Moştenitorii, for example, was the ensemble discussed in chapter 4 that was disqualified from the central zone folkloric festival and not invited to the gala performance as a special guest.

Chiper and I met in 1999 at the summer camp discussed in the introduction, which was organized by a local NGO and sponsored by the Council of Europe. When I returned to Chişinău in 2001, I sought Chiper out to get a better understanding of how material collected in the field enters an ensemble's repertoire. Thus, in July 2001 I asked Chiper to organize a field expedition that I would fund, and I asked that we include in it Afanasi Gargalik, the director of the Gagauz ensemble Altânjic. Gargalik's group had also participated in the 1999 camp; we had all met there, and he and Chiper had become friends and collaborators as a result.

Gargalik lived and worked in the village of Tomai, in the semi-autonomous region of Gagauz Yeri. He worked in the local culture house, but his primary income derived from the three stores he and his wife owned and operated in the village. I saw a weeklong expedition as a chance to discuss Gargalik's work with him and hoped the discussions would provide a view on folklore, ethnicity, and authenticity that would enrich what I was learning from Romanian-speaking ensemble directors in the capital city. Specifically, I wanted to know whether Gargalik, as the director of a southern, village-based, Gagauz ensemble, would perceive his work, the importance of folklore, and the criteria for authentic folkloric performance any differently from the way the other ensemble directors I had met perceived those things.

This extended discussion never took place, perhaps because, as other ensemble directors supposed, Gargalik was reluctant to openly express opinions that diverged from those of Chiper, on whom he relied for help and assistance in the capital. Or perhaps it was because he had already told me his views. In 1999 and again in the early spring of 2001, he had carefully and insistently told me that I needed to visit villages in order to understand real traditions. In his initial advice, Gargalik first provided a personal anecdote: villages, he said, were friendlier than Chişinău. When he had first come to Chişinău as a university student, he was surprised that no one greeted him in the streets; in villages one was always greeted. He then cautioned me against working too closely with academicians, who were concerned with theory, not practice, and who worked from books, not people. Ethnography, he insisted, was about people, not theories, and his, my, and our work as ethnographers had to come 'from the soul' and reveal the soul.

In early July, Chiper and I began discussing the possibility of an expedition. He had suggested several times in the preceding five months that we make an expedition because his understanding was that I needed field data (*material de pe teren*) for my thesis. He was willing to take me on an expedition and suggested various villages in Moldova as well as areas in neighbouring Romania and Ukraine. As the months passed, he began to remind me that we should go before very late in the summer, or people would be too busy in the fields to work with us. By late July, we mobilized.

Chiper imagined a full expedition: private vehicle with driver, cameraman with video camera, me with still camera, him with tape recorder plus spare tape recorders, and other participants, including Gargalik and as many children from his ensemble as we could take. He calculated a budget of US$300[47], keeping costs low by recruiting help from within his close personal network. He arranged for the older brother of two of the students in his ensemble to be our driver. We paid for gas (about US$50) and paid the driver 400 lei (approximately US$33) for the week's work, as well as covering his meals. We hired Chiper's teenage nephew as our cameraman, because he had a small video recorder. We bought all the videotapes and gave him 300 lei for his time. Chiper purchased pens, pencils, batteries, audiotapes, videotapes, and two rolls of film, totaling US$50, before we left Chişinău. With the rest of the money we purchased food to take to the people who housed and fed us, as well as drinks and snacks for ourselves and our informants. We slept two nights at Gargalik's house and the other nights in

[47] All costs were covered out of my stipend from IREX.

the houses of Chiper's parents and sister. Despite careful budgeting, our costs rose when a car tire needed repair during the trip, and I covered other expenses that we had not originally included, such as the cost of camera film, developing, and prints. I purchased additional videotapes on which we transcribed the original cassettes, so that Gargalik, Chiper, and I could each have our own copies of the material we collected together.

At the end of the expedition, Chiper told me that really we had operated on too stringent a budget. We had been able to make the trip as inexpensively as we did because we relied on his relatives and other close acquaintances. We should have paid the driver and cameraman more, both for their time and – especially in the case of the driver, who drove his own car – for the wear and tear on their personal equipment. Gargalik should also have been paid something. As Chiper explained it, 'We took him away from his house for a whole week, and he has a lot of work there. If you take a man from his house, he may well have an argument with his wife over his absence'. And of course Chiper thought it would have been nice if he and I had each received a small remittance, as sometimes happens in other projects that ethnographers and ensemble directors undertake. Beyond that, he said, we might also think of doing more for the people we had interviewed and videotaped. Chiper was pleased at how well hot, tired villagers had responded to our questions after we offered them something to drink, and he suggested that in the future we should consider feeding them as well.

Field expeditions can certainly be carried out for less money.[48] However, Chiper has a keen sense for doing things the right way, and his vision of an expedition thus reveals much about the ideal or standard form of expedition in Moldova. Ethnographic expeditions, as my informants have experienced them, are large undertakings. The ethnographer travels in a team, usually with private transportation. Although for personal travel ethnographers often use the regular bus service that extends even to Moldova's most remote villages, many consider an expedition inconceivable without private transportation. Recording is highly valued, so a still camera and a tape recorder are essential, and video cameras are especially coveted. The

[48] The second expedition I participated in received a grant of US$950 from the Soros Foundation to cover the full costs of a combined ethnographic expedition and art practicum for sixteen participants over ten days. This sum covered payments to two cooks (three meals per day), all food, art supplies (e.g. canvas, paper), film and film development, audio cassettes, and transportation. There was no video recording on this expedition, and costs were cut in other obvious ways. For example, the participants used the regular bus service to and from Chişinău instead of hiring private transport. Once participants were in the village, all travel was on foot, meals were simple, almost no alcohol was consumed, and informants were not offered special refreshments (although they were invited to eat with the group, if they came to the camp during a mealtime).

ethnographer works the tape recorder, but none of the other team members needs to be an active ethnographer. Students should be taken along as part of their training if possible.

We modelled our expedition on this ideal and set off from Chişinău early on a Monday morning. Chiper sat in the front seat, and I sat in the back with the cameraman and one of the young women from Chiper's ensemble. The size of the car limited the number of students we took, but Chiper wanted a girl to keep me company, so I requested one of his most active students, Tatiana, a sixteen-year-old who had been in the ensemble since before Chiper took over its direction. We gathered at seven o'clock in the morning in front of the school where Chiper taught, changed dollars into lei before leaving the city, and stopped at a market on the outskirts of town to buy snacks for the road and food for our first meal at Gargalik's house. We arrived in the village of Tomai by eleven that morning and found Gargalik at one of his stores. He gave us sodas and beers; we picked some vegetables from the garden outside the store and then headed to his house, where his wife prepared a meal for us. After we ate, the expedition began.

For the first day of the expedition, Gargalik had arranged for two women who worked at the culture house to meet us. We talked to them first, then met an elderly woman at her house. This was followed by a trip to Gargalik's parents' house in the same village and finally by a visit with an elderly man. On the second day we spent the day fishing, swimming, and eating with some of Gargalik's male relatives at the local lake. Late that afternoon we met with a women's amateur singing group at the culture house in the village of Cazaclia. Following this meeting, we were invited to a private home, and two men performed several dances for us. We considered the village to be ethnically Gagauz, but one of the men who danced for us insisted that it was a 'multi-national' village.

We travelled to Chiper's village to sleep that night, and on the third day we conducted fieldwork in the villages of Brînza and Văleni. In both cases, informants were gathered for us: we found a women's singing group in the first village, and in the evening the director of the culture house at the second village went through the village gathering people to the culture house for us. On the fourth day we worked in three villages: Slobozia Mare (with one woman), Cîşliță-Prut (Chiper's native village), and Giurgiuleşti (with two women). We returned to Slobozia Mare the same evening to work with men who had been asked during the day to join us. The five villages we visited during the third and fourth days were 'Romanian' villages, but the husband of one of the women we worked with in Giurgiuleşti was Gagauz. He gave us the name of someone we might work with on the fifth day when we travelled to Cişmichioi, another Gagauz village. We did not succeed in working with that person, but another extended family spent the day talking to us. That night we returned to Gargalik's house, where we slept, and on the sixth day we left for Chişinău.

During the course of this expedition, additional links in the folkloric community became clear. Specifically, both Chiper and Gargalik relied heavily on culture houses and their employees to identify persons who 'knew' traditions, whether music, dance, or rituals and customs. We gathered materials from other amateur ethnographers, such as the women's singing collectives in Cazaclia and Brînza, and from persons known to culture professionals for their abilities. In most cases, individuals were selected for us; we did not go knocking on unknown doors.[49] In some cases we worked with people with whom either Gargalik or Chiper had worked in the past; these included Gargalik's parents, the two women we worked with in Cîşliţa-Prut, and one of the women in Giurgiuleşti. The two women in Cîşliţa-Prut even prepared the information they were willing to tell us when they learned we were planning to come. Several of the villages we visited had long histories of interacting with ethnographers and folklorists. Giurgiuleşti, for example, was visited in 1949 by members of the state ensemble Joc, who collected and learned a dance that the local amateur ensemble had presented at a Bucharest competition in 1938 (Curbet 2005: 13).

As we worked with these people, Chiper and Gargalik made verbal notes of informants they wanted to continue working with in the future. For example, the woman in Slobozia Mare was extremely reluctant to give information about traditions, and Chiper complained about how difficult it was to work with her. He was not interested in working with her in the future. Others, especially the Gagauz family in the last village, which welcomed us even though we had no proper introduction, were favourites. Chiper and Gargalik were so excited by the possibilities of further work in this village that we made a detour by the mayor's house to propose some sort of folkloric festival there – perhaps an extension of the festival Chiper organizes the week before Easter, Duminica la Florii. Even as we were collecting, Chiper and Gargalik were thinking ahead to performances, as well as to future episodes of collecting.

---

[49] In subsequent fieldwork conducted with Varvara Buzilă, we often knocked at unknown gates. Andrei Tamazlâcaru also reports gathering songs while visiting hospital patients and over the telephone during unrelated calls. Attending weddings and occasionally funerals, uninvited, is also commonly reported. These more anonymous and random sampling approaches are considered particularly useful for locating informants in new places, but the point to emphasize in either case is that ethnographers are likely to revisit 'good' informants, incorporating them more deeply in repertoire creation, especially as the informants learn more about the interests of the ethnographers and folklorists who seek their help.

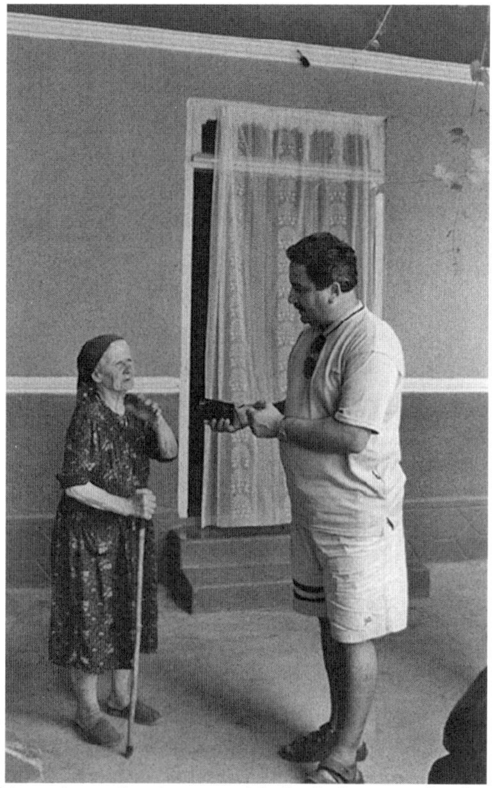

Plate 7. Valeriu Chiper interviewing an elderly informant in the ethnically Gagauz village of Cişmichioi.

Repertoire Creation

By September Chiper was including several songs from the expedition in his group's repertoire. At rehearsals I witnessed some of the mechanics involved in transforming the taped materials we had collected into elements of Mostenitorii's repertoire. As might be expected, traditions gathered in the field lost many of their local particularities almost immediately as they became the property of an organized ensemble. This was well illustrated by the song 'I Came from Work' (*De la lucru am venit*). We recorded it in Brînza, but the singer had learned it in her native village, Colibaşi. Therefore, Chiper identified it as a song from Colibaşi when teaching it to his students and said nothing of its more recent presence in Brînza. The ensemble learned another song by the same woman, intended for a boy entering the army and called 'Vasile, Mother's Dear One' (*Dragul mamei, măi Vasile*). By performance and song type, this piece would ordinarily have been sung by a single individual. Thus its rendering in multiple voices, including girls' voices, changed its form.

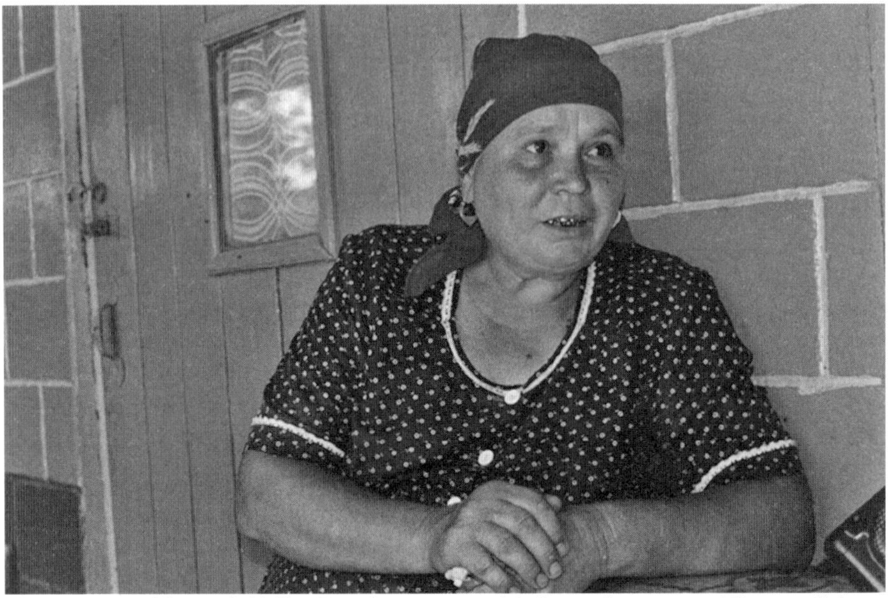

Plate 8. A resident of Cîşliţa-Prut has prepared information on wedding traditions, including vulgar jokes, to be recorded by Valeriu Chiper.

From the materials we collected in the village of Văleni, Chiper had his students transcribe and learn 'shouts' (*strigături*), short verses with satirical or humorous content that are shouted while dancing, to add interest and help the dancers keep time. The recorded musical accompaniment for the shouts was a flute, but Chiper's musicians, both students and adults, transcribed pieces for accordion, piano, and drum, creating a richer and more 'traditional' musical accompaniment for a dance involving shouts. Chiper and his musicians disagreed, however, over whether the musical form indicated by the shouts and the flute accompaniment was properly a *brîu*, *horă*, or *bătută*. These are all group dances, with differences in tempo, but at a minimum viewers distinguish them according to the way the dancers hold and move their hands and arms.

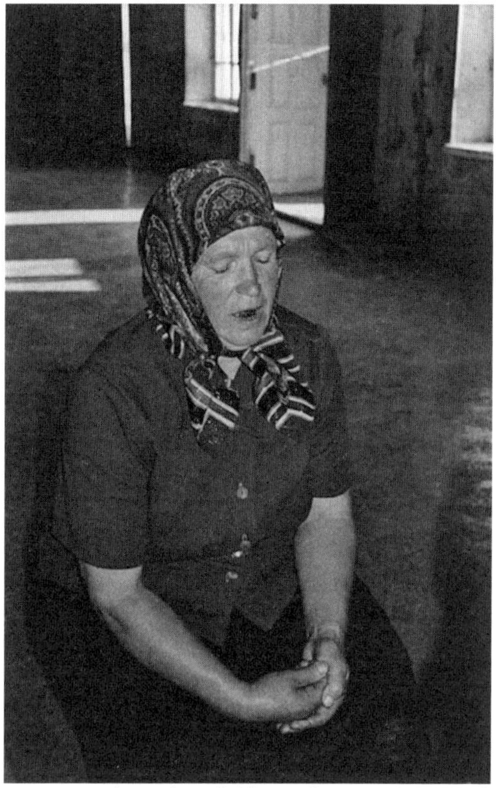

Plate 9. An elderly woman sings for visiting ethnographers at the culture house in the village of Văleni.

In the end, the piece was performed as none of these dance forms. Instead, Chiper encouraged his group to dance in place as they sang. That is, while holding hands in a large semicircle, the students were to add arm and leg movements. As they sang, they shifted a few steps to the right and then to the left, their linked arms crossing their chests. Some boys in the ensemble added irregular whistles during the pauses between refrains. In this way, a piece recorded in two voices was fleshed out into an ideal image of a village performance. The new piece was not a straightforward re-creation of what we had actually collected. Some of the transformations returned authenticity to a piece that was certainly meant to be performed in a large group, almost certainly with musicians playing multiple instruments, although these transformations were guided by Chiper's expertise and that of his musicians. Equally important, with the addition of instrumentation, whistling, and subtle group dancing, the piece also took on an outward resemblance to all the other songs performed by this ensemble. It ceased to be emblematic of the village in which it was collected, where it is performed by middle-aged and elderly men with the instruments they can afford.

Plate 10. Two men dance for visiting ethnographers in Văleni. Neither of the two had any formal training in dance, but the speed and precision of their steps drew favourable comments from Valeriu Chiper and Afanasi Gargalik.

The learning of these songs entailed some transcription. At the least, Chiper transcribed the text of a song and dictated it to his students (as in the army song just mentioned). In other instances he had students transcribe directly from the audiotapes, working singly or in small groups. He did not pose fundamental methodological questions to them in the process. Such questions might have been, How should one decide whether a piece is from Colibaşi or Brînza? When should one add instrumentation? When should a piece be performed by a small group versus a large group? When does gender or age matter in the selection of performers?

Plate 11. Ethnographers and folklorists often rely on their bodies as recording devices. Here, a member of the ensemble Moştenitorii (in white) learns a children's game from a group of kindergarten teachers in the village of Brînza.

The literal requirements of authenticity suggest that when Chiper transfers material gathered from informants in the field to his ensemble's repertoire, he should carefully scrutinize any divergences in the mode of performance. Yet in field interviews we rarely questioned informants about how a piece was performed in a 'natural' setting. Thus the confidence with which Chiper makes changes as he creates his group's repertoire indicates that the ethnographic knowledge that goes into producing an accurate repertoire involves both fieldwork and a knowledge of supposedly ideal forms and performance genres into which all field collections can be slotted (cf. Herzfeld 1982: 141).

Plate 12. Ethnographers receive a warm welcome from a women's singing group to be interviewed in the village of Cazaclia. Author in centre, holding the ensemble's gift of bread.

Plate 13. An extended family in Cişmichioi warmly welcomes the group with Chiper and Gargalik even though they had not expected visitors.

When I left Moldova in November 2001, Chiper had not yet included Gagauz materials in his repertoire. Without directly collaborating with Gargalik or another Gagauz speaker, he could not transcribe the Gagauz songs. Nor did he express interest in including such songs. He was, however, very excited about a dance we had collected in the village of Cazaclia – the eagle dance (*dansul vulturilor*) – and was considering including it. This was an erotic dance portraying the courtship, mating, and nesting of a pair of birds, which would have been performed by two men as entertainment at a wedding. While recording this dance, Gargalik had the musicians play the music without the dancers, and he tried to dance it himself. At the time, Chiper told me this dance would be a good addition to Gargalik's repertoire if he could find steps for it, but, he said, Gargalik was having difficulty dancing it because the rhythm was in fact Romanian.

This dance, then, might have been staged by two ensembles – as a Gagauz dance without the pantomime and as a Romanian dance with the pantomime. If Chiper decided to include it, he would need to decide whether the dance was from Focşani, in Romania, or from Cazaclia, the predominantly Gagauz village in Moldova where we collected it. This was because the performers had told us it was a Gagauz dance, but one of them said he had learned it from his father, who had been born in Focşani. This performer further claimed that Cazaclia was 'multi-national', not just Gagauz. Therefore, resolving the dance's origin in favour of Cazaclia would not resolve its ethnic character. However the dance might be incorporated into Chiper's or Gargalik's repertoire, the performed version would erase many of the subtleties in the dance's ethnic and even national pedigree while leaving its village origin intact.

Methods and Ideology

A basic description of our expedition indicates several other things about the practice of ethnography in Moldova. First, ethnographers use what connections they can, especially through cultural institutions and relatives, to find suitable informants. Unless amateur specialists, such as a singing group, already pursue ethnographic activities in a village, the preference is for elderly informants. Ethnography in Moldova is inherently considered a study of things done in the past, not in the present.[50] Yet ethnographers are not

[50] In this respect the ethnographic collecting that accompanies ethnographic folkloric performance has the effect, described by Deema Kaneff (2004) for folkloric activities in Bulgaria, of distancing villagers from their own past. When folklore is identified as a discrete set of practices, beliefs, and rituals distinct from everyday life, it becomes 'timeless' but also irretrievable. 'The folkloric past [consisted of] objects and activities which could be observed but were no longer "livable"' (Kaneff 2004: 152). The relationship between folklore and

necessarily interested in history as it is experienced by individuals or groups. This was well illustrated in the case of the woman in Slobozia Mare, who was ready to talk about her past experiences, particularly during World War II, and the loss of family members during the war. Chiper was interested in establishing whether Soviet deportations had taken place in the villages where we worked and whether there had been deportations in our informants' families, but he otherwise tended to hurry people, including this woman, past the details of their lives and on to discussions of tradition. Other life history details Chiper frequently elicited related to informants' years of schooling, languages known and studied in school (particularly in the case of Gagauz informants), and birth village. These were elicited data, but the mandatory data, written in notes and on cassette liners at the beginning of every interview, were the host village and county, date of interview, name of informant, and date of informant's birth. Informants tend to give more information, including their birth village and occupation, when asked to introduce themselves.

It must be said that ethnographers in Moldova have different styles, and every field expedition is unique. In addition to the range of expedition budgets, the style of collaboration within the common framework of team research varies. When travelling with Chiper, for example, we were technically three ethnographers (Chiper, Gargalik, and me), but we always travelled together. Chiper always asked the majority of the questions, but he encouraged me to ask questions as well. Gargalik almost never asked questions. During the three days when we were in Romanian villages, he was silent. On the last day, when we stopped in another Gagauz village, I expected him to ask questions again, because the material we gathered there would presumably be useful in building his ensemble's repertoire.

As Chiper ran out of questions, he turned to ask me if I had any. I deferred to Gargalik, saying that perhaps he had questions he had not yet asked. What followed was a few minutes of extreme tension in which both men insisted that they had exactly the same questions, and it did not matter which of them did the asking. I continued to pause, confused, and Gargalik did start to ask a few questions. They were indeed clarifications of questions previously asked. After our return to Chişinău, Chiper told me that if Gargalik had begun the questioning in each village, he would have asked whether the village had any dances or perhaps songs and then left it at that, because he was trained in choreography, not ethnography. Gargalik's self-presentation, however, emphasized his commitment to ethnography and to

---

everyday life is more complex in Moldova than in Kaneff's Bulgaria, because the ethnography practised by Moldova's folkloric community also has a strong revivalist investment and seeks to encourage villagers to reintegrate some traditional practices into their everyday lives.

performances informed by ethnographic study. The momentary tension in the field revealed that our collaboration involved an avowal of unity of purpose and common knowledge despite real differences in our research interests, training, and skills.

In contrast, the teamwork and collaboration of the second expedition I joined, organized by a group of university art students, was targeted towards collecting a maximum amount of data. The expedition was also intended to be a summer practicum for art students, primarily oil painters and watercolourists, so it was focused on a series of scenic villages on the banks of the Bîk River in Floreşti County. The students were accompanied by two professional ethnographers, a doctoral candidate in ethnography, and an archaeologist, all of whom supervised the students' ethnographic efforts while conducting their own research.

Plate 14. Two painters record and photograph an elderly informant in the village of Ţîra who plays a violin he received from a Romanian soldier in exchange for bread during World War II. The students will use elements of the man's life history and music to inspire their artwork and will share their recordings with ethnographers in the expedition team (Photo by Eugen Bîzgu).

The adult facilitators encouraged students to 'divide and conquer' and did the same themselves, visiting as many houses as possible in the village of Ţîra, where we stayed, and two neighbouring villages. Materials were pooled at the end of the day, although individuals retained pieces such as tapes or sketches that were of particular interest for their own projects. One of the facilitators, for example, was a doctoral student working on burial traditions. She kept her own cassette tapes but relied on others to photograph cemeteries and headstones. She kept track of who had taken the photographs and requested copies of the prints once we were back in the capital. She also recorded other information that she expected to interest other participants and notified them of her recordings.

Plate 15. A graphic design student meticulously reproduces on gridded paper the pattern in a carpet (not shown) owned by a village family in Țîra. Gridded patterns like these are used to train students in design techniques and to inspire new designs for industrially produced carpets, and they are held by museums as records of traditional carpet weaving.

A great deal of communication took place among participants at the summer camp about people already spoken to and the results of those meetings, potentially good informants, houses with interesting carpets or other artefacts, beautiful scenery, and so on. There was also a great shuttling of people back and forth. Someone who had set off with a tape recorder but no camera might ask a photographer to go back and photograph something; or after hearing an ethnographic report, a student might return to a village to sketch or paint a picture of a house, carpet, vase, or person. The expedition did not include a plan for the transcription, storage, or use of the materials gathered, so portions remained in the possession of several participants.

Although the information gathered during this expedition involved a broad range of both ethnographers' working styles and informants' responses, it was more dispersed and less easily used as a whole than the tapes from Chiper's expedition. Amid this variety, only certain constants in the data stood out: the informant's name, age, birth village, and current village.

Village Ethnography and National Identity

As suggested by the preceding description, the ethnographic fieldwork behind 'authentic' folkloric performances in Moldova bears a strong resemblance to early American and British anthropology, in two respects: it is geared towards salvaging disappearing traditions, and the interpretation of these traditions depends on and then reproduces an ideology of survivalism. The practice of local ethnography, as materials are collected in villages and performed onstage, works to suppress evidence of diversity, time, and change in villages. It also suppresses evidence of population movements and cultural exchange between villages.[51]

Even before folklore reaches the stage in Moldova, it has become part of an identity project that resembles what Michael Herzfeld (1987) identified as emblematic of Greek ethnography. The key problem for Greek ethnography and folklore, he wrote, has been to link the legacies of ancient Greece to modern practices in the Greek nation-state. The creation of textual canons of Greek folklore successfully established both national and European identity, but it did so through the erasure of history, local diversity, and the complexities of the creative processes through which the folklore was actually created.

From the late nineteenth century, Herzfeld observed, 'Greek folklorists often rejected the seemingly Turkish-derived elements that they identified in particular variants of folk texts, on the grounds that such elements were extraneous and ugly, "matter out of place" … "corruption". Their typologies and reconstructions had the effect of obliterating specific, recorded texts. They created a moralistic canon of texts that reduced diversity to uniformity' (Herzfeld 1987: 29). Similarly, the cumulative results of local ethnography in Moldova could produce a map of culturally discrete villages and regions. As in Greece, the methods currently employed by members of the folkloric community would make this a map of Moldova's culture at

---

[51] Traditions before the Soviet period were not, of course, static and unchanging. In 1935, for example, Petre Ştefanucă, a Bessarabian scholar trained by the Romanian sociologist Dimitrie Gusti, published a detailed account of changes in the dances known and danced around Iurceni, in Lăpuşna County (Ştefanucă 1990). He noted the recent introduction of new dances such as the tango, as well as the passing away of older dances that people remembered but no longer danced.

some mythic time. Folklorists explicitly acknowledge only an intention to recover pre-Soviet traditions, but their actual practice suggests also a desire to map villages and regions as they were before migrations between villages, incursions of non-Romanian speakers, and ethnic mixing began to corrupt or dissolve distinct configurations of tradition. Because of current methods of ethnographic research, the hypothetical map would also show continuity between Romanian-speaking villages in the Republic of Moldova and villages in Romania, erasing complex relations between local villages and ethnic groups. In other words, a grand mapping project of culture in Moldova, if it were undertaken by ethnographers, would indicate ethnography's support for a pro-Romanian national ideology.

The results of a village-centred methodology of ethnographic collection can therefore produce a theoretical and political orientation that is at odds with the folkloric movement's dominant goal of creating an authentic folklore that does not foreground ethnic relations. Yet the effects of collection methodology on the production of images and narratives about ethnic identity appears to be out of the direct control of its practitioners.

In an earlier work dedicated to tracing the intellectual careers of several early Greek folklorists, Herzfeld (1982) found that basic theories and methods persisted even as subsequent generations of folklorists changed their political goals and orientations. For example, in the mid-1900s a Marxist folklorist attacked earlier nationalists for interpreting epics and songs as evidence of national culture. He found fault with their basic classification system (i.e. definitions of genres), but without proposing a new classification system, he used the same materials to advance his own interpretation of folklore as evincing class conflict (Herzfeld 1982: 141). Indeed, well into the twentieth century the conceptual language of ethnology and folkloristics throughout Europe did not change to match changing research interests, which caused it often to 'sound as if nationality (ethnicity) was the ultimate and sole *explanandum* for the existence of a cultural feature' (Hann, Sarkany, and Skalnik 2005: 8). Contemporary ethnographers in Moldova similarly pursue their intellectual activities using methods and theories that they did not invent from scratch but inherited, borrowed, and modified. Therefore it is all the more important to investigate the way folklorists and ethnographers perceive their own scholarly activities. Of all the ideological positions their work can convey, which do they most intend to communicate, and which are the unintended consequences of disciplinary traditions?

In the remainder of this chapter I examine some details from life histories to understand how individuals explain their participation in the folkloric movement. I am specifically interested in understanding why 'the village' appeals to these people as a locus for research. Although some ethnographers are at least implicitly dedicated to the kind of cultural mapping that their work could generate, no one I spoke with actually claimed this kind of project for himself or other ethnographers in Moldova. If the explicitly stated goal of fieldwork is not to produce a map of Moldova's mythical 'Romanian' culture, then why do individual ethnographers and folklorists pursue a form of 'survivalist' ethnography? Why must fieldwork be done in villages, and why must *individual* villages be represented onstage?

Career Choices and Village Origins

At the level of individual ethnographers and directors of folkloric ensembles, it seems important to ask why they were drawn to their careers in the first place. As I asked people about their career histories, I found that for many ensemble directors, their training as musicians or dancers preceded their involvement in folklore. My question, for many of them, was a non-question. But when they talked about the beginnings of their careers, many of my contacts brought up their village origins. Indeed, a person's native village is common social knowledge, and people often know their colleagues' native villages as standard biographical information.

Village origins place a person and may be used to explain limitations in a specialist's knowledge or personality. The ethnographic authority inherent in jury decisions also transfers to general social life. For example, I frequently heard people complain that a friend or colleague had corrected their pronunciation. Listeners would offer consolation by replying that someone born in the north has no authority to correct the speech of someone from the south, and vice versa. From another perspective, southerners are considered to have hot tempers, and people may express their difficulty in working with someone else by noting that the colleague is from the south. A person's native village is thus a potentially important part of his or her social identity. Coming from a village seems to have shaped the career decisions of members of the folkloric community in both subtle and obvious ways.

In September 2001 I finally had the opportunity to interview Elena Osoianu, whom I had met a full year before. Osoianu is one of the founding members of the music ensemble Tălăncuța, the first *etno-folcloric* ensemble established in Moldova.[52] All members of this ensemble are involved in teaching folklore to children or adolescents, and the ensemble's founder and director, Andrei Tamazlâcaru, is known for both his work in ethno-pedagogy and his leadership of the folkloric movement. Osoianu has four sisters, all of whom are active in Tălăncuța. The five sisters also sing together as Surorile

[52] *Tălăncuța* is the diminutive form of *talancă* and *talangă*, both Romanian words for the bell put on the necks of cows and sheep.

Osoianu (the Osoianu Sisters) and are among the best-known, publicly recognized members of the folkloric movement. It was clear that Elena Osoianu and her sisters were important people to talk to, but like Andrei Tamazlâcaru himself, they were elusive. I saw them on several occasions beginning in February 2001, but it was not until September that I was able to talk explicitly with Osoianu about her work. When we finally spoke, I learned much about the limitations experienced by young adults from Moldova's villages when they tried to establish themselves in the capital city during the early 1980s.

On September 22 Elena Osoianu and her sister Maria arranged to meet Varvara Buzilă, an ethnographer and my field advisor, at her house, because they had some financial accounts to settle. Buzilă kept money for her parents at her house in Chişinău, functioning as their bank, because they did not feel safe keeping their money either in their house in the village or in a bank. Sometimes her parents send produce or recently butchered meat to be sold at the market. Buzilă kept the money from the sale and used it to purchase sugar, medicine, and other items her parents needed but could not acquire in the village. The cash was also used to pay immediate expenses for which Buzilă's family did not have money or, in some cases, for lending to close friends. Elena Osoianu's two sons had gone to Vienna to study ballet, and at least once Buzilă lent her money to help make this possible. On this day in September, Osoianu was returning money she had borrowed for one of her son's tickets to Vienna. The transaction was complicated by a loan she had given Buzilă. One of the women's loans had been made in dollars and the other in lei, and it took some time for Buzilă and Osoianu to agree on how to resolve their mutual debts. Because Buzilă knew I was eager to speak to Osoianu and her sisters but had not yet had the opportunity, she invited me to come over, with tape recorder, and wait until they arrived. After Osoianu and Buzilă worked out their loans to each other, Buzilă and I led the two sisters into a discussion of their personal histories: how they got involved in folklore, how and why they started their children's ensembles, and how their work had changed over the years.

Briefly, Osoianu had come to the State Institute for the Arts (now the University of the Arts) in 1980. Her future husband introduced her to his brother, Andrei Tamazlâcaru, who then involved her in singing folklore. Some of Osoianu's younger sisters came to Chişinău in the following few years to study, and the others came at least in part to join Osoianu in singing folklore. Tamazlâcaru was interested in staging songs that Osoianu said would suit her sisters' voices better than her own. Thus the five sisters formed Surorile Osoianu at the same time the ensemble Tălăncuța was being built. Although Tălăncuța is now state funded, it was originally composed of music students as an extracurricular club.

Osoianu and her sisters experienced multiple problems in Chişinău. Osoianu came as a student, lived in a dormitory, and experienced major bureaucratic problems only when she finished her studies. The sisters who joined her, however, had difficulty finding places to live and work because they did not have residency permits for the city. Her sister Maria, present at the interview, wanted to transfer from an institute in Bălți to the institute in Chişinău. She was accepted in Chişinău, but Bălți would not release her documents. She worked in a beauty institute in Chişinău preparing waxes in order to support herself. Another sister was assigned a teaching job outside the city. Because it was impossible for her to commute, she gave up the job so she could remain full-time in Chişinău with her sisters. When Elena Osoianu finished her studies in 1984, Surorile Osoianu had already become well known, but not having a residency permit, she had no possibility of remaining in Chişinău. Osoianu explained that she went to see at least one official at the Ministry of Culture:

> There was a respected woman at the Ministry of Culture, I don't know [Buzilă interjected here: 'I knew her']. I went to see her in 1984 when I had just finished the Art Institute, and I said, give us [a room] in the dormitory where we live – it's still a dormitory for the Art Institute today – give Surorile Osoianu a space there because we want to continue working with folklore. And she replied, you can keep doing what you are doing, but look – there are [people] coming from Russia. Lots of musicians, ballerinas are coming and we have to house them and give them apartments. You are from Moldova. You can fall back where you came [from].

The ministry official turned down Osoianu's proposal on the grounds that the ministry had to secure housing for visiting artists. Because Osoianu and her sisters were born in Moldova, the official said that the ministry could not be responsible for them.

The recollection of this event immediately evoked strong comments from Maria Osoianu (MO) and Buzilă (VB), with responses and questions from Elena Osoianu (EO) and me (JC):

> VB: Go home.
>
> MO: Go home.
>
> VB: Go back to where you came [from].
>
> MO: Go back to where you came [from]. We here in Chişinău cannot offer you anything.
>
> VB: The lady was a fighter for the ministry.
>
> MO: She was a fighter for the ministry.

VB: A fighter for the Ministry of Culture.
JC: What does fighter mean?
VB: The vice-minister of culture.
EO: That is, the vice-minister.
VB: Of culture. See the attitude? Folklore singers come to them and propose an idea.
MO: We proposed –
VB: Give us the possibility to continue this authentic folklore.
EO: Because we had to leave the dormitory at that time.
JC: And the musicians coming from Russia, they were classical musicians?
VB: Yes. (E: Exactly.) And they came here. They were not from here.
JC: They were not singing folklore?
EO: No.
MO: They were musicians, big, professional. They were coming to the Opera Theatre. Ballerinas [unclear].

The performers who would be housed instead of Osoianu were not folkloric singers but specialists in other genres – classical music, opera, ballet. The Osoianu sisters were not angered by the presence of these Russian performers per se and did not describe themselves as having been in professional competition with them. Rather, Osoianu was angry that the vice-minister at the Ministry of Culture was failing to help Moldovan citizens. She helped Russians and sent the Moldovans home – back to their native villages. That the Osoianu sisters were asking to be established as authentic folk singers only dramatized the ministry's betrayal of the local population in favour of foreigners. Not only did the official refuse to help local people, but she also refused to support autochthonous culture.

Later the same day, after the Osoianu sisters had left, Buzilă talked about her own housing difficulties. She, too, had come to Chişinău as a student. By 1983 she was twenty-eight, had studied at the university for five years and worked for three, and was about to marry. She had been in Chişinău for a total of eight years, and her husband roughly the same length of time, yet neither had been able to secure a residency permit. As in the case of the Osoianu sisters, the lack of a residency permit interfered with Buzilă's finding housing and building a career. Technically, it was not forbidden to buy a house in Chişinău without a residency permit for the city, but in practice Buzilă found that she could neither buy a house without a permit nor obtain a permit without already having a house. She spent the entirety of 1983 trying to resolve this circular problem, studying the law and the Constitution and consulting bureaucrats and lawyers. It preoccupied her thoughts and activities to such an extent that she claimed she remembered nothing about her wedding.

As these two accounts illustrate, people were deeply affected by the frustrations of being unable to secure housing, remain in the capital, begin a career related to their education, and provide for themselves. In many ways, actual jobs were the result of making do within the broader system. Although Osoianu intended to be a performer, the work she and her sisters had undertaken with children and folklore was almost certainly the result of coincidence under the difficult circumstances faced by rural Moldovans.

When I asked Elena and Maria Osoianu how they had started working with children, they did not refer to ethno-pedagogy. This was one of Andrei Tamazlâcaru's special interests (see Tamazlâcaru 1986), and the heavy involvement of Tălăncuța's members with children suggests that they likewise chose deliberately to direct their folkloric careers towards children's activities. Instead, Elena recounted that the sisters found work in a kindergarten because the director was interested in supporting folkloric activities. Elena's husband worked with a relative of the kindergarten director, who made the sisters' introduction.

This first job was in 1984 and corresponded to the birth of Elena's first son. She wanted to work at the kindergarten so that her son would be accepted into the program, and her position opened the way for all five sisters to conduct folkloric ensembles in educational establishments throughout Chişinău. In 2001, four of the five worked for the National Palace of Creativity for Children and Adolescents, but the mix of their actual positions was in continual flux. Iulia, for example, worked at both the National Palace and in a kindergarten. In September 2001 she had just arranged with the director of the National Palace to fulfil her responsibilities to the Palace by bringing a group from a kindergarten to National Palace concerts, competitions, and special events. This arrangement reduced her work load, increased her salary, and raised the official number of ensembles and children involved in folkloric performances.

The story the Osoianu sisters told about how they came to be among the most recognized folkloric performers and conductors of 'authentic' children's ensembles surprised me. As they told the story, their careers were largely accidental. Elena came to the capital to study music, and she knew folksongs from having grown up in a village, but other, more professionally advanced persons drew her into folk-singing as a career. Thereafter, her village origins made it nearly impossible for her to live or work in Chişinău, and she was willing to take any job that would help her stay. Working with children was, for her, more or less accidental.

From the perspective of individual lives, then, careers in ethnography and folkloric performance in Moldova are partly the result of both positive and negative forms of structural discrimination, and not solely the deliberate pursuit of a particular career. Positive forms of structural discrimination, for example, arose in the life histories of many ensemble directors, like Petru Dinjos, who were identified as promising musicians in childhood and sent to state training institutions, like the School for Enlightenment in Soroca, from an early age.[53] While few informants felt the state to be an unwelcome presence in their early training, they blamed the state for difficulties encountered in adulthood. In the 1980s, legislation and bureaucratic procedures hindered many people from securing housing and jobs through official channels. People relied instead on friends. Charles King (2000), too, noted the use of ethnic, regional, and sub-regional networks for personal advancement in the new Republic of Moldova. Newcomers to the capital relied heavily on co-villagers or residents from nearby villages to help them secure housing, jobs, and other necessary goods and services in the city, thereby heightening the social importance of village origins. People I talked to, however, were not always clear about exactly how and when these networks actually operated. Well-positioned persons such as Tamazlâcaru and the kindergarten director might help someone for apparently altruistic reasons, such as the recognition of talent, but like the ethnic Moldovan woman at the Ministry of Culture, they might just as easily refuse to recognize obligations on any basis. With the capital's population of ethnic Moldovans rising dramatically because of rural-to-urban migration, the social effect of village origins was heightened in the 1980s – at the same time the folkloric movement developed.

Urbanization during the Soviet Period

Urbanization generally increased after the founding of the Moldovan Soviet Socialist Republic (MSSR) in 1940. As reported by Irina Livezeanu (1981a: 335), Bessarabia's urban areas encompassed only 13 per cent of the total population in 1930. By 1959, 22.3 per cent of the MSSR's population was urban. Between 1959 and 1970, urban areas grew by 76 per cent, to account for 31.7 per cent of the republic's total population. This trend continued into the 1980s, albeit at a slower rate, with rural migrants to cities accounting for much of the urban growth. Because much of the rural population was ethnically Moldovan (i.e. Romanian-speaking), rural-to-urban migration after World War II also had the net effect of changing the ethnic composition of

[53] Indeed, folkloric festivals focused on individual competitors continue to serve this function of identifying talented youth, especially from rural areas.

Moldova's cities. For example, in 1959 Chişinău's ethnic composition was 32.3 per cent Moldovan, 32.2 per cent Russian, 19.9 per cent Jewish, 12 per cent Ukrainian, and 0.7 per cent Gagauz. By 1970 the proportions had changed to 37.2 per cent Moldovan, 30.7 per cent Russian, 14 per cent Jewish, 14.2 per cent Ukrainian, and 0.7 per cent Gagauz (Livezeanu 1981a: 334).

Although these proportional changes may seem small, they indicate substantial social change. Specifically, the increased presence of ethnic Moldovans in Chişinău challenged the capital's identity as a Russian and Jewish city, which had developed after Bessarabia's incorporation into the Russian Empire in 1812 (Livezeanu 1995: 93–97). Although the Romanian government sought to re-Romanianize Chişinău along with the rest of Bessarabia during the inter-war period, it had relatively little success, and Russian language and culture still dominated the city at the beginning of Soviet rule. By the 1960s, however, Soviet sociologists reported that ethnic Moldovans moving into urban areas maintained their rural cultural traditions, such as music and wedding styles, even when they assimilated linguistically to Russian (Livezeanu 1981b: 581). By the 1980s, when my informants came from their native villages to seek education and work in the capital city, they could interpret their difficulties as originating in the broader processes of urbanization or 'Moldovanization' then unfolding in the republic. Among members of the folkloric community, individual experiences of urbanization are equal in importance to those of ethnic discrimination in understanding professional trajectories. Firsthand experience of rural-to-urban migration also helps to explain the appeal of the village as a primary object of research among ethnographers and its unquestioned status as a locus of authentic tradition.

Social Memory and Identity

As specific places and residences of spatially defined social groups, villages in Moldova constitute what Maurice Halbwachs (1992) referred to as 'framework[s] of social memory'. Like other frameworks of memory, villages help create an experience of social unity and temporal continuity. Because the majority of Moldova's population has close family ties to villages, people weave their individual histories, memories, and experiences into a common narrative of identity. They use the trope of 'the village' as if this place corresponds to any and all of Moldova's physically existing villages. People's intimate experiences in and of actual villages lend a sense of physical reality to their shared and idealized image of the village. Moreover, the spatial and physical dimensions of real villages help anchor and organize memory so that it can be retrieved and relived.

For Moldova's folkloric community 'the village' serves as both a symbolic and a physical repository of the past. When folklorists 'go back' to villages (especially their native villages) for purposes of research and collection, they externalize the act of remembering, which otherwise occurs at the individual and collective level through discourse. When ordinary people in Chişinău talk about 'the village', they also go back to their pasts.

Recent patterns of rural-to-urban migration may have intensified the role played by the village in fostering social cohesion and communication in Moldova. For example, explaining the significance of a formerly shared house for a diasporic Jewish-Algerian family, Joëlle Bahloul (1996: 28) wrote: 'Remembering the house in which an uprooted culture originated and developed involves reversing history and sinking symbolic roots into a vanished human and geographical world. The remembered house is a small-scale cosmology symbolically restoring the integrity of a shattered geography'.

The physicality of a village, like that of a house, not only preserves memories but also helps structure social relationships in the present. Shared memories help individuals find moral orientations for new circumstances. James Ferguson (1997) for example, demonstrated that since the 1950s, workers of rural origin on Zambia's Copperbelt have engaged in dualistic schemes of moralistic thinking in which they oppose rural morality and social cooperation to urban immorality and competition.

Memory frameworks, however, must be periodically revalidated by experience (Halbwachs 1992: 183), or they will cease to feel real. Revalidation need not involve physical return to an original place, but the structural conditions of the original place must be replicated. Liisa Malkki's (1995) comparison of two groups of Hutu refugees exiled from Burundi to Tanzania in 1972 provides an excellent analysis of the way the structural conditions of life in a refugee camp supported one group's 'impassioned construction and reconstruction of their history as "a people"' (Malkki 1995: 3), whereas people in the second group, who lived in local villages, lost a collective sense of being Hutu. In the Moldovan case, village identity is salient because of the combination of experience and discrimination.

The village, as it appears in the theoretical and methodological orientations of contemporary folklorists in Moldova, thus has a new social significance because of recent trends of urbanization and rural-to-urban migration in the country. From this perspective, folkloric activity constitutes social identities not through the unilinear transmission of singular ideologies (national or otherwise) but through the polyvalent processes of memory creation and renewal. The combined process of folkloric collecting and mounting of authentic folkloric performances brings together multiple individuals and social groups in the production and renewal of 'village' memories. Folklorists, villagers, and audience members are all implicated in the process.

The emphasis on the village as the source of authentic traditions in Moldova's folkloric community derives in large part from the scholarly disciplines of ethnography and folklore. Yet the prominence given to villages in ethnography and local folkloric performances is not merely the unquestioned survival of a 'phantom' concept (Abrahams 1993).[54] As physical locations of social experience, villages are also deeply embedded in the personal lives of Moldova's ethnographers and folklorists. For this reason, villages maintain meanings for individuals, for the folkloric community, and for Moldova's population in general that contribute to the perception of authenticity when a *folcloric* or *etno-folcloric* ensemble performs.

The ethnographic methods used by members of Moldova's folkloric community are inherently political and nationalistic, but ethnographers prefer not to identify themselves as nationalists. They claim a more universal and humanistic role for their professional activities, agreeing with Gargalik that their work comes 'from the soul'. Indeed, their biographies reveal how, in the late Soviet period, folkloric activities that were focused on redefining villages as sources of authentic culture provided the possibility of 'working for the people' and working 'from the soul'. In the following chapter, I consider the implications of representing the village as the primary cultural unit of the nation and assess the degree to which the folkloric community is able to achieve its humanistic vision.

---

[54] Jane Goodman (2005) made a similar point about how the village is 'good to think' in Berber studies because it is central to both Berber social discourse about modernity, change, and migration and to social theory on the same topics. She concluded that Berbers use images of the changing village primarily to shore up anxieties about the past. My argument is that villages also provide a way to think about the present and future, even when the dominant discourse is heavily nostalgic.

Chapter 6
Inclusion and Exclusion in a Nation of Villages

On 27 August 2001, the Republic of Moldova celebrated ten years of independence. The official festivities sparked controversy. While the media encouraged citizens to be excited by the first military parade to be held in years, my informants grumbled that the festivities lacked an appropriate attention to national identity. The national anthem was not sung, and the presidential address criticized ethnic sentiments in the population. Commemorative banners in both Russian and Romanian hung around the central square, advertising the government's support for the public use of both languages. At least one of my informants feared that these facts signalled the return of Soviet-era state control. Apprehensive that his phone might have been tapped, my informant ended a call prematurely after telling me his opinion of the partial sponsorship of the event by Lukoil, Russia's largest oil company, whose local subsidiary is widely perceived as a political instrument. But despite the cynicism of some, the crowd that gathered for the day's opening ceremony was excited as the official address and military parade concluded.

A wave of young men and women then rushed from a temporary stage into the square just emptied of soldiers and began a rapid *horă*. Their white costumes shimmered in the morning sun as they danced in a pulsing circle, raising their joined hands to their shoulders, lowering them again, and quickly crossing them over their bodies as their feet carried them around. The crowd surged in behind them, forming a ring twenty people deep around the dancers. The dance lasted only three or four minutes, and then the dancers ran quickly back to the stage, leaving the spectators to disperse, reluctantly and disappointedly.

Plate 16. Dancers from multiple ensembles prepare to dance a *horă* as the Republic of Moldova celebrates ten years of independence. Choreographed by Pavel Popa.

The *horă* (pl. *hore*) performed on Independence Day was an especially striking performance, worthy of catching the public's attention as completely as it did. It was choreographed and danced by members of the several ensembles that would provide public concerts throughout the day. *Hore* are often danced in public, and it is not unusual to see several small groups of friends spontaneously begin a *horă* during the outdoor concerts open to public attendance in the capital throughout the year. The *horă* is considered the national dance, but authentic folkloric groups are expected to collect *hore*, like their other dances, from villages. The dance may be national, but if it is 'authentic' it will be danced in one of its many village variations. Thus the image of Moldova as a nation of villages is particularly well encapsulated in this dance.

In this chapter I further examine the practical consequences of the folkloric movement's criteria for authenticity. These criteria generate performances in which Moldova is imagined as a nation of villages, but what other qualities does this nation possess? Specifically, how is cultural diversity reconciled with national unity? What are the boundaries of social inclusion and exclusion in the nation of villages? How is ethnic diversity addressed?

The Metaphor of the *Horă*

Unlike other folkloric dances, the *horă* has an origin story that attributes meaning to its form and rhythm. Pavel Popa told me this version of the dance's origin:

> The *horă* is a patriotic dance. The word for it comes from the Greek *chor*. It is danced in a circle, and people dancing in a circle are invincible. The *horă* circle is like a fortress. After every battle that Ştefan cel Mare fought and won, he built a fortress. All of them are round, like the *horă* circle. All the Balkan groups, as well as Russians, have a form of *horă*. The Romanian *horă* is distinctive because it starts slow and gets faster. It's like the Romanian people. They are generally calm, do not overreact to being pushed on the trolleybus, but . . . The Moldovan people have resisted. They were originally Geto-Dacians and were then Romanized by Roman soldiers, but they kept Geto-Dacian traditions. More recently, the Russians came and the language was Russianized some, but now the Russians are gone, and the Moldovans remain.

As his story reveals, Popa claims the dance as both Romanian and Moldovan. Indeed, the *horă* is also Romania's national dance. As a patriotic dance, however, the *horă* is clearly symbolic of Moldova. Or rather, it is symbolic of two Moldovas: the medieval Moldovan state built by Ştefan cel Mare, the national hero who preserved Moldova's independence from the Ottoman Turks, and the Republic of Moldova that remains following the break-up of the Soviet Union.

Although Popa and others interpret the form of this dance as demonstrating the compatibility of national unity with cultural heterogeneity, this meaning is not inherent to the dance itself. Popa ascribed much of the dance's meaning to its circular form, but circle dances may have other meanings. This is made clear by a comparison with Stanley Brandes's (1990) account of Catalonia's national dance, the *sardana*, which is also circular in form.

Brandes wrote that the *sardana* was a prototypical 'invented tradition'. Precursors of the dance existed from as early as the sixteenth century, but a modern *sardana* emerged in 1850 and has been danced identically since then, except for the single, hotly debated feature of being danced with arms either up or down. Investigating the power of the *sardana* to symbolize Catalan identity, Brandes concluded that the power of the dance resided in its form. As a circle, the *sardana* reflected key Catalan values: harmony, uniformity, democracy, brotherhood, and the elimination of class distinctions. Moreover, the dance's complex steps had to be counted. Not only did this counting reflect Catalonia's involvement in capitalism, but it also reflected the voluntary nature of Catalan identity: a person had to be able to do the steps to join the circle of dancers, but learning them required only practice and counting, so no one was pre-emptively excluded.

Different national qualities are ascribed to the same circular form in the Moldovan *horă*. Instead of symbolizing equality and brotherhood, the *horă* circle symbolizes cultural survival; the importance of the form is its wholeness and unbrokenness. Additionally, the Romanian or Moldovan *horă* is only one circle dance among many, because the Balkan peoples and the Russians have their own circle dances. In another conversation with Popa, this time about dancing in the south of the country, he told me that every village there had its own version of the national dance:

> In the south, every village has its own *horă*. On Saturday nights, there are dances in Cahul [the county seat].[55] When you go, you look for the group that is dancing the way you know how to dance, and join them. In this way you meet other people from your village. If you join another group but dance with your own steps, they will not hold your hand, and you have to leave the group. At a wedding, if a bride and a groom are from different villages, there will be separate circles for each village. Guests from other villages will also form a separate circle from each village. If one circle is made for everyone, then every dancer will dance the steps from his own village.

Popa's discussion acknowledges that there are situations when village identities are not symbolized and maintained in dancing the *horă*. He says that as a general rule, however, it is the village's identity and solidarity that are manifested in the *horă*, even if the dance is a 'national' genre. In the context of a wedding, the dance symbolizes not the union of two families but the separateness of two villages. Similarly, when dancers gather at the county seat, they group together with co-villagers, and the *horă*s being danced symbolize the distinctiveness of the villages incorporated within a larger administrative area.

Brandes's (1990) interpretation of the *sardana* and Popa's discussion of the *horă* indicate that one must already know the key aspects of national character before being able to see it expressed in the form of the dance. In the case of the *sardana,* the opposition between Catalonia and Spain is the important story to tell in dance, along with other expressions of national

---

[55] These Saturday night dances were mentioned to me by other people as well, but I could never verify whether they were things of the past or ongoing. Some local administrations have recently been reviving village dances, though this is not a uniform or coordinated effort across the country. Most adults also remember a gradual tapering off of public dancing, both at weddings and in all-village settings, during their lifetimes, but no one could provide fixed dates or time periods.

identity. In the case of the Moldovan *horă*, the important story is about the survival of a people. In addition to Moldovan continuity through the parallel symbolism of the dancing circle and Ştefan cel Mare's fortresses, the *horă* comments on the way Moldovans have survived. They are united in their survival through their diversity, and the national dance is always being danced by villages. Popa's interpretation of the *horă* envisions the Moldovan nation not as a single large village but as a collection of unique villages, all 'dancing' to a common rhythm but using different steps. In his roles as ensemble director, frequent jury member, dance historian, and specialist at the National Centre for Folk Arts, Popa shares and transmits his vision widely.

Insider and Outsider Views of Villages

Folklorists and ethnographers in Moldova look to villages further to supply local models for political behaviours and values at the state level. For example, in the course of the second ethnographic expedition in which I participated in 2001 – the summer practicum for art students – I found expedition members and villagers engaged in lively discussions of the local villages' social composition.[56] Under Ottoman suzereinty, three types of villages composed of free peasants existed in Bessarabia.[57] One type was villages established by simple free peasants who did not own land but leased it from monasteries or landlords. Another was villages inhabited by *răzeşi,* or free peasants who owned their own land, paid no taxes, and were obliged only to perform military service. The third was villages pertaining to another privileged social class, the *mazili,* or boyars who had been released from service to the state and received land as compensation. The primary village we visited, Ţîra, was a *răzeşi* village. Its neighbors were either *răzeşi* or *mazili* or a combination of the two. *Mazili* and *răzeşi* villages are said today to be prouder than those established by simple free peasants. Indeed, locals distinguish the different villages according to the degree of pride (*mîndrie*) manifested by their contemporary inhabitants, pointing to a wide range of behaviours, including habits of greeting and other elements of etiquette and demonstrations of elegance.

---

[56] The second ethnographic expedition was organized as a summer practicum by university art students, primarily oil painters and watercolorists, to a series of scenic villages on the banks of the Bîk River in Floreşti County. The students were accompanied by two professional ethnographers, a doctoral candidate in ethnography, and an archaeologist.

[57] Even landless peasants in Bessarabia were personally free (unlike Russian serfs) and could move to new places (Hitchins 1994: 241), which adds to a general pride in contemporary Moldovan villages.

In the case of Țîra, villagers told us that in the early decades of the twentieth century, men from their late teens onwards had carried walking sticks (*bastoane*) and worn fedora hats, like gentlemen in major European cities. As in most other villages in Moldova, Țîra's roads are unpaved even today, so such elegance of individual person must have been particularly striking nearly one hundred years ago. Even in 2001 old men greeted each other using their ranks from military service, performing the prestige of their individual identities and distinguishing the village from others with its aura of aristocratic and chivalrous behaviour. Members of the ethnographic expedition I joined were fascinated by this image, telling and retelling it to themselves and other visitors from Chişinău. The ethnographers were also fascinated by the village's manifestation of pride in the seriousness with which its inhabitants upheld their historic liberties and freedoms.

The ethnographers were struck, for example, by the fact that residents of Țîra allowed their pigs to roam freely through the streets during the day, without fear of their being stolen. During a group interview on a national radio station made after the team's return to Chişinău, one student mentioned that his strongest impression of the village was that 'even the pigs wander freely' (*chiar porcii umblă liber*). The ethnographers saw this as the ultimate demonstration of freedom and even democracy, because pigs are considered lowly animals. If even they could walk around freely, then Țîra was indeed a village that granted enfranchisement to all. That villagers would not steal one another's pigs (as was said to happen in almost any other village in Moldova) was taken to mean that this village also maintained extraordinary respect for personal property, coupled with scrupulous morality. Finally, members of the expedition played with their own interpretation of Țîra's 'free pigs', hinting, through the ethnic slur of calling a Russian a *porc* (pig), that this Romanian-speaking village extended rights even to Russians. In this way they juxtaposed village administration with state policies on the linguistic, cultural, political, and other rights of ethnic minorities. Playing with the idea of 'free pigs' enabled participants in the expedition to imagine this village as a good model for the national government.

Although it was never explicitly acknowledged among the expedition members, the play in conversation asked whether the enfranchisement of Russians should be valued positively or negatively.[58] Țîra's commitment to equal enfranchisement was viewed positively, but the difference between a positive and a negative evaluation turned on questions about what rights Russians actually had, and how they had achieved them. In Țîra, it was clear

[58] That expedition members were aware of the play in conversation became clear when other expedition members became briefly afraid of censure following their team member's comment on radio.

that the (Romanian-speaking) village had *given* freedom and liberties to their pigs. This was a different situation from the one Romanian speakers usually described for Romanian-Russian relations in Moldova, in which Russians were seen as having *taken* liberties or having been granted them by an illegitimate authority.

Members of the ethnographic expedition to Ţîra saw evidence in the details of daily life that this village was a strong moral actor in the field of political issues that they themselves, as Romanian-speaking intellectuals from the capital, took seriously: democratization, language rights, and ethnic relations. Even though they publicly represented their professional activities as being disinterested in regard to politics, these artists and ethnographers closely tracked signs of political change in the capital and elsewhere. In other aspects of daily life, these visitors from the capital were disappointed. Although I had been told that *răzeşi* and *mazili* villages throughout Moldova had been the first to decollectivize land (and that villages where serfdom had been legal were among the last to privatize land), we found that most of Ţîra's inhabitants had returned their land to a cooperative farming arrangement. Moreover, the people we talked to about their participation in the new collective arrangement were dissatisfied. Their particular disappointment in August 2001 was that they were being paid for their labour and land share in wheat rather than cash. When I asked the local teachers who were cooking for the expedition whether villagers would change anything in the association's functioning, they said probably not, because people were afraid. This vision of Ţîra from the inside, as its inhabitants talked about their fears and incapacity to act in concert with one another, was very different from the vision that the village's visitors from the outside talked about and promoted, both to themselves and villagers while in the village and to others after they returned to the capital.

Critique of Ethnicity or Ethnic Exclusion?

By focusing temporarily on village identity and ignoring intersections between ethnic and village identities, it is possible to see how 'authentic' folkloric performances do actually convey images of Moldova as a culturally diverse nation and state. The examples in this chapter further indicate that the specialists I worked with believed that the value they placed on cultural diversity was implicitly shared by Moldova's general population. Popa's discussion of *horă* dancing, for example, focused on the ordinary occasions on which Moldova's citizens danced. At weddings, county gatherings, and other public occasions, he noted, as many variants of a dance were performed as there were villages represented. When he talked about weddings, Popa further suggested that Moldova's citizens perceived no conflict between diversity and unity. Wedding symbolism generally commented on the union of individuals and groups, and Popa described *horă* dancing at weddings as reflecting the distinctive qualities of the individuals and villages who came together to help create a new family.

In previous chapters I demonstrated how the focus on villages in new folkloric ensembles contested Soviet ideologies of ethnic and national identities. Since 1994, successive governments have recognized Moldova's ethnic diversity as one of its strengths and sought to promote and protect minority rights. By continuing to emphasize villages instead of ethnic groups as the sources of authentic traditions and culture, the folkloric community offers a powerful and authoritative argument against the country's post-Soviet governments. As in the ethnographers' depiction of Țîra, the asserted authenticity of villages can reveal the way post-Soviet governments have misconstrued, poorly applied, and perhaps even manipulated the population's ordinary valuing of cultural diversity by championing ethnic minorities. If the folkloric movement is correct, then the state's insistence on building national identity on an ethnic (or even a multiethnic) core may create more ethnic problems than it resolves. Indeed, local citizens often insist that there are 'no ethnic problems' except those created by successive state governments, and that daily life provides numerous examples of people overcoming ethnic differences. Yet the folkloric movement's model of Moldova as a nation of villages does not wholly address the problem of ethnic inclusiveness.

In most cases, the focus on village identities incorporates an ethnic dimension. As I discovered while accompanying local ethnographers on field expeditions, villages themselves usually have ethnic identities. Villages are known as 'Moldovan' or 'Gagauz', for example, without necessarily indicating that the inhabitants are ethnically homogeneous. Members of other ethnic groups may marry or move into these villages without changing their identity; for example, we met an elderly Gagauz man in the Moldovan village of Giurgiulești, and ensemble director Afanasi Gargalik's wife retained her Moldovan identity while living in the Gagauz village of Tomai. But villages such as Lebedenca, whose *etno-folcloric* ensemble performs local versions of Romanian, Bulgarian, Ukrainian, Russian, and Gagauz traditions, are rare in publicly acknowledging and being known for their multiethnic populations. Ethnographers may also deny villagers' assertions of multiethnicity, as in the case of Cazaclia, where an informant with a Romanian father argued that the village was 'multinational' rather than Gagauz. Thus, village-nation relations have implicitly ethnic dimensions, based on the overlap between the ethnic and village identities of most villagers.

Moreover, the folkloric movement's criteria for authenticity tend to exclude urban, industrialized, highly market-oriented, and 'mixed' cultural traditions. If applied rigidly, the criteria would contribute to the exclusion from folkloric performances of Russians, Jews, Gypsies (Roma), and a number of other minorities historically present in what is now the Republic of Moldova.[59] At present, the exclusion of such groups is potential rather than actual, because few ensembles have been organized to perform the folklore of these groups. The importance of ethnographic collection, however, also offers a route to inclusion, subverting the rural emphasis in the criteria for authenticity, as I describe next for the Jewish case. It is 'mixed' cultures that are more difficult to include and that pose a greater challenge to national identity as it is represented in folkloric performance.

Urban or Mixed? The Jewish Example

Barely three weeks into my field research, I received a phone call from a German woman I had never met. Sabine, an engineer and amateur clarinettist, had been told she needed to meet me. Several years previously, she had chanced upon some rare recordings of klezmer music from Bessarabia and since then had spent her holidays and spare time seeking the origin of this music in contemporary Moldova.[60]

In March 2001 Sabine made her second visit to Chişinău. She rented a room with a family and met the daughter's classmates from the University of the Arts, who promptly took her to their teacher, Varvara Buzilă. Buzilă and Sabine had difficulty communicating across languages, so Buzilă gave Sabine my phone number, hoping that we would talk in English. As a result, I met Sabine for a day of touring the capital, which included a stop in the artists' park to talk to Liubomir Iorga, an instrument maker and former dancer whom Sabine had met previously at a convention in Germany. Sabine's original interest in klezmer music had expanded to include contemporary Moldovan folk recordings, and she was in search of a particular recording, which we could not find. The next time I met with Buzilă, I summa-

[59] Interestingly, the criteria for authenticity are shared by at least some of the organizers of Moldova's two festivals of minority folklore, sponsored by the Department for National Relations. At a performance of Polish dance, for example, Tatjana Levandovschi expressed disappointment that none of the dances came from local Polish villages in Moldova. She also missed the accented *temperament* of Moldovan dances.

[60] Sabine remembered being introduced to klezmer music by a radio program broadcast from Chicago to Germany in the mid-1980s, but she had difficulty finding recordings in local stores and met few Germans who were acquainted with the music either. The first recording she found for sale was a compilation of early twentieth-century performers that she discovered in an alternative book and record shop.

rized Sabine's interest in Jewish folk music in Moldova. Sabine called it 'klezmer', and this was the term I used when explaining it to Buzilă. 'Klezmer?' she asked. 'How do you spell it?'

Buzilă's field experience and participation in ethnographic expeditions was unparalleled by many of her colleagues. Her research on the ritual uses of bread (Buzilă 1999) had taken her to villages in Romania and Ukraine and through the related literature on Italy and Bulgaria, and she actively followed the currents of European ethnology. Although she did not consider herself an expert on musical texts, she collected them as a matter of course during field expeditions. Between her field experience, theoretical and comparative knowledge of European ethnology, participation on juries at folkloric festivals, and other professional interactions with folklorists and folk performers, Buzilă might well have known something about Jewish traditions in Moldova. But she did not, and so she telephoned the Musicians' Union to speak with Andrei Tamazlâcaru.

Reading off the piece of paper on which I had spelled 'klezmer', Buzilă asked Tamazlâcaru if he knew what it was. 'Klezmer?' he confirmed. Yes, he did know it. Klezmer, he said, was actually a musician, not a type of music. The word was used specifically for musicians who played certain instruments (including the violin) and who were carriers (*purtători*) of Jewish musical traditions. Klezmer, he finished, could also refer more broadly to singers.

Tamazlâcaru is widely recognized as the primary expert on folk music in Moldova and is considered the father of the folkloric movement. But when it came to the question of Jewish folk music in Moldova, he admitted knowing very little. As the phone conversation continued, he acknowledged that some areas of Bessarabia were known for their Jewish musical traditions, but these had never really been studied. When he was a professor at the State Institute for the Arts in the late 1970s, he had some Jewish students who began documenting Jewish musical traditions in Moldova. The tapes made by the students had been lost, however, and Tamazlâcaru knew of no research conducted recently on Jewish musical traditions. But, he added, Jewish music was a mixture of other national musics. A particular piece might contain elements of Polish, Romanian, and Hungarian music. A Jewish song might keep the melody of a Romanian song but give the melody sad lyrics instead of cheerful ones, or vice versa.

In October 2001 Sabine made another trip to Chişinău. This time she had two weeks and wanted to take some clarinet lessons. She really wanted to learn some Bessarabian klezmer pieces, of course, but she was also interested in learning any Moldovan folk music. I helped her arrange private lessons with Petru Dinjos, a flute and clarinet teacher at a children's music school, the director of the children's folk ensemble Buciumaşii, and a long-time member of Tălăncuța and participant in the folkloric movement. Although Dinjos had received specialized folk music training since early adolescence, first at the School of Enlightenment in Soroca and then at the University of the Arts in Chişinău, and had a broad personal repertoire, he knew no 'Jewish' music. He had, however, played at some Jewish weddings and was quick to dismiss the cultural value or even distinctiveness of Jewish practices. Jewish weddings, he said, were basically like Russian weddings. When pushed for further clarification, he explained that a Russian wedding was like a *bal* (ball): a lot of eating and drinking, without any other traditions. Ethnic Moldovan weddings also involve lavish displays of food and prolonged eating and drinking, but feasting is punctuated by 'traditions' as gifts are presented from one family to the other, money is collected for the young couple, successive courses are brought to the tables, and so on.

These anecdotes reveal how Moldova's Jewish population and its traditions receive scant attention from local ethnographers, despite widespread evidence and common knowledge of the Jewish community's social, cultural, and historical importance in Bessarabia. Outside of Moldova, the existence of a Jewish community in the region is plainly visible. At the turn of the twentieth century, nearly 12 per cent (that is, 228,168 persons) of Bessarabia's population was Jewish, as was more than half of Chişinău's (50,000 persons) (King 2000: 24). Jews had become the primary trading and manufacturing class as urbanization increased during the 1800s (Livezeanu 1995: 94). During the period of Russian imperial rule in Bessarabia, Jews, together with Russian bureaucrats, constituted the local urban elite. Moldova's Jewish population decreased during Soviet rule, from 95,107 in 1959 to 65,672 in 1989 (King 2000: 174), yet even in Moldova it is common knowledge that a large Jewish population once existed.

'Common knowledge' of Jews appears in a variety of guises. For example, Rîşcani, one of Chişinău's five districts, is known as a neighbourhood that had a large Jewish population in the 1960s and 1970s. Common stereotypes identify Jews as good employers, and Jews are also known for their skills in commerce through a number of insulting jokes. The brother-in-law of a former bass player in the Joc ensemble orchestra told a joke about Jews buying wormy apples. The punch line conveyed the common combination of admiration and denigration directed publicly towards the Jewish community: 'The Jew buys wormy apples because the worms always choose the best apples'. More bitter jokes effectively blame Moldova's worsening economy on the latest exodus of Jews in the 1980s and 1990s.

Despite common knowledge about Moldova's once large population of Jews, specialists have little knowledge of Jewish folklore and traditions and have done little ethnographic research to acquire such knowledge. Research on Jewish folklore was discouraged during the Soviet period (Zemtsovsky and Kunanbaeva 1997: 15), and much may be blamed on institutionalized forms of Soviet anti-Semitism. Yet local scholars are still surprised when foreigners ask about Jewish history and traditions or even the current status of the Jewish community, and they may discourage research attempts because they believe there is nothing to be found. Even, and perhaps especially, specialists in tradition deny the existence of documentable and recoverable traditions. The Jewish community is described as 'gone', with those remaining being indistinguishable from Russians. Jewish culture is likewise described as Russian or as a mix of other 'national' traditions. Thus, if Jewish traditions did exist, they would have to be studied from the perspective of how, as 'mixtures', they combined these other traditions, rather than as pure cultural products.

The case of Jewish culture in Moldova is particularly complex because it is the object of increasing attention from abroad, and local specialists are confronted by growing demands for information about traditions they have assumed to be non-existent. In Chişinău, a Jewish community centre is now housed in the Jewish branch of the municipal library, which has the most extensive cultural and social programming among all of Chişinău's five 'ethnic' libraries.[61] The Jewish library receives substantial funding from foreign Jewish organizations to support English, Hebrew, and Yiddish language lessons and a number of special interest clubs. It offers music lessons, too, but only in Israeli folk music – not in Bessarabian-derived traditions. Jewish émigré communities have recently hired Moldovan musicians and dancers, including Petru Dinjos, Victor Botnaru, and Nicolae Gribincea – all members of the ensemble Tălăncuţa – to teach dances and music from Jewish Bessarabia at special workshops in Germany. Whereas Dinjos's self-reported response was to pragmatically teach 'Moldovan' music, Nicolae Gribincea began to seek out Jewish traditions during village-based fieldwork before his first engagement in 2005. Gribincea reports limited access and ongoing skepticism about the possibility of recovering Jewish traditions in Moldova, but he is nevertheless committed to trying. He has not yet openly questioned the fundamental assumptions embedded in local practices for collecting and performing folklore regarding the "purity" or "mixed" nature of traditions.

The skepticism expressed by the folkloric community towards Jewish culture reflects what the criteria for authenticity ordinarily hide – namely, that Moldova's ethnic groups have historically been co-implicated in the

[61] The other libraries with special language collections are the Ukrainian, Russian, Bulgarian, and Gagauz (Kulikovski 1998).

production of cultural traditions. Certainly, in recent decades rural and urban musicians alike have played with and for members of multiple ethnic and religious groups. The social structure has not limited music-making or other forms of cultural production to some groups who play for the other, nor have ethnic communities been closed to interactions with others. Although specialists know this from their lived personal experiences, they nevertheless expect cultures to be pure, and this expectation is widely shared. Hence, the local Jewish community seeks its cultural traditions from abroad, even as émigrés seek to elaborate what they have 'lost'.

Lost or Borrowed? The Gagauz Example

The persistent expectation that each ethnic group should have distinct cultural traditions can have political ramifications. This is made explicit in the way members of the folkloric community respond to the presence of the few Gagauz ensembles that participate in folkloric festivals and competitions and to the Gagauz dances, music, and costuming that remain in the repertoires of many *popular* groups, including those striving for authenticity.

Many versions of ethnogenesis exist for the Gagauz, but suffice it to say that they have lived in the southern regions of the current Republic of Moldova since at least the beginning of the 1800s. Specialists in ethnography deny, however, that the Gagauz have more than a few distinct traditions of their own.

At least one Gagauz ensemble promotes itself as a folkloric group and strives to meet the generally accepted definitions for authenticity. Altângic is a 'model' ensemble. As I described in chapter 3, a group holding the 'model' title regularly participates in and wins local, national, and international contests. It receives extra money from the government to hire specialists to help improve the quality of its repertoire and performances, and the ensemble director usually has a special mentoring and training relationship with specialists at the National Centre for Folk Arts. In other words, even though Altângic is designated a *popular* ensemble, its model status means that it is also considered a high-quality folkloric ensemble, even if its repertoire is not entirely 'authentic'. Indeed, the ensemble's director, Afanasi Gargalik, does participate in ethnographic expeditions, such as the one we took together in 2001 (chapter 5), and uses the material he gathers from Gagauz villages to build his ensemble's repertoire.

Plate 17. At the festival Duminica la Florii, the ensemble Altângic performs a version of the ritual 'Lazarelul' collected in the ethnically Gagauz village of Tomai.

Gargalik is a personal friend of Valeriu Chiper, who promotes Altângic's activities in Moldova and Romania. For example, Chiper organizes the folkloric festival Duminica la Florii, at which Altângic is a featured participant with a Gagauz version of the combined song and dance ritual 'Lazarelul'[62]. The friendship and collaboration between Chiper and Gargalik were also demonstrated when Chiper invited Gargalik's group to perform in a celebration marking the ten-year anniversary of Chiper's group. This celebration was videotaped and then shown some six months later to parents and other guests who attended Chiper's end-of-school performance and

[62] The tradition is an enactment of the biblical story of Lazarus rising from the dead, which is performed by children who go from house to house requesting eggs immediately before Easter. Variations were performed by both Moldovan and Gagauz ensembles at the Duminica la Florii festival in 2001. Duminica la Florii, or Flower Sunday, is the Sunday before Easter. Willow branches are blessed during the church service, and there are multiple traditions related to willows, grasses, and plants, including the making of flower crowns, which are exchanged to make blood brothers and sisters and are raced in streams.

celebration. Gargalik had been invited but was unable to attend, and his name was brought up by several of the guests. Then, while the videotape played as background to our meal, Chiper and a specialist who worked in Chişinău's municipal Department of Culture called attention to one of the dances performed by Altângic. This dance, they said, was actually a Romanian dance from the Banat, a historical region now divided between Romania, Serbia, and Hungary.

Chiper recounted the way Romanians had commented that Gargalik's group danced the dance better than they did, but the implication was that something needed to change in Gargalik's ascription of the dance to Gagauz culture. A third man, seated next to the specialist from the Department of Culture, then asked what Gargalik had to say about this dance being Romanian. The specialist replied that Gargalik insisted it was Gagauz. It was an old discussion. He had known Gargalik for many years, and Gargalik had never changed his response. It was pointless to argue with him, the man said.

As in the case of Jewish traditions, local specialists tend to ignore or downplay the existence of Gagauz traditions. Gargalik's ensemble participates in folkloric competitions and commands a certain level of appreciation within the folkloric community for authenticity and artistry. At the same time, definitions of culture employed by local ethnographers redefine 'authentic' Gagauz traditions as Romanian. This procedure recognizes the existence of other ethnic groups in Moldova but denies the existence or legitimacy of non-Romanian cultures in the region.

The question of whether folkloric ensembles can locate any distinctly Gagauz traditions reveals implicit definitions of culture used by members of the folkloric community. The translated text that follows comes from an interview I conducted with Pavel Popa in late September 2001. I interviewed him in the context of his position as specialist at the National Centre for Folk Arts, but I also asked questions about the children's ensemble he directed as a hobby. The translated portion begins with a discussion of how dance reflects the ways of life of its innovators. Popa draws a contrast between the dances of villages of the plains and the mountains in Ardeal, Romania, and I ask whether the differences between dances in the northern and southern regions of the Republic of Moldova could also be explained by differences of terrain and way of life. We specifically discuss the greater prevalence of pair dancing in the north than in the south. Popa asserts that pair dances are relatively new for Moldovans, in comparison with an older tradition of dancing communally. He connects this difference not to terrain but to the incursion of larger numbers of non-Romanian speakers in the north of the country than in the south. I then ask about the non-Romanians in the south, and it is his response to this question that I examine further:

JC: So with the differences in the dances of the three zones [north, center, and south of Moldova]. Do they also reflect differences in way of life?
PP: Yes, yes. Of course. For example, in Romania, in Ardeal, there are dances from the plains and dances from the mountains.
JC: And those [people] from the plains don't dance –
PP: – dances from the mountain? No. There are slower dances, faster dances … it's also a communal dance, that is the people of the plains also dance a *horă*, but they are distinguished a little bit by the steps. It's the character of the steps. Character. Dance is distinguished by its character. Dance from the mountains … is more spectacular in technicality. Dance is distinguished through technique, interpretations, movements of dance, through virtuosity. And these [people] from the plains have their own virtuosity, because they have limpid movements – a great expertise. But look, the basic steps of a dance distinguish it. We [in Moldova], our terrain is flatter than in the mountains, of course, and we resemble each other a little more. That is, there isn't such a big difference. (JC: Between the north and south? PP: Yes.) We have differences of style, of character. Those in the south dance with more technique, with more virtuosity, and with more rhythm.
JC: But why? Is there something unique about life in the south?
PP: No. They have – the majority lives in steppe land. The land is flatter in the south. The ground is – because it is dry. And they [in the south] have always danced with smaller steps – smaller, but more accentuated. All the movements in a dance are boiling, more – that is – more accented. And they dance more often in communal dances, together. Pair dances are less developed in the south because the south was more preserved. More has been kept in the south than in the centre and the north. Even other populations came into the south less than into the centre and north. Other families, of other nationalities, other people, strangers.
JC: But there are Bulgarians and Gagauz there.
PP: Yes. There are Bulgarians who came even before the First World War. Even in 1812 [there were those] who formed their own villages and maintained their own culture, which was embellished by the culture of the Moldovans, and they had this culture of interference [i.e. cultural mixing] – a Romanian village alongside a Bulgarian village. These incidences [are] very interesting. Because they speak Bulgarian using many Romanian words, dancing Romanian [dances], and singing songs in Bulgarian with Romanian melodies.

JC: When did they come?
PP: Beginning in 1812.
JC: With the Russians?
PP: Yes, yes. When Catherine II brought Bulgarians, the Gagauz who are [here] now came from Bulgaria, but they are of Turkic origin. The Bulgarians and Gagauz came into Moldova from the region of Dobrogea, parts of which are now in Romania and Bulgaria, but then it was all Ottoman territory. The Bulgarians are also of Turkic origin, but they were Slavicized long ago. There were also German villages. (JC: They also came after Catherine? PP: Yes, yes.) They were deported here.
JC: From Germany?
PP: No, not from Germany. From Russia, yes. There were Jewish villages. There were Czech villages.
JC: But there were more foreigners in the north?
PP: Even now there are more foreigners in the north. [There are more] Ukrainian, Russian villages than in the south. Because when the Gagauz came, they settled on the land. They didn't extend through all of Bessarabia. They took land exactly where they settled. They are thus a, that is, [there are] Moldovan villages next to Gagauz villages. Bulgarians the same. The villages are together, one next to the other. And in this way they preserved some of their traditions. Only some. But in general they lost their culture. The Gagauz do not have their own culture. They have borrowed. From neighbouring villages. From the Bulgarians and from the Moldovans. They borrowed. And so they believe that they have formed their own culture, but it isn't true. They do not have a national costume [*port popular*]. They don't know it. They did not keep their own tradition. They are religious traitors. They changed their religion. But changing religion, you then have to change folk tradition. Religion is based, formed on the basis of folk tradition. To not do evil, to not commit adultery, to not steal, to not murder, to respect those who are older, to love, to do good, to give *pomană* [charity, but also offerings given in rememberance of the dead], to study well, to love your wife, to respect children, to respect the elderly, to respect. Look this is our religion, Orthodoxy. But they, in their religion, would have had other points of reference, other criteria. When they changed religion like this, borrowed our religion, then they automatically borrowed out of folk tradition as well. They braid *colacul* [a ring-shaped bread used in many rituals] just like we do. We make *colac* out of bread, right? [Their] food technology is like ours.

They make soups like we do. Wine technology, the preparation of wine, they do like we do. Because they borrowed our tradition.
JC: So language is the only difference?
PP: Only language distinguishes them a little. More – no. Language distinguishes them.
JC: But a little with dances, or not even with dances?
PP: No, the dances are Romanian. The Gagauz don't have dances. They do not have their own dances. They don't realize this. They don't know this, but the dances are Romanian. The dances from Gagauzia, from the Gagauz, are the same dances that are danced in Romania, in [the region of] Dobrogea.[63] The same dances. For example, researching the dance *kadînească*, the Gagauz say *kadînja*. Romanians say *kadînească*. I found similar variants among the Gagauz. I found in Romania, in Dobrogea, twelve variations of *kadînească*. That is, they have variations and twelve *kadînja* there. It's clear to whom the dance belongs. This is because they even dance the *horă* like we do.
JC: But how did they take dances from Dobrogea? Did they pass through there?
PP: They passed through there, yes. Because Dobrogea is on the Danube. When they came from Bulgaria, they crossed the Danube.
JC: And from there they took the dance?
PP: Yes. And we are neighbors with Dobrogea. The south, the southern part of Bessarabia borders Dobrogea. We are at the Danube's delta, the bed of the Danube. And that's how they got established.
JC: But here when an ensemble of *dans popular* dances *kadînja*, is it called a Gagauz dance or a Dobrogean dance?
PP: Truthfully, it should be Dobrogean dance.
JC: Yes.
PP: But it's still called a Gagauz dance. Before, we didn't know that this is a Dobrogean dance. Only in 1989, when the gates to Romania were opened and we began folkloric research, then we realized that they [the Gagauz] do not have their own culture. They borrowed. Both from us and from the Dobrogeans. Both music and dance. But a costume, they didn't have. There is not a national costume. This one [worn on stage] is work clothing. But a national costume is seen on holidays. That is a difference from our dress. They should have an apron like this – one in front and one in back, with the skirt un-

[63] Dobrogea was gradually incorporated by the Kingdom of Romania through a series of cessions from the Ottoman Empire beginning in 1878 (Hitchens 1994: 50).

> derneath. This is beautiful. Boys with embroidered clothing. But here is a dress with only a single color. It looks Gypsy. Or American, huh? With a dress of this type.

To summarize, Popa dates the migration of Bulgarians, Gagauz, Czechs, Germans, and others into the southern portion of Moldova from the year 1812. The Bulgarians and Gagauz, he says, came from Dobrogea, which he considers to be part of a larger Romanian cultural region, despite the region's complex political history. The Gagauz, before being in Romania, had been in Bulgaria. He does not specify a length of time for these transits but notes that it was in this migration away from their homelands that both Gagauz and Bulgarians began to lose their traditions, their own culture. In Bessarabia, both groups (like other ethnic groups) settled in villages and continued to borrow cultural elements from neighbouring Moldovan villages. Thus, today one finds Bulgarian villages that speak Bulgarian with many Romanian words. These villages dance Romanian dances, and their songs, while having Bulgarian lyrics, are based on Romanian melodies. Popa refers to this 'culture of interference' as 'interesting'. He offers a stronger and more negative comment on the situation of Gagauz culture. In short, the Gagauz do not have a culture. Everything they have except language is borrowed from Romanians.

At other points in this interview, Popa clearly identified language as the one element that a people must have if it is to remain a distinguishable people. Thus, even by his own terms the Gagauz are a people with a culture distinguishable from the Romanian people and their culture. I do not want to focus, however, on the logical flaws in Popa's discussion of the relationships between language, culture, and 'people-hood' as if they are unique to him. His discussion of these relationships is important because it reflects the range of discussions of these topics I had with other informants, both inside and outside the folkloric community in Moldova. In our interview, Popa speaks primarily as a specialist in dance and ethnography, but there are also moments when he is simply telling me what is 'common knowledge' for all Romanian speakers in Moldova and at these points, his language becomes more emotionally charged, reflecting widely shared political frustrations. I prefer therefore to focus on a moment when he was clearly speaking as a specialist.

Importantly, Popa claims that the Gagauz borrowed the dance *kadînja* (Gagauz variant) from Romanians in Dobrogea. But, he says, this fact was unknown to ethnographers in Moldova before 1989, when they gained access to Romania and began to conduct ethnographic research there. This fact is still unknown to the Gagauz, who persist in believing that *kadînja* is their dance. Yet as Popa attempts to articulate for me, political and ethnic histories in southeastern Europe are poorly matched, and it is difficult to know which ethnic group, if any, originated many of the dances.

Cultural borrowings in Dobrogea have been even more complex than Popa described. The region has long had an ethnically mixed population including Bulgarians, Romanians, and Turks. The cultural history of the region is so complex that Jan Harold Brunvand (1976: 79) concluded that a 'national' perspective was not enough; ethnographers working in the region needed a Balkan and European perspective. Yet Moldova's folkloric community has recently encountered only the Romanian ethnographic literature on the region, which was itself produced as part of a national identity project. Indeed, Romanians undertook substantial research in 1977 precisely to commemorate the centennial of the region's 'reunification' with Romania from its long incorporation in the Ottoman Empire, glossing over the fact that modern Romania had not existed when the Ottoman Empire first acquired Dobrogea.

Plate 18. Does the dance belong to a region or an ethnic group? The ensemble Moldovița performs a dance from the region of Dobrogea, a dance known by both the Gagauz name *kadînja* and the Romanian name *kadînească*.

Following the taped portion of our interview, I gave Popa copies of several photographs I had taken of his ensemble. I pointed out one in which his dancers were costumed in what is ordinarily represented as Gagauz clothing. Women's dress most markedly distinguishes Gagauz from Romanian costume. The Gagauz costume is a knee-length dress in a solid colour, usually bright pink or green, with a white apron and often a necklace of metal coins.[64] I showed Popa this photograph and asked whether the dance was Gagauz. No, he said, the dance was Romanian. I persisted in asking about the costumes, and he agreed – the costumes were Gagauz and should be changed.

Popa continued to explain that the Gagauz had no 'national costume'. The costumes he had finally agreed were 'Gagauz' still did not count as national dress. They were 'work' clothes, as signalled by the single colour, absence of ornamentation, and single apron. A non-specialist would most certainly have identified the dance as Gagauz. If it was not an exact copy of dances in the repertoires of other Gagauz ensembles, it nevertheless shared certain easily recognizable diagnostic elements. In particular, circular hand movements initiated from the wrist, with a slight pulse as the palm pushes away from the body, appeared in the photographs. Such arm movements do not appear in the Romanian dances performed onstage in Moldova, but they are a common posture in the dances of Turkic groups.

For some observers, Gagauz dances certainly suggest a closer cultural affiliation between the Gagauz and other Turkic groups than between the Gagauz and Romanians. On the basis solely of research in Romania, however, a local ethnographer feels confident asserting that this dance, like almost all other aspects of Gagauz culture, comes from an implicitly pure and aboriginal Romanian culture. There is nothing particularly unusual about this kind of situation, in which minority cultures are imagined as 'variants' of the majority culture. In China, for example, it is a part of official minority policy (Diamond 1993). In Moldova this confidence rests on the kind of survivalist and salvage ethnography described by Herzfeld (1987) and discussed in the previous chapter. Not only do Moldovan ethnographers posit the existence of a pre-Soviet culture that can be recovered and reconstructed in the present, but they also rely on the recovery and reconstruction of a pre-Ottoman culture in the Romanian-speaking lands to accomplish this task.

Although members of the folkloric movement have worked to purify culture (i.e. folkloric performance) of politics by shifting attention away from the 'ethnic question', their art still conveys a subtle politics of national belonging for some ethnic groups and exclusion for others. This is so even

[64] Black dresses are featured in museum displays.

though ensembles specializing in minority repertoires participate in and win folkloric competitions. In the following section I illustrate how the concept of cultural borrowing gives rise to a discourse of political obligation.

Cultural Borrowing and Political Obligations

The notions held by my informants concerning how culture is created, mixed, borrowed, and lost by ethnic groups imply relations of obligation between certain groups. The foregoing discussions reflect an understanding that ethnic groups have pure cultures, and so commonalities between groups indicate borrowing, which essentially goes one way. Both Jews and Gagauz are considered to have 'mixed' Romanian culture with their own and are therefore culturally indebted to Romanians. The conversation recorded in what follows demonstrates how easily cultural debt can be converted to political debt. In this case, a belief that some minorities have borrowed culture from Romanian speakers supports a politically oriented argument that these minorities have received other 'gifts', which they should repay through political and linguistic unity with Romanian speakers.

Although definitions of culture generally have the power to establish a hierarchy of national belonging and establish obligations between Moldova's ethnic groups, members of the folkloric movement rely on specialists to make the final pronouncements on ethnic relations. Although the ensemble directors I worked with were specialists in traditions, culture, and the practice of ethnography, they deferred to other specialists when pushed on particular questions, especially when their answers about culture had political implications. In the first example given in this chapter – that of Jewish traditions – Petru Dinjos deferred to 'specialists' even though he was personally confident that Jewish tradition was a mixture, that Romanian and Jewish weddings differed, and that Jewish weddings were more similar to Russian weddings than to Romanian ones. Several months earlier, Dinjos and I had discussed my upcoming field expedition (chapter 5), in which I would go to several Gagauz villages. The tension between culture and its political implications were evident in his comments regarding Gagauz rights and obligations. Although he was initially confident in telling me who the Gagauz were, Dinjos ultimately suggested that I seek the opinion of a colleague trained in history. He suggested Valeriu Chiper, the very ensemble director with whom I was going to do fieldwork.[65] It was clear to me that he

[65] Chiper's professional training was as a history teacher. Institutionally, ethnography is organized in Moldova as a specialization within history, except at the Academy of Sciences. Like the Osoianu sisters, whose career path I described in chapter 5, Chiper did not set out to organize and direct a folkloric performing ensemble but arrived at that role indirectly.

already knew Chiper's position on the Gagauz and expected that it would support his own – which it did, despite Chiper's personal friendship and collaboration with the Gagauz ensemble director, Gargalik. Nevertheless, it is significant that Dinjos placed on a historian the responsibility for connecting an ethnic group's cultural and political statuses relative to those of Romanian speakers. In response to my upcoming expedition to Gagauz villages, Dinjos commented that the Gagauz were not really a nation (*națiune*), and Gagauz was not really a language. It's Turkish, he said. Are they an ethnic group (*grupa etnică*), I asked?

PD: No.

JC: Well, are they not an ethnic group or a nation because they speak Turkish? Is a *națiune* based on language?

PD: No, it's not language. Because there are cases in which two different nations speak the same language. For example, English is spoken by Americans and by the English. The Gagauz and Turks understand each other just fine, but Turkish is a scientific language, and Gagauz is degraded and has a reduced stock of words.

JC: Because it is spoken only at home?

PD: Yes. Because it is spoken only at home. But do you know who the Gagauz are? The Gagauz are Turks who were in Moldova, and when they could not go home after some wars, Ştefan cel Mare offered them land and houses.

It was at this point in our conversation that Dinjos suggested I ask Chiper, a historian, these questions, including the first one I had asked, about whether the Gagauz were an ethnic group or nation. Dinjos's historical presentation is almost certainly inaccurate, because he places the Gagauz in Moldova during the reign of Ştefan cel Mare, three hundred years before Moldova was split, Bessarabia was taken into the Russian Empire, and Catherine the Great encouraged settlement of the empire's frontiers. But he referred me to a historian to learn what Ştefan cel Mare did. In other words, Chiper was meant to tell me about the obligations that Gagauz had incurred, not about historical facts. This became especially clear as Dinjos continued to explain that it was 'unnatural' for Gagauz not to have learned Romanian. As a counter-example, he said that if he were to go to America, he would learn English. And he would 'be together' with the Americans; after all, he would be in their home (*acasă la dînşi*). This, he said, was not what the Gagauz had done, and so it was clear that they did not respect the country (*țară*).

Two months earlier I had witnessed Petru Dinjos in a similar conversation. Although professionals in their own right, he and another musician, a man in his late twenties whom I call Andrei, played in the *muzică populară* ensemble sponsored by the culture house at the state university. The ensemble rehearsed twice a week while the university was in session, though it was rare for every member of the group to attend. On this occasion, in early May, I was invited to watch the group's rehearsal as well as that of the culture house's dance group. Both groups were preparing for the end-of-year concert. My visit came on a night in which a core group of friends – the director, Dinjos and Andrei, and a male and a female university student – all came to rehearsal and had time to spare afterwards. This was a rare occasion for them, and the two students quickly gathered a few lei from everyone (except me, the guest) and went to buy wine, bread, pâté, mayonnaise, and lunchmeat from a nearby store. When we left this gathering, Dinjos, Andrei, and I were headed towards the same neighbourhood, and one of them suggested prolonging the evening. We went first to a sidewalk café for beer and then to a second café for coffee.

Language had been a topic of conversation in the first portion of the evening, giving way to a series of off-colour jokes. The two colleagues returned to the topic of language over coffee. My notes include a brief summary of this discussion:

> [A. said that] the language spoken by people didn't matter. He said when he was a student at the university, some Gagauz students came to his room one night, and they played music together. He liked them so much that he went to Comrat [the main city in Gagauz Yeri] for two years. He lived in a dorm there but told his parents he was staying in a hotel. He even learned some Gagauz. Petru asked if they had stopped speaking Romanian to him as soon as he started to speak some Gagauz. A. tried to avoid this question. P. insisted. He said that the Gagauz should speak Romanian, and not Russian. They are not grateful that Ştefan cel Mare gave them the piece of land in which they are now living. There was more – in which P. agreed that it was okay for them to speak Gagauz but also said they needed to speak Romanian. Ideally, there would be schools, books, and newspapers in Gagauz so everyone could study in their own language. But the country is poor. Therefore, they should work with the Romanians for a while, to build Moldova. A. was visibly agitated by this discussion. He rarely made eye contact with P., looked for the waitress, and generally shifted his body position a lot. P. asked A. if he disagreed, and A. said that had not been the point. We left soon after this discussion.

In this conversation, Dinjos maintained his previous position. That is, having received land from 'Moldovans', the Gagauz should speak Romanian and work with Romanian speakers to build the Republic of Moldova. He stopped short of saying that the Gagauz should assimilate, but he placed the common economic good of all citizens before the cultural rights of minorities.

Yet his colleague meant to make another point, which was that ethnicity need not be a barrier to friendship or even to living together. The important thing was for a person to be able and willing to learn another language. On many other occasions I heard people make positive comments about immigrants who had learned the language of their host country. According to this perspective, A. did the right thing when he learned some Gagauz while living with Gagauz people. The problem, from Dinjos's perspective, was that this situation implied that A. was living in Gagauz territory, whereas Dinjos believed the Gagauz were living in Moldovan (i.e. Romanian-speaking) territory. A. might have done the right thing, but did his Gagauz friends do the right thing by continuing to speak Romanian to him? Did they acknowledge their debt to Moldovans, a debt established when Ştefan cel Mare founded Moldova?

If the perspective on landownership and political rights that emerged in this discussion represents the majority view among Romanian speakers, then there may be significant differences in the way Moldova's ethnic groups ground their concepts of basic political rights. For example, Hülya Demirdirek (2000: 69) argued that among the Gagauz, 'when it comes to legitimizing access and claims to land, prior ownership of property is not regarded as an important value whereas hard work is'. By extension, she explained, historical narratives and myths of ethnogenesis are not the primary ways in which contemporary Gagauz argue for the right to local political autonomy. Rather, having laboured and lived on a particular piece of land is what people believe is important. The Gagauz do not perceive themselves as ungrateful members of the Moldovan state because they meet their own criteria for social and political recognition.

The conversations on the topic of Gagauz culture from which I have quoted indicate that the traditions, languages, and cultures of ethnic groups in Moldova can be understood as establishing and expressing relationships of obligations, rights, and responsibilities between these groups. Folkloric performance provides one perspective on these relations, but the instances in which specialists defer to others, as if they are not themselves authorities on culture, history, language, or musical style, make it clear that the relationships could be understood otherwise.

None of the conversations quoted here represents the full complexity of Dinjos's or Popa's views on cultural property, borrowing, or social debt. Their personal lives, for example, testify to close relations as kin, neighbours, and friends with many non–ethnic Moldovans. My intent is to draw attention to what they know as specialists, the conclusions they draw from that knowledge, and the limitations they recognize.

As Popa hints in the interview quoted earlier, local specialists do recognize that cultures may share common elements without having 'mixed' or 'borrowed' from their neighbours in ways that imply debt. He notes, for example, that all Balkan groups – like Romanians – dance *hore*, without having taken the dance from Romanians or vice versa. Yet specialists in Moldova rarely discuss the conditions under which two or more groups may have equal claims to similar traditions. Even similarities between villages are usually treated as an historical problem for which the direction of cultural borrowing should be worked out and an original version established. While current definitions of culture in Moldova provide many principles for exclusion, they provide few principles for inclusion.

Chapter 7
Conclusion: Authenticity, Ethnographic Authority, and Nation-Building

> People find money to buy all sorts of things – ice cream, bananas – but very rarely find the money to buy a book. This is bad because books can be read and studied over and over again. A book of folklore is valuable because what is published in a book cannot be forgotten. All of our culture is based on folklore. Folklore is the base of Romanian literature. Folklore is the calling card of a people. People abroad are not interested in pop music (*muzică de stradă*) from Moldova; they want to know the folklore.
>
> – Valentina Oglindă, director of Mioriţa, speaking at her book launch, 18 April 2001

> Very often, politicians can ruin the relations between countries, but musicians and artists never can; they cannot do anything but unite peoples. The goal of any musician is to create a feeling of calmness and peace above all. If an audience feels this peace, it does not matter who sings or plays. Ah, but he is a Jew, or he is a Russian – it does not matter. The message of calmness and peace that an interpreter carries must be put out and understood by the audience.
>
> – Trofim Suruceanu, head of the Department for Theatre, Music, Concert Halls, and Cinema, Ministry of Culture, 29 June 2005, reflecting on Moldova's recent success at a North Korean music festival

> Everyone here is involved in culture. I am Gagauz but will speak in Russian so that everyone will understand. The government made a mistake in the question of nationalities and politics. There are similarities between Gagauz culture and Moldovan culture – e.g. the Lazarel tradition is known to the Gagauz and even has the same mu-

> sic as among Moldovans.[66] Culture must be separate from politics. Culture is the face of the nation. If Moldova does not use its traditions, it will end up like America – with money, but no culture. Culture is the face of a nation, and culture and traditions have to be the foundation of the state.
>
> – Afanasi Gargalik, toasting fellow participants at the folkloric festival Duminica la Florii, 7 April 2001

These three quotations capture many of the themes raised in the preceding chapters, where I have evaluated the contradictions, inconsistencies, and paradoxes in the work and vision of the folkloric community in Moldova. In this chapter I briefly summarize those findings and then discuss the interplay between ethnographic authenticity and authority in Moldova and in American anthropology.

Authenticity and Ethnicity in Moldova's Folkloric Movement

Folcloric and *etno-folcloric* ensembles began to emerge as distinct folkloric genres in Moldova in the 1980s. They distinguished themselves from the previously existing *popular* ensembles by means of self-consciously 'authentic' repertoires. During the Soviet period, *popular* ensembles performed stereotyped images of ethnic Moldovans, as well as others, in narratives of inter-ethnic friendship. Like *popular* ensembles, most *folcloric* and *etno-folcloric* ensembles are nowadays organized and supported through the state's system of amateur performance formations. The songs, dances, and other traditions presented by *folcloric* and *etno-folcloric* groups are collected in villages, and an ensemble's authenticity is considered greater the more restricted its zone of collection. Festivals and competitions have been created to evaluate the authenticity of ensembles' repertoires and performances, to select and promote some groups for national, televised festivals and for travel abroad, and to encourage the further refinement of authentic repertoires and performances. The result of all this activity is an ideology and representation of the Republic of Moldova as a nation of villages.

In creating ensembles and the system to support them, members of the folkloric movement see their work as contesting Soviet ideology, especially as it related to ethnic and national identities. Like other culture workers, members of the folkloric community consider their work apolitical, and believe that it generates a better foundation for the state than ethnic politics can do. As indicated in the second quote, culture workers believe that their

[66] This is a reference to the ritual enactment of the biblical story of Lazarus rising from the dead, discussed in chapter 6.

work calls attention to beauty and creativity, and that it generates peace, calmness, and mutual understanding and appreciation. This positioning remains relevant in the post-Soviet context because of both the state's official pronouncements of multiethnicity since the early 1990s and the Communist Party's continued political strength.

The preceding chapters elaborate many of the ways in which the representation of traditional culture and values in Moldova is neither simple nor, in fact, apolitical. Village-based traditions are necessarily transformed by procedures used in their collection, recording, transcription, selection, performance, and attribution. Even ensembles that court visual chaos in their performances through a maximal display of social diversity in performers' ages, genders, and costumes nevertheless flatten the historical dimensions of cultural production. Onstage, Moldova's villages appear as unchanging cultural isolates and holistic moral worlds, undisturbed until the Soviet period. Indeed, even though they often depict sorrowful brides and young wives, folkloric performances erase the effects of inter-village marriages on cultural production – effects that are abundantly clear to ethnographers in the field.

Although they aspire to avoid commenting on ethnic relations, members of the folkloric movement nevertheless convey messages about ethnic identity and national belonging. Judges of folkloric competitions, especially, elaborate and apply criteria of authenticity in ways that effectively deny public representation to many ethnic groups. Ethnic groups that have historically predominated in urban areas, such as Russians and Jews, are obvious candidates for exclusion. Yet hierarchies of authenticity that privilege the traditions of ethnic Moldovans also work to exclude other ethnic groups, such as the Gagauz, who do live in rural areas. The few ensembles that collect and mount village-based repertoires for the Gagauz are thus regularly informed that 'their' traditions are really borrowed from the dominant Moldovans. Also, though nearly all villages include some persons of different ethnic backgrounds, few ensembles claim this multiethnic heritage in their performances. Ensemble directors, like visiting ethnographers and folklorists, may ignore villagers' claims to a multiethnic heritage, rendering the village monoethnic onstage when lived reality and historical memory include interethnic relationships. In this way the multiethnic dimensions of Moldova's national culture and traditions are severely curtailed while appearing to be adequately represented.

The exclusionary effects of Moldova's *folcloric* and *etno-folcloric* ensembles stand in strong contrast to their efforts to maintain authenticity in moving traditions "from the field to the stage". Moving folklore onto the stage often erases many of the complexities of lived social experience, including the realities of cultural diversity. In this respect, there is nothing unusual in the state of folklore and folkloric ensembles in Moldova. The exclusion of several ethnic groups from equal representation on the stage is only noteworthy because they occupy an extreme position on the continuum of authenticity in folkloric performance, alongside ensembles from countries such as Croatia (Shay 2002) and Portugal (Holton 2005).

What is noteworthy about Moldova's ensembles is precisely the earnestness with which folklorists and ethnographers pursue authenticity, struggling to define and locate the "authentic" without recourse to the language of ethnicity. At the most immediate level, the definition of authenticity used by ethnographers and folklorists in Moldova's folkloric ensembles challenges the view taken by the former Soviet state – that ethnic groups are the primary sources of cultural identity and therefore the basis of national formation. Second, this assumption was not specific to the Soviet Union, but underpins all modern nation-states and the 'national order' of suprastate organizational relations. This is true, as Liisa Malkki (1995) has shown, even among organizations and legal infrastructures meant to protect and assist refugees and other stateless persons. Third, the 'authentic' folklore performed by groups in Moldova also challenges the multiculturalism of the post-Soviet state, something the international community encourages through a variety of transition programs, consultations, and advisory relations. In short, the alternate vision of "authentic" culture promoted by Moldova's *folcloric* and *etno-folcloric* ensembles challenges participants and observers to think critically about the very nature of collective identities.

Audience Interest and the State

Most strikingly, the contextualization of these ensembles within a "folkloric movement" points to the fluidity of identity. Because identity emerges through boundary-making processes, it changes overtime. Boundary-making also responds to structural constraints. In the case of national and ethnic identities, the ideologies, policies, and institutions of the state provide an important reference point for identity personnel, precisely because of the state's power to influence the course of individual lives according to collective criteria such as language, religion, or place of origin. When states change – as they have done so repeatedly and dramatically in Moldova – identity personnel become acutely aware of the tenuousness of their own roles.

Even as I studied Moldova's folkloric community and its successes in 2001, members began to tell me about the loss of public interest in their work. For example, in April 2001, during the Duminica la Florii festival, Gheorghe Obreja, a specialist in the Department of Culture in Cahul County, expressed surprise that I was studying children's folkloric ensembles. What could I, as an American, possibly find interesting about these ensembles? I explained that, among other things, they were interesting for their scale of involvement relative to the size of the population. He responded, 'In terms of scale, interest in traditions is decreasing. In 1990 there was a lot of interest: people in Chişinău would cry during folkloric performances'. The initial interest, he thought, had to do with the large number of people in the city who had been born in villages and knew the traditions being performed. As our conversation continued and I tried to probe for the causes of declining interest, Obreja found it difficult to provide an explanation. He did not think that the loss of interest was directly connected to the country's economic difficulties or migration, and he ultimately concluded that people's attention had simply turned 'elsewhere'.

Months later, on 14 October 2001, I attended a small festival that coincided with the capital's celebration of its patron saint. The 'Pie Festival' featured newly fermented wine and savoury pies along with folk music performances and folk craft vendors. It was meant to reflect traditions such as pie-baking contests between women that typically accompanied saint's day celebrations in villages. Having reached its second anniversary, it represented yet another festival, albeit not a performance-based one, that might be added to the list of the folk movement's successes. As evening fell, I left the festival with Elena Osoianu, one of the original members of the ensemble Tălăncuţă, and conversation turned to the fact that the ensemble had recently held fewer concerts. Why, I asked? She responded:

> There are fewer public gatherings now. They are not gone – you will see tomorrow on City Day, with the folk groups. And there is more folkloric presence – for example on television there used to not be any folkloric broadcasts [and now there are many]. But there was a time when there were more gatherings. There were demonstrations for language. Tălăncuţă performed at these. For a time people were more united. They believed that through language, through culture, life would be better. Now they are *dezamăgit* [disillusioned, disenchanted] and less united.

When I asked when the change had taken place, Osoianu could not fix a date on it, saying only that it had come in the previous few years.

By 2005, when I returned to Moldova, this sense that the movement had foundered was more pronounced, and by 2006, not only members of the folkloric movement but also culture workers more generally felt defeated by political and social changes in the country. Poverty, high rates of migration, and the renewed power of the Communist Party left culture workers feeling that their work was not only impossible, because of tight funding, but also futile, under-appreciated, and vulnerable to changes of political mood. They remained committed to their work, and members of the folkloric movement continued to build on their existing activities, but with little hope.

This sense of declining public interest in folklore points to the real possibility that folkloric performance is no longer an effective vehicle in Moldova for expressing and creating the immediate sense of collective experience and identity that galvanizes public action. As I discussed in chapter 5, when folkloric ensembles performed village traditions in the 1980s, they evoked powerful memories associated with the experiences and lifeworlds of actual villages for audiences dominated by first-generation rural-to-urban migrants. These people had recently arrived in Moldova's Russian-dominated cities and were suffering institutional discrimination as 'peasants' as much as they suffered from ethnic and linguistic forms of discrimination. As Obreja's and Osoianu's comments suggest, almost everything they believe accounted for the appeal of folklore in the 1980s is still present – public performances, large percentages of first-generation rural-urban migrants, experience of village life, and knowledge of village traditions. What is missing is the Soviet state and the discrimination it engendered. The meaning of folkloric performance is thus changing again, as the political context changes. This is not unusual; it follows the usual course of a folkloric revival (Ronstrom 1996; cf. Robbins 2001). But despite the continuing points of relevance that I have identified in their work, throughout the 2000s, the folkloric community in Moldova had difficulty rearticulating a new goal for its activities, beyond its outdated protest against the Soviet state, because of the ambiguous combination of change and continuity in its relationship to the state.

The folkloric community continues to depend on state support for organization, financial viability, and recognition. The transition from socialism, however, has changed the formal relationship between politics and culture, and thus the contextual relationship of folklore to the state, in two obvious ways. First, the state budget devotes less money and fewer resources to cultural activities than did that of the Soviet Union, leading professionals in the cultural sphere to question the state's commitment to supporting the arts and education in general. Second, broad efforts to dismantle state socialism have effectively legalized and authorized private and individual initiatives in the cultural sector, as in other areas of the economy. Performance opportunities have become available through organizations that are unaffiliated with any of the state's ministries and do not depend on state funding. And even the individuals and institutions that continue to be formally supported by the state, such as the majority of folkloric ensembles, expect greater freedom in their professional activities than they did in the past.

Nevertheless, the formal continuity in arts organization through the Ministries of Culture and Education means that the state retains the ability to infuse official ideology directly into arts training programs. In theory, the state could attempt to shape the public representation of national identity and the portrayal of ethnic relations through folkloric performances, just as it has intervened in the curricula of history courses.[67] To date, however, folklorists have maintained control over the definition of authenticity, resulting in the continued and increasing 'performance of villages' on national stages.

The political vulnerability and dependence of the folkloric community on the state was made clear again in the fall of 2009, when optimism was cautiously restored. In late summer, a coalition government formed, replacing the Communist Party. With ministerial reorganizations in process, the community felt it was regaining sympathetic ears. During a launch of compact discs prepared under a special grant from the United States Embassy for the Preservation of Intangible Cultural Heritage, performers, directors, and folklorists including Elena Oca, Nicolae Gribincea, Valeriu Chiper, Andrei Tamazlâcaru, Nina Negru, the Osoianu sisters, and Vasile Chiseliţa gathered around a festive table in the National Museum of Ethnography and Natural History to toast and celebrate the continued success of the folkloric movement.

Multiculturalism, Multiethnicity, and National Culture

Even as the folkloric community's relationship to the new state remains ambiguous, the commitment to articulating an alternative ideology to multiethnicity and multiculturalism has strengthened more generally among culture workers. In the summer of 2005, interest in cultural policy appeared to be growing among institutions and individual culture workers. On 23 June, for example, a conference entitled 'The Development of Culture: A Condition for the Democratization of Society and European Integration' was organized by the Department of Artistic Management and Culturology at the University of the Arts in Chişinău, with additional support from the Ministry of Culture and the Institute of Philosophy, Sociology, and Law at the Acad-

---

[67] Vladimir Solonari (2002) analyzed two competing history curricula in Moldova. The 'History of Romanians' was introduced as the compulsory history curriculum in public elementary schools in 1999–2000. In December 2001, the government attempted to replace this curriculum with a 'History of Moldovans', which, as Solonari demonstrated, partly resurrected old Soviet paradigms. Several months of public protest persuaded the government not to require the new materials. Both curricula, however, advanced ideologies that Solonari argued to be incompatible with the basic value orientations of a democratic and civil society. Anderson (2005, 2007) provides further details about how school teachers and professional historians have negotiated a common stance during curriculum reforms.

emy of Sciences. The Communist Party's second term of government had just begun, and the Ministry of Culture had recently been renamed the Ministry of Culture and Tourism and given a new mandate to prepare vigorously for European integration. The conference drew a wide range of cultural administrators and academics included in the category 'culture people' (*oameni de cultură*). They spoke on a large variety of topics and held contradictory opinions about greater or lesser state support, the recentralization of culture houses, the renewed state-based production and distribution of teaching materials for amateur ensembles, and other such practical questions. They agreed, however, on the fundamental relationship of culture to politics and the state. In particular, they agreed on the relationship between national culture, identity, and multiethnicity (or in the words of some, still using Soviet rhetoric, multinationalism). Following are some telling remarks made by a few of the conference-goers:

> There is a category of people for whom European integration is incompatible with the development of national culture … nor do these people want to promote authentic national culture.
>
> – Viorica Aderov, organizer, during her opening comments

> Out of love for culture, we came here today. … Only culture can make our people more cultivated, more tolerant.
>
> – Paulina Zavtoni, words of welcome

> Why do we need culture? Any country has problems with culture if the capital has become a centre for politics. … Our society is multicultural, but not multinational.[68] … We should respect those who have other cultures.
>
> – Ana Pascaru, sociologist

> Culture needs to be placed very strategically. Without culture, no state can exist. … Culture must be used in politics as a source of unity and not division.
>
> – Tihon Chilimar

These people's comments suggested that highlighting 'multiethnicity' was a political concern, rather than one that arose from an interest in cultural identity, heritage, or development. As such, multiethnicity was suspected of being politically divisive. The proposed alternative was to emphasize cul-

[68] Pascaru used the Soviet term for 'multiethnic'.

tural unity as the foundation for politics, recognizing that diversity existed within unity.

That same summer, the vice-director of Chişinău's municipal Department of Culture spoke more explicitly about how culture could be used effectively as a foundation for the state's political activities. A writer himself, Ianoş Ţurcanu was also a key organizer of many city events involving children, including several with folkloric orientations, and so he should be considered a culture worker and a peripheral member of the folkloric community. On 4 July 2005 he said in an interview:

> Culture people work from the soul. We work at all times, Saturday and Sunday. When a person works like that it has to be out of love. Culture people have an intuition about right and wrong. The French know this. Mitterand used to meet with artists for four to five hours a week. Others criticized him for this, asking how he could spend time talking about art when there was so much else that needed to be done. But it's clear – artists, people of culture, would tell him the truth about what was happening in the country. I am not a parrot. I do not have to speak for someone else, and so I would say, look Mr. President, this is the way I see it. People of culture are not concerned with politics themselves, but they see.

Although multiculturalism theoretically envisions cultural diversity as stemming from social communities that are not ethnic groups, in its practical applications and export, ethnic groups are assumed to be the primary and principal sources of cultural diversity in any society. This is especially true in Moldova, and European reviewers of Moldova's cultural policy urge that the country's multiple ethnic groups be taken as 'a self-evident cultural strength'. The activities of Moldova's folkloric community, however, draw attention to the existence of many other models for describing, theorizing, and ordering local forms and experiences of cultural diversity. European reviewers may be unable to see these, but ethnographers and folklorists continually call attention to them. The 'nation of villages', the *horă*, weddings, and even local livestock-tending practices (free pigs) in the village of Ţîra have all served as ways to imagine the balancing of cultural diversity and unity.

In the following sections, I take a bold turn to consider how the practices and reoccupations of Moldova's folkloric community bear the perceived crises of ethnographic authority in American anthropology over the past decades. In particular, the social role of the ethnographer, as understood in Moldova, may be a 'missed alternative' in the discipline's recent developments.

Authenticity and Authority

> When you try to explain to people what is happening in the country, they call you a nationalist. It hurts.
>
> – Petru Dinjos, 17 October 2001

Members of the Moldovan folkloric community consider themselves authorities on tradition and its interpretation. But who should listen to them? Do the alternative models they see to the state's concern with ethnicity matter at all? To whom should they listen?

Folklorists and ethnographers in Moldova claim authority on the basis of having conducted fieldwork in the country's villages. As individuals, they also claim personal authority on the basis of their village origins. Yet despite seeing villagers as idealized sources of authenticity, ethnographers often criticize them. On several occasions I witnessed 'experts' from the city – both ethnographers on expeditions and members of folkloric competition juries – correcting villagers on the name by which they referred to their language, on the way they wore costumes, on the authenticity of their repertoire materials or performance styles, on the way they evaluated carpets or taught children to select colours and designs for art projects, and on how much value they assigned to their traditions. Following the logic of my informants' statements, villagers should have held the ultimate authority in these matters, but they did not.

The villagers usually acquiesced verbally, but one wonders what their full reaction was.[69] Did anything in their behaviour change as a result of these encounters with professional ethnographers? Indeed, beyond the narrow confines of professional workshops, seminars, and festivals, does it matter whether one can correctly identify 'authentic' and 'inauthentic' traditions? Do the practice of fieldwork, the exploration and study of multiple locales, and the intimate and formative experience of growing up in a village possessed by members of the folkloric movement confer a kind of

---

[69] On two occasions I was able to talk at length with women whose favourite personal folkloric items had been criticized. In one case, carpets with large pink and red roses had been at issue, and the woman explained to me that she liked them anyway, because they were cheerful. In the second case, the owner of an 'inauthentic' costume defended the design; she considered it attractive, but more important, she had completed the sewing and embroidery by hand, as had all the young women in her ensemble, and they were proud of their work. In both cases the women's reasons for valuing their possessions mirrored the kinds of values promoted by the folkloric community. Yet these women were also teachers and identity personnel in their own right, drawing attention again to the public silence of people who are not identity personnel by profession.

knowledge, perspective, or authority that should be recognized as valuable in public debates? Is that perspective valuable beyond the immediate social and political context of the late Soviet period, when it provided a powerful critique against the effects of Soviet modernization, urbanization, and nationalities policies? Are the skills in which members of the folkloric community are trained valuable to anyone? All these questions point to a crisis in ethnographic authority relevant well beyond Moldova's borders.

The key issues of authenticity and authority in the Moldovan folkloric community resonate with dominant concerns in American anthropology over the past few decades concerning the validity and viability of ethnographic research. James Clifford (1988), for example, explored the dilemmas perceived and experienced by anthropologists conducting ethnography in the postcolonial world, precisely through the concepts of authenticity and authority. He saw a cluster of related dilemmas: 'pure products' seemed to have 'gone crazy'; 'traditions' were continuously disappearing while cultural differences remained and even emerged; urbanization and modernization were ongoing throughout the world; 'exotic' populations were moving into 'Western' spaces; the West itself was becoming more culturally diverse; and ethnography no longer seemed clearly distinguishable from fiction, autobiography, and other written genres. These developments posed dilemmas for anthropologists because they challenged fundamental assumptions regarding ethnography's subject matter – that is, 'authentic' cultures, artefacts, traditions – and the ethnographer's authority to speak on behalf of another population in the capacity of scientist.

Approached from any number of directions, the dilemmas raised by 'reflexivity' took precedence in the 1980s over previous theoretical concerns in sociocultural anthropology. In his review of these developments, George Stocking (1992: 369) expressed surprise that ethnography had not become 'so problematic psychologically, morally, and politically' that new cohorts of graduate students chose simply to conduct library research. Instead, new generations of anthropologists continued to go 'to the field' and conduct ethnography, despite their intense training in questioning ethnography's doability, viability, and validity. For this reason, Stocking concluded that 'the ethnographic impulse that helped to define modern anthropology has not spent its force' (1992: 372), but he challenged new generations of anthropologists to rediscover and reassign significance to the ethnographic enterprise that lay at the heart of professional anthropology: 'There can be little doubt that students entering the field today face unprecedented problems of professional self-definition. In a very real sense, they must each, in becoming anthropologists, reinvent the field for themselves – rebounding it, if not rebinding it, in the process' (1992: 372). The question, then, is what ethnography offers, methodologically and theoretically, that makes it both distinct and valuable.

The origins of Moldova's folkloric movement were contemporaneous with the period of intense concern for reflexivity in American anthropology. The two ethnographic discourses can thus be seen as alternative responses to the common problem of a shifting world. Moldova's folklorists, too, sensed that under Soviet-led modernization and nationalities policies, 'pure products' had 'gone crazy', and visual depictions of traditions were no longer accurate but had become 'kitsch'. In this, Moldova's folkloric community reflects the shared dilemmas of ethnography and anthropology everywhere. The shared nature of these dilemmas is revealed as members of the folkloric community speak about fieldwork, folklore, and ethnography.

Once, while riding to a folkloric festival with jury members, I asked Andrei Tamazlâcaru why there were so many folk singers in Moldova. I expected him to confirm what I had been learning about the Soviet Union's extensive investment in amateur performance and the economic and practical advantages of folk genres relative to classical ones. But Tamazlâcaru paused for a long time before responding. He answered: Because Moldova is such a small country, people are crowded and lift their voices to define themselves.

As always, Tamazlâcaru's words sounded like poetry. In response to a question I had imagined primarily in the causal language of history, politics, or economy, he conjured up another vision of the world, one in which people respond to hardship – in this case the physical, social, and emotional compression of crowding – by creating something beautiful. And through this creative act they define themselves, coming to the attention of others through their creation. Is this really why Moldova has so many folksingers? Maybe. But whether or not it is factually true, Tamazlâcaru's response draws attention to his role and authority as an interpreter of tradition. As he paused, long and carefully, before answering, Tamazlâcaru reminded me that his authority carried with it a moral obligation to call attention to the forms of beauty created by his crowded compatriots. In the rest of this concluding chapter, I want to bring this vision of ethnographic authority into discussion with recent debates in sociocultural anthropology.

The Ethnography of Ethnographers as Critical Ethnography

In American anthropology, the problem of ethnographic authority has often been treated as a combined textual and methodological problem, to be solved through increased reflexivity. 'Reflexivity' has come to mean many things, but it is always, at a minimum, connected to the written products of ethnographic research.

In the following section, I juxtapose the main arguments in two works by George Marcus and Clifford Geertz – each a leading proponent for a reflexive approach in anthropology. The intent is not to provide a comprehensive account of the debates on reflexivity, which has been done elsewhere (e.g. most recently by Zenker and Kumoll 2010), but to illustrate the sense of impasse that the debates have generated, and to propose – or rather, to reinvoke, another approach to the problems of constructing ethnographic knowledge and authority.

For George Marcus (1998), the term reflexivity was indistinguishable from experimental ethnographic writing. As he saw it, the hallmark of an experimental, 'multi-sited', or 'messy' text was 'its contingent openness to the boundaries of the object of study (which emerge in the heterotopic space of the work, whose connections by juxtaposition are themselves *the* argument), its concern with position, and its derivation/negotiation of its analytic framework from indigenous discourse, from mappings within the sites in which the object of study is defined and among which it circulates' (Marcus 1998: 188, original italics). Although Marcus presumably thought some experimental ethnographies were better written than others, he expressed no particular concern for quality. In this way, he departed significantly from Clifford Geertz (1988), who expressed great ambivalence about ethnographies that deliberately problematized the relationship between fieldwork and text construction.

For Geertz, fieldwork and writing remained fundamentally two separate activities, even though anthropologists, as authors, gain authority among their readers by constructing texts that collapse the distinction. The overt problematization of fieldwork as a textual strategy was exemplified, for Geertz (1988: 91), by what he called 'Malinowski's Dilemma', 'Participant Description', the 'Diary Disease', and 'I-Witnessing' – all writing strategies that turn ethnography into an excessive description of the ethnographer's activities and situational responses. In contrast to Geertz, who urged caution in adopting reflexive writing strategies, Marcus generally championed reflexivity and experimental works to liberate anthropology from a constraining 'ideology of objectivity, distance, and the transparency of reality', because he thought such experimentation would result in the 'recognition of the need to explore the ethical, political, and epistemological dimensions of ethnographic research as an integral part of producing knowledge about others' (Marcus 1998: 190). Geertz thought it was possible to proceed the other way around – reflexive writing should make an ethnographically centred anthropology more feasible, not less so.

For Marcus (1998: 193), the simplest form of reflexive ethnographic writing was the 'self-critique, the personal quest, playing on the subjective, the experiential, and the idea of empathy'. This was, in short, the same type of writing that Geertz (1988) referred to as 'I-Witness' accounts. Geertz was ambivalent towards ethnographies of this type because he recognized that they were essentially extensions of the same kind of writing for which Bronislaw Malinowski was renowned. Indeed, Malinowski was responsible for the model of participant observation that underlies all contemporary ethnography. Why would ethnography that carried Malinowski's injunctions to their logical conclusions be poorly appreciated by the anthropological community? Geertz was not alone in his ambivalence; Marcus also indicated that this simple form of reflexivity (compared, for example, with his more elaborate notion of 'multi-sited' ethnography) was the one that 'most often evokes nervous responses or dismissals of reflexivity as dead-end self-indulgence, narcissism, and so on' (Marcus 1998: 193). But he did not think such dead ends should deter further experimentation with reflexive strategies.

Marcus argued, too, that although subjectivist accounts of fieldwork performed an important function in opening up critical discussion in anthropology, they could also become dead ends. I leave him to speak for himself on the importance of foregrounding the ethnographer's subjectivity:

> In anthropology, elaborate subjectivist accounts of fieldwork experience became the primary means of destabilizing the notion that fieldwork could be a method on a par with, say, surveys. Such reflexivity, previously limited to confessionalist framings of functionalist ethnography, exposed the epistemological and ethical grounds of anthropological knowledge to full critical discussion and opened the way for hermeneutics to become a major influence on anthropological theory and research practice. But here is where the main contribution of this kind of reflexivity has remained, and once its critical function became well absorbed, it lost its power and fell prey to those who would nervously dismiss reflexivity altogether. At most, such reflexivity opens up the possibility for the so-called polyphonic text or the completely collaborative project, but more often than not, it merely reinforces the perspective and voice of the lone, introspective fieldworker without challenging the paradigm of ethnographic research at all – to the contrary (Marcus 1998: 193).

For Marcus, reflexivity was important precisely because it enabled ethnographers to challenge existing paradigms of knowledge and authority. At the moment when subjectivist accounts reinforced rather than challenged existing paradigms, they lost their reflexive power.

Although he concentrated on the destabilizing effects of reflexive ethnography within anthropology, Marcus neglected a parallel consideration of ethnography's destabilizing effects on academic knowledge in general.

When Geertz (1988) pointed to the connection between contemporary exercises in reflexivity and Malinowski's work, he revealed how deeply the notion of subjectivity was embedded in one of anthropology's charter myths. It was Malinowski's work, as we learn from the history of anthropology, that finally and decisively delegitimated the 'armchair anthropologist'. When Marcus called for ethnography to challenge 'the perspective and voice of the lone, introspective fieldworker' (1998: 193), he was also calling on ethnographers to challenge the very figure who initially created their authority and established them as the 'true' anthropologists. Marcus was so eager to challenge ethnography's authority and to build a better ethnography that he did not seriously consider the repercussions such a challenge might have on anthropology's authority among other intellectual disciplines.

Since these publications, the shortcomings of reflexive approaches have been well argued to restore the discipline's legitimacy. In particular, critics note that proponents of reflexivity overemphasize the problem of "knowing" a culture as a logical, cognitive, emotive or moral problem, and easily identify logical and empirical flaws with each conceptualization (e.g. Lindholm 1997; Salzmann 2002). Critics also argue that the greater problem is that reflexive approaches generally fail to realign their findings with anthropology's mission as a social science (e.g. Kuper 1994). One conclusion from debates about reflexivity is clear: it is dangerous for an ethnographer to foreground her own subjectivity when she writes. If she does it well, she further legitimates the method of participant observation and extends the authority of ethnography. If she does it poorly, then she may jeopardize that same legitimacy and authority with repercussions for all.

There is, however, another way to approach the problem of ethnographic authority which somewhat reconciles reflexivity with its critics. Instead of attempting to resolve the problem only through the classic formulation of anthropologist versus foreign culture, it is also possible to invoke the findings of critical ethnography of another ethnographic tradition. As I found, other foreigners working and travelling in Moldova often know a great deal about local culture, politics, mentality, social relations, roles, and behaviour, without engaging in extensive research. Early in my research I found myself asking, what it was, that distinguished my knowledge as an ethnographer? I found my answer as I slowly began to learn what was expected of me by members of the folkloric community that I was studying. The strength of participant observation as a research methodology is to be located not in what can be known, but in how things are known more generally. Knowledge is inseparable from experience, socialization, social structures and roles, and moral stances. Ethnography is done as the ethnographer takes up this very role, learning what is expected of her by the communities with which she has contact, and learning to negotiate agency and authority from within this role. Other anthropologists have already theorized ethnography from this direction.

As early as 1950 Claude Lévi-Strauss advanced a sophisticated critique of objectivity and subjectivity as key methodological issues in the practice of ethnography. In his *Introduction to the Work of Marcel Mauss* (1987), originally published in 1950, Lévi-Strauss illustrated several aspects of Mauss's work that seemed especially significant for later anthropologists. For example, Lévi-Strauss expanded the conceptual utility of Mauss's notion of the 'total social fact' beyond its usual interpretation: 'To call the social fact *total* is not merely to signify that *everything observed is part of the observation*, but also, and above all, that in a science in which the observer is of the same nature as his object of study, *the observer himself is a part of his observation*' (Lévi-Strauss 1987: 29, original italics).

Lévi-Strauss acknowledged that the observer's presence changes the social fact he observes (as is the case in all sciences), but he emphasized a much less recognized dimension of the relationship between subjectivity and objectivity. It is the un-italicized section of the foregoing quote, however, that is critical to today's debates: 'the observer is of the same nature as his object of study'.

In other words, the ethnographer is a social being, a 'social fact' himself. In his professional capacity as an observer, the ethnographer is always a 'subject', and things different from him are always 'objects'. But this would be the case for any individual in the society that ethnographer is observing; that individual would also define himself always as a 'subject', distinct from the 'objects' (including other people) that he is not. To grasp the totality of a social fact, an ethnographer must perceive it both objectively (from his own perspective) and subjectively (from the insiders' perspective[s]).

But how does one actually achieve this balanced perspective, either in the course of fieldwork or in conveying it through writing? Certainly Lévi-Strauss's vision of 'total' ethnographies encourages us to ask questions about how we can 'know' what others think, perceive, and experience. To satisfy his reader, Lévi-Strauss gave two answers. On the one hand, he pointed to Marcel Mauss's concept of the unconscious as a 'fourth dimension of the mind' (Lévi-Strauss 1987: 34). On the other, he asserted that ethnography was possible for a simpler reason: 'The thousands of societies which exist or have existed on the earth's surface are human, and on that basis we share in them in a subjective way; we could have been born into them, and so we can seek to understand them as if we were' (1987: 32). As this quotation suggests, if the anthropologist had been born into the society under study, he or she would have learned about the group's culture through the socialization that encouraged him or her to conform to (or rebel against) its rules, values, and normative behaviours.

Lévi-Strauss is not typically considered a model ethnographer, but his half-hidden insights into the ethnographer's own social role and socialization are key to 'rebinding' field-based anthropology. Quite simply, the ethnographer is a social and socializable being. From this perspective, 'participation' is a powerful methodology because it promotes the ethnographer's socialization. The ethnographer learns about others' lives by understanding – viscerally – how to enter into socially acceptable roles and relationships. The ethnographer may also learn much about the interplay between individuality and sociability as she learns to negotiate ascribed roles. And she will learn what it takes to remain part of the community even when she breaks the rules. Socialization is an ongoing process. As Anya Peterson Royce (2002: 5) reminds us, ethnographers enter the field as if they were children, but they have to 'grow up' quickly in order to understand the community they have entered:

> We come into other people's lives, *in media res*, always. And this is how we learn, *in media res*, always. Despite the fact that we are trained in all the latest techniques, have carefully chosen a research problem with its appropriate methods, have read everything we could find about the people and the place, in terms of being a functioning adult in that society, we are hopeless. We rely totally on the kindness of strangers. Just as they look out for three year olds in their own society, they look out for us. They help us to learn how to see and how to listen. If we stay long enough, they teach us humility.

In this passage, Royce emphasizes that the 'objects' of ethnographic study actively train the 'subject'. The childlike ethnographer is trained to be an adult, and often a particular kind of adult. As Royce further indicates, most societies have roles for highly knowledgeable individuals, and foreign ethnographers may find themselves being trained by their hosts to occupy just such a role.

As an example, the Zapotec of Juchitan, Mexico, among whom Royce has worked, recognize two categories of highly knowledgeable persons, the *binni nanna,* a 'person with a lot of words', and the *binni guendabianni,* or wise person. Neither category corresponds to a list of actual professions, and an individual ethnographer or anthropologist could be placed in either or both categories. Technical skills, higher education, and professional credentials make one a *binni nanna*, whereas the Zapotec recognize a *binni guendabianni* on the basis of his or her stance toward community: '[Being] a *binni guendabianni*, a wise or enlightened person, means not only being a repository of wisdom and knowledge but also having the willingness to use it for the good of the community and to be transformed by it. This is very far from the experience of even the most good-hearted fledgling ethnographer, and it is legitimate to ask whether or not we would take that first step knowing this possibility' (Royce 2002: 31).

Even in the long term, the ethnographer's identity is shaped by the host community, and she has only limited choice in defining her own roles. Royce, for example, is clear that her role as an interpreter of Zapotecs' lives to themselves and the outside world has been shaped by Zapotecs' assessments of their needs and desires, as well as their assessments of her strengths, talents, and possibilities:

> Ta Feli [a healer and friend], along with other [Zapotec] friends and family, has identified particular qualities I can contribute to the larger community. Every Zapotec has them and, when you make a commitment to *guendalisaa* [a sense of kinship, relatedness, and cooperation that is central to making community], you agree to use them for the common good. I am not asked to do extraordinary things. I am asked to view Juchitan with the eyes of my heart, to turn my particular kind of wisdom to enlighten, to speak the truth, to come back (Royce 2002: 33).

In other words, Royce has allowed the Zapotec to transform her into 'their' ethnographer. Whatever she writes or says or does, she is aware of belonging to that community.

As an 'ethnography of ethnographers', my account of folkloric ensembles in Moldova should suggest some broad areas of similarity and difference between ethnography as it is currently practiced in Moldova and in American sociocultural anthropology. But my affiliation with local ethnographers has also sensitized me to the processes through which ethnographers are always socialized into local roles.

For example, I found it exceedingly difficult to gain access to my informants outside of their professional activities. From my first visit to Moldova in 1999, being an ethnographer, even if only a student, was my primary social identity. Most people thus expended significant effort to see that I was able to be a proper ethnographer – but according to their own definitions of what ethnographers were supposed to be and do, not according to mine. My landlady regularly sent me out of the house in the morning 'to study'; her daughter introduced me almost immediately to a local ethnographer, who introduced me to other ethnographers and took me to museums, local conferences, university classes, academic gatherings, and the Academy of Sciences. Ethnographers and other academics were eager to see me go on field trips – and so on. From one perspective, all this activity merely indicates that my contacts wanted to help me succeed in my research. They did, but had I followed the schedule that most of my professional contacts laid out for me, my time would have been spent almost completely in the capital's academic institutions. That is how ethnographers in the capital spend their time, with the exception of the occasional, extremely important village field trips, which they also urged me to undertake. There were many activities on which I was not supposed to 'lose' my time – for example, observing food preparation, whether for celebrations or for winter provisioning. Food was considered a legitimate topic for field research, but only by surveying cuisine in villages, not by helping to shell walnuts for a cake with my landlady or canning vegetables for winter.

In the last three months of my fieldwork, I finally learned to argue my way into the kitchen, because I could tell that the professional lives and activities of local ethnographers and folklorists were constrained and enabled by the routines of daily living, material resources, and gendered divisions of labour and behaviour, and I had been unable to document these patterns. In the harsh economic conditions of the late 1990s and early 2000s, the constraints were particularly severe, as individuals worked multiple jobs and attempted to live with very little money. In order to participate in and observe these aspects of life, I had to learn to insist that these activities were also 'of interest' and 'beautiful' – the same terms my informants used in fieldwork. In other words, I acquired social roles and gained the social knowledge and skills necessary to achieve and enact those roles over time, in partial form, and only with the subtle pushing and pulling of people around me. By virtue of the people with whom I interacted most often, the social role I developed most highly was that of ethnographer.

Social Responsibilities of Ethnographers, There and Here

> We do not know what happened. We were all crowded inside the house, but the lady refused to lament. So Andrei Tamazlâcaru sent us all outside. What happened then, we do not know. It was quiet for a long time. Did he make love to her? Then, we heard the lament, louder and louder. A neighbour passing by stopped to ask what had happened – had the woman's husband died?
>
> – Mayor of the village of Goteşti, at a CD launch, 13 November 2009, retelling the story of the field expedition to his village undertaken by members of Moldova's Society for Ethnology

> I am a terrorist. If I have an old lady on the telephone, like the landlady for the Osoianu sisters, I ask her, 'Don't you know any old songs?' Or if I am at a funeral, I get right up by the mourners with

> my tape recorder in my pocket and urge them on. 'Wail louder. Don't cover your mouth with your scarf'. When I could not get official leave to do fieldwork last year, I went to the hospitals in Chişinău and talked to the villagers there. I speak *limba populară* [colloquially] when I am doing fieldwork, not Romanian. Fieldwork is an art. You must be insistent. You have to be attentive to the small things and know how to value the small things.
>
> – Andrei Tamazlâcaru, encouraging me as I began fieldwork in the village of Răscăieţi, 13 November 2009

In the chapters in this book, I have recounted a number of things I learned about being an ethnographer in Moldova. What is an ethnographer there responsible for? At a bare minimum, an ethnographer in Moldova should be able to distinguish objects of kitsch from objects of value, in material as well as expressive culture. An ethnographer should be able to distinguish the relative ages and values of ethnographic objects. He or she should also be able to distinguish patterns of regional variability, which at the very least means distinctions between northern, central, and southern Moldova and between Moldova and neighbouring countries and ethnic groups. He or she should also be able to describe the distinguishing characteristics of these regions, countries, and peoples.

It is easy for American anthropologists to dismiss eastern European ethnographic traditions because of perceived traces of 'survivalism' in the dominant methods, theories, and concerns in the work of eastern European ethnographers (Hofer 1968). Yet the attention devoted to amassing collections of material culture and folklore and attempting to document regional, ethnic, and national histories through these collected materials should not be dismissed as merely an outdated, and probably nationalistic, approach. Rather, it is important to see how the styles and concerns of research are connected to the social roles held by ethnographers in Moldova, which the ethnographers manifest through their professional activities.

Ethnographers in Moldova see their professional role as that of recovering and preserving traditional material, as has been done in other European countries. More broadly, though, an ethnographer in Moldova is responsible for training others to see distinctions in human groups, behaviours, and material culture. The ethnographer is responsible for teaching others to see beauty and to value objects that are locally produced. He or she is responsible for validating traditional knowledge, skills, and ways of living in the face of industrialization, urbanism, and, possibly, global capitalism and consumerism. Finally, the ethnographer has the right and the duty to speak on behalf of 'the people'.

The ethnographer is responsible for a body of knowledge, but being an ethnographer also entails moral responsibilities to teach and to speak. The ethnographers I worked with sought to train me in both sets of responsibilities. Non-ethnographers did too, and I was interviewed by radio and television announcers far more frequently than I liked. Initially I saw these interviews as ethical dilemmas, but I was repeatedly urged on and told, 'This is one of things we do as ethnographers'.

What I learned to do in interviews, as in making toasts, was to comment on the values people held in common. I learned from other ethnographers to see the beauty of villages, to comment favourably on the hospitality of people I met, to value culture above material wealth, and to appreciate the human labour and creativity that was expressed by traditions and traditional artefacts, both material and performative. In other words, I, too, learned to craft a stance towards a set of issues – language, culture, and lifeways – that could be politicized under other circumstances. Yet the stance I took was appropriate for my social role as an ethnographer, and in refusing to see the potential incompatibility of cultural diversity with social or political unity, I, too, became a fledgling 'Moldovan' ethnographer.

I am not arguing that sociocultural anthropologists should take on exactly the same objective concerns as Moldovan ethnographers. Rather, I mean to call attention to the fact that ethnography, wherever it is practised, is a social endeavour. Ethnographers are identity personnel who learn, study, teach, and live within complex systems of constraint. American anthropology has recently recognized the tremendous influence nineteenth-century imperialisms exerted on its basic theories, methods, and choices of research sites and topics. Similarly, ethnographers in the Republic of Moldova operate in fields heavily defined by state socialism, Soviet ideology, and more general European intellectual trajectories. Ethnography in Moldova, as in the United States, is clearly political. Instead of advancing and contesting the politics of empire and now globalism, however, Moldovan ethnography advances and contests the politics of nationalism, above and beyond all else. In the context of a nationalizing state, it should come as no surprise that ethnographers, too, contribute to a society-wide debate on the connections between culture and politics through the public representation of 'national' culture. Ethnographers in Moldova represent a particularly ambivalent kind of nationalist, however, and their ambivalence deserves further attention.

Through their professional and everyday activities and statements, my informants regularly contradicted themselves regarding the value of cultural diversity, ethnic relations and rights, and the legitimacy of a multiethnic national identity for Moldova. They reconciled the contradictions by insisting that their work sought to transcend the limitations imposed on human activity by the institutional, economic, and ideological dimensions of the state. They did not escape the state's structural power, but they did encourage those who would listen not to allow political ideas to dictate artistic and cultural production and expression. They also sought, repeatedly, to locate new models from within tradition, for political behaviour that promoted unity rather than division.

Local ethnographers struggle, usually in good faith, to locate authentic manifestations of art and culture and to promote authoritative voices to speak about the local and universal dimensions of human experience. When we have looked into their social roles and aspirations, it seems particularly unhelpful to critique to the point of condemning ethnographers and anthropologists in Moldova or anywhere else for relying on such politically implicated terms as *authenticity*; for failing to achieve, consistently and without contradiction, their stated goals of objectivity, cultural relativism, and the protection of cultural diversity; or for the resonances, parallels, and intersections of their ideas and theories with political ideologies such as imperialism and nationalism. As Charles Briggs (1996) and Dorothy Noyes (1999) have both pointed out, folklore's language of authenticity and tradition is one of the few languages that identity personnel in marginal areas of the world have for representing and protecting themselves vis-à-vis the nation-state. As they suggest, it is more helpful to engage the 'people who still care about folklore' (Noyes 1999: 256) in dialogue.

Critical ethnography of our own and other traditions will broaden our perspective on ethnography to reveal its emergence, innovations, and weaknesses in the context of larger social discourses and power relations. The critical study of ethnographers in Moldova, for example, points towards a more general dilemma in multiethnic societies today, which no ethnographic tradition has yet been able to resolve alone. In the Republic of Moldova, as throughout the world, ethnographers and many other individuals and institutions champion cultural diversity while still participating in exclusionary practices. If critical ethnography can reveal why these practices persist among ethnographers in Moldova, despite their best intentions, we will have a better understanding of why exclusionary forms of national identity continue to have such wide appeal. When we critically engage the assertions of local ethnographers that authenticity matters, that certain ethnic groups do not have culture, and that authority is located in villages, we stand to gain a better understanding of locally salient identities, and how they inflect citizenship and nation-building. From there, as we unravel the assumptions embedded in the key concepts discussed in each of the preceding chapters, we will come closer to understanding how to replace institutions and ideologies based on inequality with new forms rooted in equality.

APPENDICES

Figure 3.1. Organization of folkloric ensembles and festivals

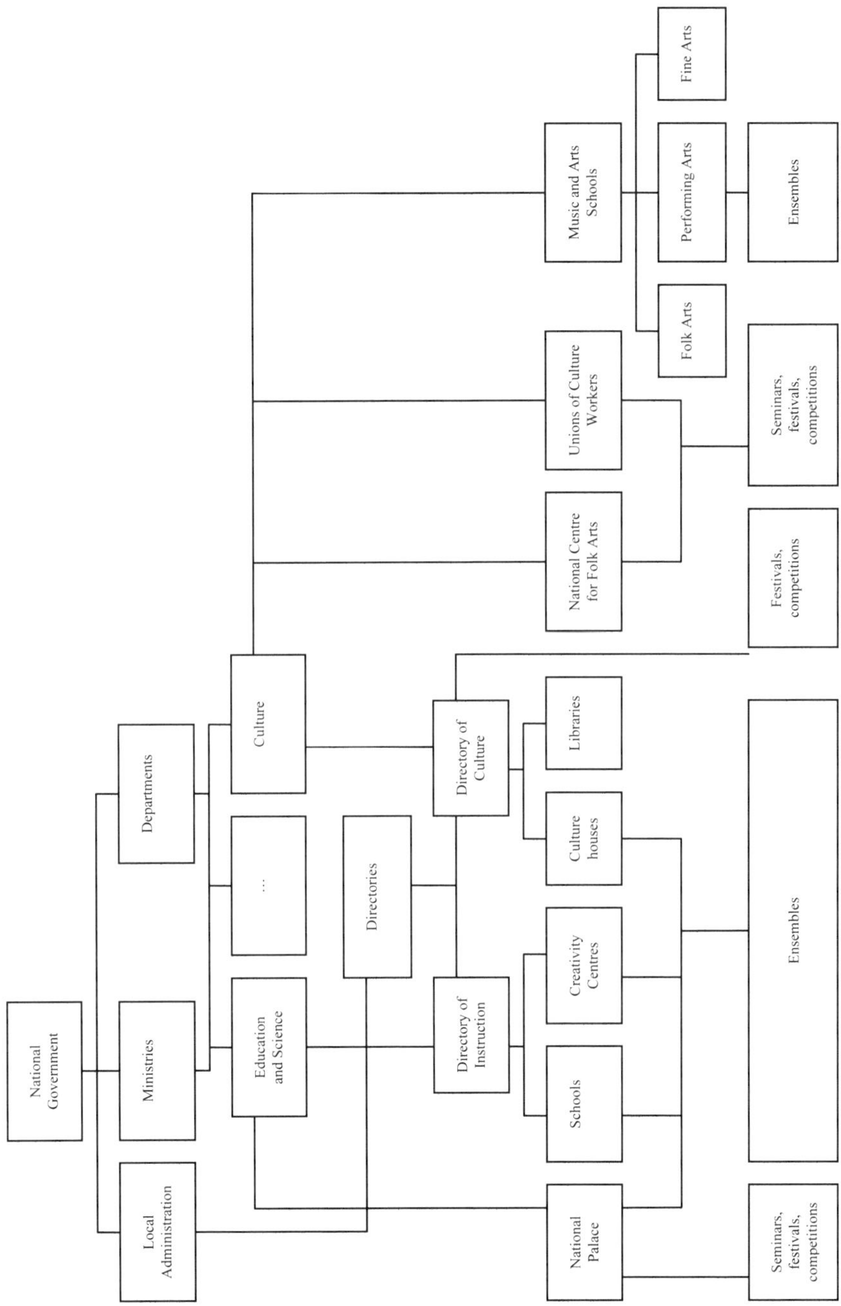

Figure 3.2. Official performance categories in 2001. *Folcloric* and *etno-folcloric* ensembles exist within all *popular* genres, but are not officially recorded.

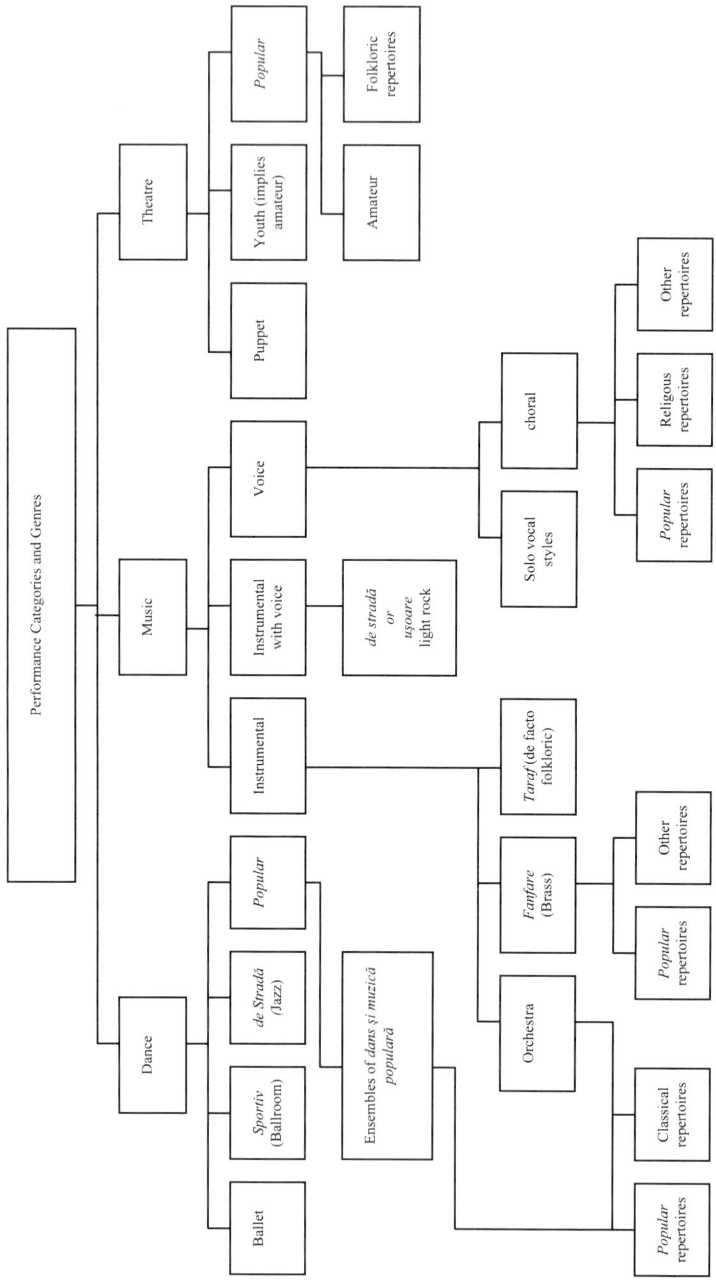

Bibliography

Abrahams, R. 1993. Phantoms of Romantic Nationalism in Folkloristics. *Journal of American Folklore* 106 (419): 3–37.

Ali, T. 2002. The Limits of Multiculturalism. In E. R. Larreta (ed.), *Identity and Difference in the Global Era,* pp. 476–486. Rio de Janeiro: UNESCO.

Anderson, A. 2005. Backward, Forward, or Both? Moldovan Teachers Relationship to the State and Nation. *European Education* 37 (3): 53-67.

——. 2007. "They Are the Priests": The Role of the Moldovan Historian and Its Implications for Civic Education. *Compare: A Journal of Comparative and International Education* 37 (3): 277-290.

Anderson, B. 1991. *Imagined Communities: Reflections on the Origin and Spread of Nationalism*. New York: Verso.

Appadurai, A. (ed.). 1986. *The Social Life of Things: Commodities in Cultural Perspective.* Cambridge: Cambridge University Press.

Applebaum, A. 1994. *Between East and West: Across the Borderlands of Europe*. New York: Pantheon.

Arbore, Z. 1899. *Basarabia în Secolul XIX-lea (Obiceiuri, Cîntece*). Bucharest.

——. 1906. *Graiul Nostru*. Bucharest.

Bahloul, J. 1996. *The Architecture of Memory: A Jewish-Muslim Household in Colonial Algeria, 1937–1962*. Cambridge: Cambridge University Press.

Banks, M. 1996. *Ethnicity: Anthropological Constructions*. London: Routledge.

Barker, A. M. 1999. *Consuming Russia: Popular Culture, Sex, and Society since Gorbachev*. Durham, North Carolina: Duke University Press.

Barth, F. 1969. *Ethnic Groups and Boundaries: The Social Organization of Culture Difference*. Boston: Little, Brown.

Bauman, R. 1992. Genre. In R. Bauman (ed.), *Folklore, Cultural Performances, and Popular Entertainments: A Communications Centered Handbook*, pp. 53–59. Oxford: Oxford University Press.

Bendix, R. 1997. Of Names, Professional Identities, and Disciplinary Futures. *Journal of American Folklore* 111 (441): 235–246.

Benk, L. 1999. Autonomy in Gagauzia: A Precedent for Central and Eastern Europe? *Journal of the Turk World* 9 (16). (Distributed through Turkistan-N listserve, 10 February 1999).

Berdahl, D. 1999. *Where the World Ended: Re-Unification and Identity in the German Borderland*. Berkeley: University of California Press.

Beuf, A. 1977. *Red Children in White America*. Philadelphia: University of Pennsylvania Press.
Bîrlădeanu, V. forthcoming. Wine and Speed: The Post-Soviet Holidays in the Republic of Moldova (2001–2009). *History and Anthropology* 23 (2012).
Bíró, A.-M., and P. Kovács. 2001. *Diversity in Action: Local Public Management of Multi-ethnic Communities*. Budapest: LGI/OSI.
Brandes, S. 1990. The Sardana: Catalan Dance and Catalan National Identity. *Journal of American Folklore* 103 (407): 24–41.
Bremmer, I. 1997. Post-Soviet Nationalities Theory: Past, Present, and Future. In I. Bremmer and R. Taras (eds.), *New States, New Politics: Building the Post-Soviet Nations*, pp. 3-26. Cambridge: Cambridge University Press.
Briggs, C. 1996. The Politics of Discursive Authority in Research on the 'Invention of Tradition'. *Cultural Anthropology* 11 (4): 435–469.
Bröcker, M. 1996. Folk Dance Revival in Germany. *World of Music* 38 (3): 21–36.
Brubaker, R. 1999. *Nationalism Reframed: Nationhood and the National Question in the New Europe*. Cambridge: Cambridge University Press.
Brunvand, J. H. 1976. A Fieldtrip in Dobrogea. In L. Dégh, H. H. Glassie, and F. J. Oinas (eds.), *Folklore Today,* pp. 65–80. Bloomington: Indiana University Press.
Buchannan, D. 2006. *Performing Democracy: Bulgarian Music and Musicians in Transition*. Chicago: University of Chicago Press.
Bulger, P. 2003. Looking Back, Moving Forward: The Development of Folklore as a Public Profession. *Journal of American Folklore* 116 (462): 377–390.
Buzdugan, I. 1922. *Cântece din Basarabia,* vol. 1. Chişinău: Luceafărul.
——. 1928. *Cântece din Basarabia,* vol. 2. Craiova: Ramuri.
Buzilă, V. 1999. *Pâinea, aliment şi simbol: Experienţa sacrului*. Chişinău: Ştiinţa.
Cantwell, R. 1993. *Folklife and the Representation of Culture.* Chapel Hill: University of North Carolina Press.
Carpenter, I. G. 1996. Festival as Reconciliation: Latvian Exile Homecoming in 1990. *Journal of Folklore Research* 33 (2): 93–124.
Cash, J. 2004. Reviving Moldova: Social and Political Dimensions of Contemporary Folkloric Performances. *Anthropology of East Europe Review* 22 (1): 61–76.

------. 2007. The Social Role of Artists in Post-Soviet Moldova: Cultural Policy, Europeanisation, and the State. *Europe-Asia Studies* 59 (8): 1405–1427.

------. 2008. Building New States in Old Societies: Minority Policies in Post-Socialist Eurasia. *Identities* 15: 2, 240–260.

------. 2009. 'The Communists Cannot Take Us to Europe': Negotiating Moldova's Place in the Post-socialist World. *Journal of Cultural Geography* 26 (3): 259–279.

Chamberlain-Creangă, R. 2008. The 'Transnistrian People'? Citizenship and Imaginings of 'the State' in an Unrecognised Country. In M. Heintz (ed.), *Weak State, Uncertain Citizenship: Moldova,* pp. 103–124. Frankfurt am Main: Peter Lang.

Chinn, J., and R. Kaiser. 1996. Moldova. In J. Chinn and R. Kaiser (eds.), *Russians as the New Minority: Ethnicity and Nationalism in the Soviet Successor States*. Boulder, Colorado: Westview Press.

Chinn, J., and S. D. Roper. 1998. Territorial Autonomy in Gagauzia. *Nationalities Papers: The Journal of Nationalism and Ethnicity* 26 (1): 87–101.

Ciscel, M. 2007. *The Language of the Moldovans: Romania, Russia, and Identity in an Ex-Soviet Republic*. Lanham, Maryland: Lexington Books.

------. 2010. Reform and Relapse in Bilingual Policy in Moldova. *Comparative Education* 46 (1): 13–28.

Čiubrinskas [Ciubrinskas], V. 2000. Identity and the Revival of Tradition in Lithuania: An Insider's View. *Folk* 42: 19–40.

------. 2010. Forging (Ethno) Nationalist Sentiment through Time and Space: Revivalist and Diasporic Ways of Accommodating Multiculturalism in East Europe and the USA. In F. Ruegg and A. Boscoboinik (eds.), *From Palermo to Penang: A Journey into Political Anthropology*, pp. 103–118. Berlin: LIT Verlag.

Clifford, J. 1988. *The Predicament of Culture: Twentieth-Century Ethnography, Literature, and Art*. Cambridge, Massachusetts: Harvard University Press.

Cockcroft, E. 1974. Abstract Expressionism: Weapon of the Cold War. *Artforum* 12 (10): 39–41.

Codreancu, A., and G. Ştefănescu. 1931. *Comorile Satelor (Cântece, Doine, Strigături, Proverbe)*. Craiova.

Cohen, R. 1978. Ethnicity: Problem and Focus in Anthropology. *Annual Review of Anthropology* 7: 379–403.

Cojocari, L. 2007. Political Liturgies and Concurrent Memories in the Context of Nation-Building Process in Post-Soviet Moldova: The Case of 'Victory Day'. *Interstitio: East European Review of Historical Anthropology* 1 (2): 89–121.

——. 2011. Festivalul "Mărţişor" (1967–2009): între celebrarea primăverii şi mitologii naţiunii. In T. Nicoara (ed.), *Disciplinarea socială şi modernitatea în societatea modernă şi contemporană (sec. XVI-XXI)*, pp. 529-543. Cluj-Napoca: Accent.

Colac, T. 1987. *Hronic de familie*. Chişinău: Literatura artistică.

Cole, J. 1977. Anthropology Comes Part-Way Home: Community Studies in Europe. *Annual Review of Anthropology* 6 (1): 349–378.

Council of Europe. 2001. *Cultural Policy in Moldova: Report of a European Panel of Examiners*. European Programme of National Cultural Policy Reviews. Strasbourg: Council of Europe, Council for Cultural Co-operation, Culture Committee.

Creed, G. 2011. *Masquerade and Postsocialism: Ritual and Cultural Dispossession in Bulgaria*. Bloomington: Indiana University Press.

Crowther, W. 1991. *Exploring Political Culture: A Comparative Analysis of Romania and Moldova*. Report Submitted to the National Council for Soviet and East European Research on Surveys Conducted in 1991. Unpublished report in the possession of the author.

——. 1997. The Construction of Moldovan National Consciousness. In L. Kürti and J. Langman (eds.), *Beyond Borders: Remaking Cultural Identities in the New East and Central Europe*, pp. 39–62. Boulder, Colorado: Westview Press.

——. 1998. Ethnic Politics and the Post-Communist Transition in Moldova. *Nationalities Papers: The Journal of Nationalism and Ethnicity* 26 (1): 147–164.

Curbet, V. 1989. Avem acum oameni care ştiu să deosebească mazeri de griu şi orez de secară. *Tinerimie Moldovei* (newspaper), 28 April.

——. 2005. *La vatra jocului străbun*. Chişinău: Pontos.

Daftary, F., and F. Grin (eds.). 2003. *Nation-Building, Ethnicity and Language Politics in Transition Countries*. Budapest: Local Government and Public Service Reform Initiative (LGI) andEuropean Centre for Minority Issues (ECMI).

de Cuellar, J., et al. 1997. *Our Creative Diversity*. Paris: UNESCO.

de Martonne, E. 1919. *What I Have Seen in Bessarabia*. Paris: Imprint des Arts et des Sports.

Demirdirek, H. 1999. The Painful Past Retold: Social Memory in Azerbaijan and Gagauzia. *Journal of the Turk World* 9 (16).

——. 2000. Living in the Present: The Gagauz in Moldova. *Anthropology of East Europe Review* 18 (1): 67–71.

Diamond, N. 1993. Ethnicity and the State: The Hua Mio of Southwest China. In J. D. Toland (ed.), *Ethnicity and the State,* pp. 55–78. New Brunswick, New Jersey: Transaction Publishers.

Doi, M. M. 2002. *Gesture, Gender, Nation: Dance and Social Change in Uzbekistan.* Westport, Connecticut: Bergin and Garvey.

Dorian, F. 1964. *Commitment to Culture: Art Patronage in Europe, Its Significance for America.* Pittsburgh, Pennsylvania: University of Pittsburgh Press.

Dorson, R. M. 1966. The Question of Folklore in a New Nation. *Journal of the Folklore Institute* 3: 277–298.

——. 1976. Folklore, Academe, and the Marketplace. In R. M. Dorson, *Folklore and Fakelore: Essays Toward a Discipline of Folk Studies,* pp. 1–29. Cambridge, Massachusetts: Harvard University Press.

Dubinskas, F. 1983. *Performing Slavonian Folklore: The Politics of Reminiscence and Recreating the Past.* Ph.D. dissertation, Stanford University.

Dunn, E. C. 1998. *Privatization and Personhood: Transforming Work in Postsocialist Poland.* Baltimore, Maryland: Johns Hopkins University Press.

Dyer, D. L. (ed.). 1996. *Studies in Moldovan: The History, Culture, Language and Contemporary Politics of the People of Moldova.* Boulder, Colorado: East European Monographs.

——. 1998. What Price Languages in Contact: Is There Russian Language Influence on the Syntax of Moldovan? *Nationalities Papers: The Journal of Nationalism and Ethnicity* 26 (1): 73–86.

Ejofor, P. 1984. *Cultural Revival in Igboland.* Onitsha, Nigeria: University Publishing Company, Varsity Industrial Press.

Engerman, D. C., N. Gilman, M. H. Haefele, and M. E. Latham (eds.). 2003. *Staging Growth: Modernization, Development and the Global Cold War.* Amherst: University of Massachusetts Press.

Eriksen, T. H. 2001. Between Universalism and Relativism: A Critique of the UNESCO Concept of Culture. In J. Cowan, M.-B. Dembour, and R. Wilson (eds.), *Culture and Rights: Anthropological Perspectives*, pp. 127–148. Cambridge: Cambridge University Press.

Ferguson, J. 1997. The Country and the City on the Copperbelt. In A. Gupta and J. Ferguson (eds.), *Culture, Power, Place: Explorations in Critical Anthropology,* pp. 137–154. Durham, North Carolina: Duke University Press.

Fisher, W. A. 1980. *The Soviet Marriage Market: Mate-Selection in Russia and the USSR.* New York: Praeger.

Fitzpatrick, S. 1992. *The Cultural Front: Power and Culture in Revolutionary Russia.* Ithaca, New York: Cornell University Press.

Friedwagner, M. 1927. Rumänische Volkslieder aus Bessarabien. *Revista Filologică* 1 (1–2).

——. 1931. *Graiul Nostru: Prin Sate şi Mănăstiri Basarabene (cântece).* Bucharest.

Geertz, C. (ed.). 1963. *Old Societies and New States: The Quest for Modernity in Asia and Africa.* London: Free Press of Glencoe.

——. 1988. *Works and Lives: The Anthropologist as Author.* Stanford, California: Stanford University Press.

Gellner, E. 1983. *Nations and Nationalism.* Ithaca, New York: Cornell University Press.

Giurchescu, A. 1987. The National Festival 'Song to Romania': Manipulation of Symbols in the Political Discourse. In C. Arvidsson and L. E. Blomqvist (eds.), *Symbols of Power: The Esthetics of Political Legitimation in the Soviet Union and Eastern Europe,* pp. 163–172. Stockholm: Almqvist and Wiksell International.

Glazer, N. 1997. *We Are All Multiculturalists Now.* Cambridge, Massachusetts: Harvard University Press.

Goodman, J. 2005. *Berber Culture on the World Stage: From Village to Video.* Bloomington: Indiana University Press.

Gorton, M., and J. White. 2003. The Politics of Agrarian Collapse: Decollectivisation in Moldova. *East European Politics and Societies* 17 (2): 305–331.

Grillo, R. D. 1998. *Pluralism and the Politics of Difference: State, Culture, and Ethnicity in Comparative Perspective.* Oxford: Clarendon Press.

Gupta, A. 1995. Blurred Boundaries: The Discourse of Corruption, the Culture of Politics, and the Imagined State. *American Ethnologist* 22 (2): 375-402.

Gupta, A., and J. Ferguson (eds.). 1997. *Culture, Power, Place: Explorations in Critical Anthropology.* Durham, North Carolina: Duke University Press.

Guss, D. M. 2000. *The Festive State: Race, Ethnicity, and Nationalism as Cultural Performance.* Berkeley: University of California Press.

Habeck, J. O. 2011. Introduction. Cultivation, Collective, and the Self. In B. Donahoe and J. O. Habeck (eds.), Reconstructing the House of Culture: Community, Self, and the Makings of Culture in Russia and Beyond, pp. 1-25. New York: Berghahn.

Halbwachs, M. 1992. *On Collective Memory.* Chicago: University of Chicago Press.

Halpern, J. M., and D. A. Kideckel. 1983. Anthropology of Eastern Europe. *Annual Review of Anthropology* 12 (1): 377–402.

Hamm, M. F. 1998a. Chronology. *Nationalities Papers: The Journal of Nationalism and Ethnicity* 26 (1): 165–175.

——. 1998b. Kishinev: The Character and Development of a Tsarist Frontier Town. *Nationalities Papers: The Journal of Nationalism and Ethnicity* 26 (1): 19–37.

Hann, C., M. Sárkány, and P. Skalník. 2005. Introduction: Continuities and Contrasts in an Essentially Contested Field. In C. Hann, M. Sárkány and P. Skalník (eds.), *Studying Peoples in the People's Democracies: Socialist Era Anthropology in East-Central Europe,* pp. 1–20. Münster: LIT Verlag.

Haraszti, M. 1987. *The Velvet Prison: Artists under State Socialism.* New York: Basic Books.

Hayden, R. 2007. Moral Vision and Impaired Insight: The Imagining of Other Peoples' Communities in Bosnia. *Current Anthropology* 48 (1): 105–131.

Heintz, M. 2006. Tolerance, Conformity, and Moral Relativism: Cases from Moldova. In C. Hann & the "Civil Religion" Group, *The Postsocialist Religious Question: Faith and Power in Central Asia and East-central Europe*, pp. 193-212. Berlin: Lit Verlag.

Herzfeld, M. 1982. *Ours Once More: Folklore, Ideology, and the Making of Modern Greece.* Austin: University of Texas Press.

——. 1987. *Anthropology through the Looking-Glass: Critical Ethnography in the Margins of Europe.* Cambridge: Cambridge University Press.

——. 2003. Localism and the Logic of Nationalistic Folklore: Cretan Reflections. *Comparative Studies in Society and History* 45 (2): 281–310.

——. 2005. *Cultural Intimacy: Social Poetics in the Nation-State.* New York: Routledge.

Hirsch, F. 2005. *Empire of Nations: Ethnographic Knowledge and the Making of the Soviet Union.* Ithaca, New York: Cornell University Press.

Hitchins, K. 1994. *Rumania 1866–1947.* Oxford: Clarendon Press.

Hobsbawm, E. J., and T. O. Ranger (eds.). 1983. *The Invention of Tradition.* Cambridge: Cambridge University Press.

Hofer, T. 1968. Anthropologists and Native Ethnographers in Central European Villages: Comparative Notes on the Professional Personality of Two Disciplines. *Current Anthropology* 9 (4): 311–315.

Holton, K. 2005. *Performing Folklore: Ranchos Folclóricos from Lisbon to Newark.* Bloomington: Indiana University Press.

Kallberg, J. 1996. *Chopin at the Boundaries: Sex, History, and Musical Genre*. Cambridge, Mass.: Harvard University Press.

Kaneff, D. 2004. *Who Owns the Past? The Politics of Time in a 'Model' Bulgarian Village*. Oxford: Bergahn.

Karghin, A. 1995. *A Modern Festival of Folklore: Experience, Problems, Prospects*. Moscow: State Republican Centre of Russian Folklore.

Kaufman, S. J. 1996. Spiraling to Ethnic War: Elites, Masses, and Moscow in Moldova's Civil War. *International Security* 21 (2): 108–138.

Kenney, P. 2002. *A Carnival of Revolution: Central Europe 1989*. Princeton, New Jersey: Princeton University Press.

Keough, L. 2006. Globalizing 'Postsocialism': Mobile Mothers and Neoliberalism on the Margins of Europe. *Anthropology Quarterly* 79 (3): 431-461.

King, C. 1994. Moldovan Identity and the Politics of Pan-Romanianism. *Slavic Review* 53 (2): 345–368.

------. 1995. *The Politics of Language in Moldova, 1924–1994*. Oxford: Oxford University Press.

------. 1998. Ethnicity and Institutional Reform: The Dynamics of 'Indigenization' in the Moldovan ASSR. *Nationalities Papers: The Journal of Nationalism and Ethnicity* 26 (1): 57–72.

------. 2000. *The Moldovans: Romania, Russia, and the Politics of Culture*. Stanford, California: Hoover Institution Press.

Kligman, G. 1998. *The Politics of Duplicity Controlling Reproduction in Ceausescu's Romania*. Berkeley: University of California Press.

Kolstø, P. (ed.). 2002. *National Integration and Violent Conflict in Post-Soviet Societies: The Cases of Estonia and Moldova*. Lanham, Maryland: Rowman and Littlefield.

Kolstø, P., and A. Malgin. 1998. The Transnistrian Republic: A Case of Politicized Regionalism. *Nationalities Papers: The Journal of Nationalism and Ethnicity* 26 (1): 103–127.

Konrád, G., and I. Szelényi. 1979. *The Intellectuals on the Road to Class Power*. New York: Harcourt Brace Jovanovich.

Koroleva, E. A. 1989. *Unde joacă moldovenii*. Chişinău: Timpul.

Kulikovski, L. 1998. *Library Services for the National Minorities in Chişinău*. Online publication of the American Library Association. www.ala.org/work/international/intlpprs/kulikovs.html (Accessed 28 May 1999).

Kuper, A. 1994. Culture, Identity and the Project of a Cosmopolitan Anthropology. *Man (New Series)* 29 (3): 537-554.

Kutrzeba-Pojnarowa, A. 1982. The Traditions, Present State, and Tasks of Ethnographic Science in the Polish People's Republic. *Soviet Anthropology and Archeology* 20: 3–40.

Landis, K. 1974. Russian Colonialism and Bessarabia: A Confrontation of Cultures. *Nationalities Papers: The Journal of Nationalism and Ethnicity* 2 (2): 19–38.

Lerman, Z., and D. Cimpoieş. 2006. Land Consolidation as a Factor for Rural Development in Moldova. *Europe-Asia Studies* 58 (3): 439–455.

Lévi-Strauss, C. 1987 [1950]. *Introduction to the Work of Marcel Mauss.* London: Routledge and Kegan Paul.

Levin, T. 1996. Dmitri Pokrovsky and the Russian Folk Music Revival Movement. In M. Slobin (ed.), *Retuning Culture: Musical Changes in Central and Eastern Europe*, pp. 14–36. Durham, North Carolina: Duke University Press.

Lindholm, C. 1997. Logical and Moral Dilemmas of Postmodernism. *The Journal of the Royal Anthropological Institute* 3 (4): 747-760.

Livezeanu, I. 1981a. Urbanization in a Low Key and Linguistic Change in Soviet Moldavia: Part 1. *Soviet Studies* 33 (3): 327–351.

------. 1981b. Urbanization in a Low Key and Linguistic Change in Soviet Moldavia: Part 2. *Soviet Studies* 33 (4): 573–592.

------. 1995. *Cultural Politics in Greater Romania: Regionalism, Nation Building and Ethnic Struggle, 1918–1930.* Ithaca, New York: Cornell University Press.

------. 2007. Nationalism and Internationalism in Moldova, 1917–1990. *Interstitio: East European Review of Historical Anthropology* 1 (2): 11–49.

M'Closkey, K. 2008. *Swept under the Rug: A Hidden History of Navajo Weaving.* Albuquerque: University of New Mexico Press.

MacKinnon, N. 1994. *The British Folk Scene: Musical Performance and Social Identity.* Maidenhead, U.K.: Open University Press.

Madan, G. 1897. *Suspine.* Bucharest: Carol Müller.

------. 1932. Obiceiuri şi Rânduieli la Naştere, Rodină, Botez, Nuntă şi Înmormântare în Părţile Codrilor din Basarabia. *Cuvînt Moldovenesc* 8: 36–41.

Maday, B. C. 1968. Hungarian Anthropology: The Problem of Communication. *Current Anthropology* 9 (2–3): 180–184.

Malkki, L. 1992. National Geographic: The Rooting of Peoples and the Territorialization of National Identity among Scholars and Refugees. *Cultural Anthropology* 7 (1): 24–44.

——. 1995. *Purity and Exile: Violence, Memory, and National Cosmology among Hutu Refugees in Tanzania*. Chicago: University of Chicago Press.

Mallinson, G. 1987. Rumanian. In B. Comrie (ed.), *The World's Major Languages*, pp. 303–321. New York: Oxford University Press.

Mally, L. 1990. *Culture of the Future: The Proletkult Movement in Revolutionary Russia*. Berkeley: University of California Press.

——. 2000. *Revolutionary Acts: Amateur Theater and the Soviet State, 1917–1938*. Ithaca, New York: Cornell University Press.

Maners, L. 1995. *The Social Lives of Dances in Bosnia and Herzegovina: Cultural Performance and the Anthropology of Aesthetic Phenomena*. Ph.D. dissertation, University of California, Los Angeles.

Marcus, G. E. 1998. *Ethnography through Thick and Thin*. Princeton, New Jersey: Princeton University Press.

Mardar, M. 1971. *Studiu choreografic pentru amatori*. Chişinău: Cartea Moldoveanească.

Marriott, M. 1963. Cultural Policy in the New States. In C. Geertz (ed.), *Old Societies and New States: The Quest for Modernity in Asia and Africa*, pp. 27-56. London: Free Press of Glencoe.

Martin, T. 2000. Modernization or Neotraditionalism? Ascribed Nationality and Soviet Primordialism. In D. Hoffman and Y. Kotsonis (eds.), *Russian Modernity: Politics, Knowledge, Practices,* pp. 161–184. New York: St. Martin's.

——. 2001. *The Affirmative Action Empire: Nations and Nationalism in the Soviet Union, 1923–1939*. Ithaca, New York: Cornell University Press.

McGuigan, J. 2004. *Rethinking Cultural Policy*. Maidenhead, U.K.: Open University Press.

Miller, T., and G. Yudice. 2002. *Cultural Policy*. London: Sage.

Ministry of Culture. 1988. *Scena Artistului Amator: Sugestii Repertoriale*. Chişinău: Literatura Artistică.

Motyl, A. 2001. Inventing Invention: The Limits of National Identity Formation. In R. G. Suny and M. D. Kennedy (eds.), *Intellectuals and the Articulation of the Nation*, pp. 57–75. Ann Arbor: University of Michigan Press.

Muiznieks, N. 1997. Latvia: Restoring a State, Rebuilding a Nation. In I. Bremmer and R. Taras (eds.), *New States, New Politics: Building the Post-Soviet Nations*, pp. 376-403. Cambridge: Cambridge University Press.

Netzer, D. 1978. *The Subsidized Muse: Public Support for the Arts in the United States*. Cambridge: Cambridge University Press.

Neukirch, C. 1999. National Minorities in the Republic of Moldova: Some Lessons Learned, Some Not? *South-East Europe Review* 3: 45–64.

Noyes, D. 1999. Provinces of Knowledge: Or, Can You Get Out of the Only Game in Town? *Journal of Folklore Research* 36 (2–3): 253–258.

Ohana, Y. 2008a. *Supporting Cultural Actors of Change in Belarus, Moldova, and Ukraine: A Regional Review.* Washington, D.C.: German Marshall Fund of the United States and European Cultural Foundation.

——. 2008b. *Culture and Change in Moldova.* Washington, D.C.: German Marshall Fund of the United States and European Cultural Foundation.

Oinas, F. J. 1961. Folklore Activities in Russia. In R. M. Dorson (ed.), *Folklore Research Around the World: A North American Perspective*, pp. 76–84. Bloomington: Indiana University Press.

Olson, L. 2004. *Performing Russia: Folk Revival and Russian Identity*. New York: Routledge Curzon.

Opalski, M. (ed.). 1998. *Managing Diversity in Plural Societies: Minorities, Migration and Nation-Building in Post-Communist Europe*. Nepean, Ontario: Forum Eastern Europe.

Oshurko, L. V. 1957. *Narodnii tansii Moldavii.* Chişinău: Gosudarstvenni izdate.

Panici, A. 2003. Romanian Nationalism in the Republic of Moldova. *Global Review of Ethnopolitics* 2 (2): 37–51.

Parekh, B. C. 2000. *Rethinking Multiculturalism: Cultural Diversity and Political Theory*. Basingstoke, U.K.: Macmillan.

Popescu, G. 2006. Geopolitics of Scale and Cross-Border Cooperation in Eastern Europe: The Case of the Romanian-Ukrainian-Moldovan of Borderlands. In J. W. Scott (ed.), *EU Enlargement, Region Building and Shifting Borders of Inclusion and Exclusion*, pp. 35-51. Aldershot: Ashgate Publishing.

Porter, J. 1971. *Black Child, White Child: The Development of Racial Attitudes*. Cambridge, Mass.: Harvard University Press.

Prevots, N. 1998. *Dance for Export: Cultural Diplomacy and the Cold War.* Middletown, Connecticut: Wesleyan University Press.

Raun, T. 1997. Estonia: Independence Redefined. In I. Bremmer and R. Taras (eds.), *New States, New Politics: Building the Post-Soviet Nations*, pp. 404-433. Cambridge: Cambridge University Press.

Rex, J. 2004. Multiculturalism and Political Integration in the Modern Nation-State. In J. Rex and G. Singh (eds.), *Governance in Multicultural Societies.* Aldershot, U.K.: Ashgate.

Roach, S. 2005. *Cultural Autonomy, Minority Rights, and Globalization.* Farnham, UK: Ashgate.

Robbins, J. 2001. Whatever Happened to Revival? From Charsimatic Movements to Charismatic Church in a Papua New Guinea Society. *Journal of Ritual Studies* 15 (2): 79-90.

Roberts, J. 1999. Hidden Right Out in the Open: The Field of Folklore and the Problem of Invisibility. Presidential address to the American Folklore Society, 1998. *Journal of American Folklore* 112 (444): 119–139.

Rogers, K. 1983. Moldavian, Romanian, and the Question of a National Language. In M. Manoliu-Manea (ed.), *The Tragic Plight of a Border Area: Bassarabia and Bucovina,* pp. 167–174. Humboldt, California: Humboldt State University Press.

Ronstrom, O. 1996. Revival Reconsidered. *World of Music* 38 (3): 5-20.

Rowland, R. 2009. Population Trends in Europe's Poorest Country. *Eurasian Geography and Economics* 50 (4): 480–495.

Royce, A. P. 1982. *Ethnic Identity: Strategies of Diversity.* Bloomington: Indiana University Press.

------. 1984. *Movement and Meaning: Creativity and Interpretation in Ballet and Mime*. Bloomington: Indiana University Press.

------. 2002. Learning to See, Learning to Listen: Thirty-Five Years of Fieldwork with the Isthmus Zapotec. In R. V. Kemper and A. P. Royce (eds.), *Chronicling Cultures: Long-Term Field Research in Anthropology*, pp. 8–33. Walnut Creek, California: AltaMira Press.

Royce, A. P., and R. V. Kemper. n.d. *Who Is 'Indian' in Mexico: Perceptions and Performances*. Manuscript.

Rus, I. A. 2007. The Rise of Moldovan-Romanian Nationalism in Bessarabia (1900–1917). *Interstitio: East European Review of Historical Anthropology* 1 (2): 51–66.

Said, E. W. 1994. *Representations of the Intellectual.* New York: Pantheon.

Salzmann, P. C. 2002. On Reflexivity. *American Anthropologist* 104 (3): 805-813.

Schwarz, B. 1995. The Diversity Myth: America's Leading Export. *Atlantic Monthly,* May 1995, pp. 57–67.

Senn, A. 1997. Lithuania: Rights and Responsibilities of Independence. In I. Bremmer and R. Taras (eds.), *New States, New Politics: Building the Post-Soviet Nations*, pp. 352-369. Cambridge: Cambridge University Press.

Shay, A. 2002. *Choreographic Politics: State Folk Dance Companies, Representation, and Power.* Middletown, Connecticut: Wesleyan University Press.

Shevchuk, G. 1982. *Cultural Policy in the Ukrainian Soviet Socialist Republic*. Paris: UNESCO.

Simon, G. 1991. *Nationalism and Policy toward the Nationalities in the Soviet Union: From Totalitarian Dictatorship to Post-Stalinist Society*. Boulder, Colorado: Westview Press.

Skortova, A. 2006. The Impact of EU Enlargement on Moldovan-Romanian Relationships. In J. W. Scott (ed.), *EU Enlargement, Region Building and Shifting Borders of Inclusion and Exclusion*, pp. 133-148. Aldershot: Ashgate Publishing.

Skvortsova, A. 2002. The Cultural and Social Makeup of Moldova: A Bipolar or Dispersed Society? In P. Kolstø (ed.), *National Integration and Violent Conflict in Post-Soviet Societies: The Cases of Estonia and Moldova*, pp. 159–196. Lanham, Maryland: Rowman and Littlefield.

Slezkine, Y. 1994. The USSR as a Communal Apartment, or How a Socialist State Promoted Ethnic Particularism. *Slavic Review* 53 (2): 414–452.

Smidchens, G. 1996. *Baltic Music: The Folkloric Movement in Lithuania, Latvia, and Estonia: 1968–1991*. Ph.D. dissertation, Department of Folklore, Indiana University.

Smith, A. 1991. *National Identity*. Reno: University of Nevada Press.

Socor, V. 1994a. *Five Countries Look at Ethnic Problems in Southern Moldova*. Radio Free Europe/Radio Liberty (RFE/RL) Research Report. Electronic document.

------. 1994b. *Gagauz Autonomy in Moldova: A Precedent for Eastern Europe?* Radio Free Europe/Radio Liberty (RFE/RL) Research Report. Electronic document.

Solonari, V. 2002. Narrative, Identity, State: History Teaching in Moldova. *East European Politics and Societies* 16 (2): 414–445.

------. 2003. Creating a 'People': A Case Study in Post-Soviet History-Writing. *Kritika: Explorations in Russian and Eurasian History* 4 (2): 411–438.

Solonar [Solonari], V., and V. Bruter. 1994. Russians in Moldova. In V. Shlapentokh, M. Sendich, and E. Payin (eds.), *The New Russian Diaspora: Russian Minorities in the Former Soviet Republics*, pp. 72–90. Armonk, New York: M. E. Sharpe.

Ştefanucă, P. 1990 [1935]. Hora în Reguinea Iurcenilor. In P. H. Stahl (ed.), *Les Roumaines Orientaux, Romanii din Răsarit*. Paris: Sociétés Européenes.

Stocking, G. W. 1992. *The Ethnographer's Magic and Other Essays in the History of Anthropology*. Madison: University of Wisconsin Press.

Stoica, G., and P. Petrescu. 1997. *Dicționar de artă populară*. Bucharest: Editura Enciclopedică.

Stolcke, V. 1995. Talking Culture: New Boundaries, New Rhetorics of Exclusion in Europe. *Current Anthropology* 36 (1): 1–24.

Stoeltje, B. 1992. Festival. In R. Bauman (ed.), *Folklore, Cultural Performances, and Popular Entertainments: A Communications Centered Handbook*, pp. 261–271. Oxford: Oxford University Press.

Suny, R. G. 1995. State, Civil Society and Ethnic Cultural Consolidation in the USSR: The Roots of the National Question. In A. Dallin and G. W. Lapidus (eds.), *The Soviet System: From Crisis to Collapse*, 351–364. Boulder, Colorado: Westview Press.

——. 1998. *The Soviet Experiment: Russia, the USSR, and the Successor States*. Oxford: Oxford University Press.

Suny, R. G., and M. D. Kennedy (eds.). 1999. *Intellectuals and the Articulation of the Nation*. Ann Arbor: University of Michigan Press.

Svet, A. 2009. *Politico-Economical Markers in the Project of Transnistrian Regional Identity Construction. New and Ambiguous Nation-Building Processes in South-Eastern Europe*. Working Paper Series, http://www.oei.fu-berlin.de/nation-building/resources/wp/svet_02 (accessed October 2009).

——. n.d. *Constructing Identities in State-Building of Transnistria: Heritage of the Past and Its Repercussion in the Present. New and Ambiguous Nation-Building Processes in South-Eastern Europe*. Working Paper Series, http://www.oei.fu-berlin.de/nation-building/resources/wp/svet_01 (accessed October 2009).

Tamazlâcaru, A. 1986. *Tepuşele, Tepuşele*. Chişinău: Literatura artistică.

Taylor, C. 1994. The Politics of Recognition. In A. Gutmann (ed.), *Multiculturalism: Examining the Politics of Recognition*, pp. 25–74. Princeton, N.J.: Princeton University Press.

Tcacenco, V. (ed.). 2009. *Viziuni de viitor: Politică culturală a Republicii Moldova de la schimbări la viabilitate*. Chişinău: Arc.

Teodorescu-Kirileanu, S. 1922. *Poveşti basarabene*. Bucharest: Cultura Națională.

Thompson, P. 1998. The Gagauz in Moldova and Their Road to Autonomy. In M. Opalski (ed.), *Managing Diversity in Plural Societies: Minorities, Migration and Nation-Building in Post-Communist Europe*, pp.128–147. Nepean, Ontario: Forum Eastern Europe.

Timiras, N. 1983. The Idiom of Bassarabia: Its Latinity and Identity with the Romanian Language. In M. Manoliu-Manea (ed.), *The Tragic Plight of a Border Area: Bassarabia and Bucovina*, pp.143–166. Humboldt, California: Humboldt State University Press.

Tishkov, V. 1997. *Ethnicity, Nationalism, and Conflict in and after the Soviet Union: The Mind Aflame*. London: Sage.

Tishkov, V., and E. Filippova (eds.). 2002. *Local Governance and Minority Empowerment in the CIS.* Budapest: Local Government and Public Service Reform Initiative.

Tismaneanu, V. 1998. *Fantasies of Salvation: Democracy, Nationalism, and Myth in Post-communist Europe*. Princeton, New Jersey: Princeton University Press.

Trouillot, M.-R. 2001. The Anthropology of the State in the Age of Globalization: Close Encounters of the Deceptive Kind. *Current Anthropology* 42 (1): 125–138.

van Meurs, W. P. 1994. *The Bessarabian Question in Communist Historiography: Nationalist and Communist Politics and History-Writing*. New York: East European Monographs.

Verdery, K. 1991. *National Ideology under Socialism: Identity and Cultural Politics in Ceausescu's Romania*. Berkeley: University of California Press.

------. 1996. *What Was Socialism, and What Comes Next?* Princeton, New Jersey: Princeton University Press.

Voight, V. 1976. Towards a Theory of Theory of Genres in Folklore. In L. Degh, H. Glassie, and F. Oinas (eds.), *Folklore Today*, pp. 485-496. Bloomington: Indiana University Press.

White, A. 1990. *De-Stalinization and the House of Culture: Declining State Control over Leisure in the USSR, Poland and Hungary, 1953–89*. London: Routledge.

Williams, B. 1989. A Class Act: Anthropology and the Race to Nation across Ethnic Terrain. *Annual Review of Anthropology* 18: 401–444.

Wilson, W. 1976. *Folklore and Nationalism in Modern Finland*. Bloomington: Indiana University Press.

Wolf, E. R. 1999. *Envisioning Power: Ideologies of Dominance and Crisis.* Berkeley: University of California Press.

Yurchak, A. 2006. *Everything Was Forever, Until It Was No More: The Last Soviet Generation*. Princeton, New Jersey: Princeton University Press.

Zelenciuc, V. C., and M. N. Guboglo. 1979. *Natsional'noye i internatsional'noye v sovetskom obraze zhizni*. Chişinău: Ştiinţa.

Zemtsovsky, I., and A. Kunanbaeva. 1997. Communism and Folklore. In J.Porter (ed.), *Folklore and Traditional Music in the Former Soviet Union and Eastern Europe,* pp. 3–23. Los Angeles: University of California–Los Angeles, Department of Ethnomusicology.

Zenker, O., and K. Kumoll (eds.). 2010. *Beyond Writing Culture: Current Intersections of Epistemologies and Representational Practices*. New York: Berghahn Books.

Zipes, J. D. 1988. *The Brothers Grimm: From Enchanted Forests to the Modern World*. New York: Routledge.

Zvorykin, A. A. 1970. *Cultural Policy in the Union of Soviet Socialist Republics*. Paris: UNESCO.

Index

Academy of Music, Theatre, and the Plastic Arts 76n
Altângic 16, 16n, 100, 149-51
aesthetics 46n, 95, 96, 103
amateur; artistic activity (formation) 4, 19, 60, 76; new legislation for 68-9; (performance) ensembles 2, 3, 13, 19, 54, 57, 60, 63, 65, 69, 73-4, 114, 164, 170
anthropology 23, 106-7, 125, 164, 171, 173-80, 183, *see* ethnography; ethnology
art 9, 19, 35, 55, 63, 71, 73, 78, 95, 100, 103, 157, 168, 169, 171, 182, 184; classification of 64; modern 55n; under socialism 53; visual and plastic 56, 76n, *see also* national art forms; performing arts
art schools 61-2, 78
artists 15, 52-3, 61, 123, 129, 143, 163, 171; folk 41, 42, 79, 145; unions 61, 79
audience; role of 20, 67-9, 75, 77-8, 81-2, 90, 95-103 *passim*, 166-8
authenticity 4, 7, 8, 67, 184; criteria for/in folkloric performance 13, 20, 49, 64, 79, 81, 86-7, 90, 95, 103, 108, 135, 138, 145, 148, 165-6; and emotion 7, 12; and ethnicity 88-90, 103, 148-9, 151; and ethnographic authority 7, 84, 87, 89, 164, 173; and folklore 12, 13, 66, 89, 166, 184; and morality 12, 95; and personal experience 7, 8; of villages 107, 135, 144, 172

ballet 57, 73, 91, 96, 128, 130
bands 63, 65
beauty 165, 174, 182, 183
Bessarabia 26n, 27-36, 40, 43n, 48, 57, 57n, 125n, 132-3, 141, 141n, 145-8, 153-5, 159
boundary; and construction of identity 6-7, 166; double 7-8, 17, 52, 103
bread 1, 75, 77, 123, 146, 153, 160
Buciumaşii 16, 94, 100n, 147
Bucurie 59
Bukovina 29, 66n, 93
Bulgarians 5, 8, 25, 33, 39, 44-6, 74, 152-3, 155-6

careers 4n, 76, 102, 126-7, 131-2
casă de cultură, *see* culture house(s)
census data 42n, 42-3
child development 57-8, *see also* ethno-pedagogy
choir(s) 63-4, 64n-5n, 68
citizenship 9, 26, 37, 47, 184; Soviet 34, 36, 56, 75
civic nation 25, 47
communism 56, 100-1, *see also* socialism
Communist Party 40-1, 99-101, 165-70
competition 15-6, 19, 40, 62, 71, 74, 79-90 passim, 93, 97, 114, 130-1, 134, 149, 151, 158, 164-5, 172, *see also* festival
constructivism 48
Colac, Tudor 76-7
costume(s) 13, 57n, 68, 72-3, 78, 86, 89, 96-7, 124, 137, 153, 154, 157, 165, 172; costuming 71, 90-3, 149
Council of Europe 2, 10, 41, 54, 58, 58n, 110
creativity centres 15, 61-2, 92
critical ethnography 11, 15, 20, 107, 177, 184
culture; concept of 9; organization of 19, 54, 59-62, 78; role of 51, 59
culture house(s) 15, 54, 56, 60, 62-3, 76, 78, 80, 108, 110, 113-4, 117, 160, 170
culture producer 51-3, 58n, 98, 102

culture workers 52, 60n, 78, 81, 164, 167, 169, *see oameni de cultură*
cultural; activity 56-7, 61, 64, 80; diplomacy 58; enlightenment 54; institutions 41, 51-2, 77, 121; intimacy 17-8, 77; policy 9-11, 54-6, 58, 68, 169, 171; pluralism 9, 11-2
cultural diversity 6-8, 13, 14, 17, 20, 55, 138, 143, 144, 166, 171, 183-4; 'missed alternatives' 10-1, 171; and multiculturalism 8-11
cultural revival 55
cultural specialists 7, 13, 21, 41, 52, 58

dance; classical 57; composition of 73-4, 78, 85, 116; ensembles (professional) 59; folk 57, 66, 75; Gagauz 2, 121, 149-51, 157; national 71, 73; in the field 92, 113, 114, 121; Jewish 148; qualities of 92, 96, 152, *see also dans popular, horă, kadînjă*
dans popular 64, 66, 68, 72, 73, 91n, 96
decollectivization 14, 42, 143
democracy 55, 139, 142
Department for the Functioning of Languages and National Relations 39, *see* Department of National Relations
Department of National Relations 5n, 15, 58n
discrimination 18, 106, 132-4, 168
diversity; political 9; social 92, 165; *see also* cultural diversity, ethnic diversity
Dnestr Republic, *see* Transnistria
Dobrogea 153-6
Duminica la Florii 80, 88, 92-4, 114, 150, 150n, 164, 166

eastern Europe 9-10, 14, 39, 52-3, 98, 101, 106, 182
economy 17, 24, 42, 91, 93, 98, 147, 168, 174
education; aesthetic 54; cultural 4, 56; history courses 169n; and language 41, 43, 48; and multiculturalism 9 169n; reform 45-6, *see also* language, training
ethnic; conflict 37; diversity 7, 32, 138, 144; group (definitions of) 5-8, 11, 14, 17, 20, 23-6, 31, 31n, 35, 39-48 *passim*, 58n, 69, 72-3, 88-90, 126, 144, 148-9, 151, 155-9, 161, 165-6, 171, 182, 184; identity 6, 19, 23, 26, 33, 40, 43, 45-8, 126, 165; relations 5, 5n, 10, 18-20, 25, 40, 55, 67, 73, 126, 143, 158, 161, 165, 169, 169n, 183
ethnic minorities; Armenians 33; Czechs 33, 155; Germans 33, 39n, 45-6, 145n, 155; Greeks 33; Gypsies 42, 72n, 145 (see Roma); Kazakh(s) 45; Lithuanians 2, 5, 5n, 7; Poles/Polish 33, 106, 145n, 146; Romanians 25-6, 43, 46; in Soviet Union 34, 35, 36, 39, 45; Swiss 33; Turk(s) 39n, 156, 159, *see* Bulgarians, Gagauz, Jews/Jewish, Russians, Ukrainians
ethnic; nation 25, 40, 47; nationalism 12-4
ethnicity 5-6, 11, 18, 20, 23, 25, 32, 46-7, 72-3, 79n, 88-90, 110, 126, 160, 166, 172
ethno; choreology 73; pedagogy 127-8, 131; mimesis 12; musicology 73
ethnographic authority 12, 21, 69, 86-7, 87n, 98, 103, 106-8, 127, 164, 171-178 *passim*, 184
ethnographic zones 83, 85, 152
ethnography 15, 35, 62, 106, 107, 110, 111, 121, 122, 125, 126, 127, 132, 135, 149, 157, 158, 173-80,

183; of ethnographers 180; (ethnographic) collection 126, 145; (ethnographic) expeditions 87, 110-4, 122-4, 146, 149; salvage 157, *see* critical ethnography
ethnology 126, 146, 181
etno-folcloric ensemble(s) 63-4, 66-72 *passim*, 78-9, 88-92, 127, 135, 144, 164-6
European Union 41
exclusion 5n, 11, 12, 17, 18, 47, 106, 138, 145, 157, 162, 165-6, 183

fanfar 63-4
festival(s); in former Soviet Union 56, 58, 80; juries and judging 58n, 68, 69, 72, 79n, 81, 88, 92, 174; organization of 79-81
Festivalul Folcloric 80, 82
fieldwork 7-8, 20, 57n, 67, 78, 86-8, 108, 113, 114n, 119, 125, 127, 148, 158, 172, 174-8, 181-2, *see also* ethnographic expeditions
Fluieraş 59, 110
folcloric ensemble(s) 63-7, 71-2, 78-9, 88-90, 97, 135, 164-6
folklore; discipline of (folkloristics, folklore studies) 2, 3, 12, 14, 54, 62, 64, 76, 78, 106, 125-6, 135, 184; in education 4, 60, 66, 127, 131; Soviet uses of 19, 54, 57, *see also* ethnography
folkloric activity 54-5, 57-9, 61, 64, 106, 134
folkloric community 15, 19-21, 52n, 53, 58n, 60, 68, 72n, 79, 81, 86-90, 93, 95-7, 100, 102-7, 114, 125, 127, 133-5, 144, 148-51, 155, 164, 166, 168-74, 177
folklore clubs 4, 57, 60, 74, 78, 129, 148
folklore ensembles 2-5, 8, 11, 13-20, 41, 51, 54, 57, 60-3, 67-71, 77, 85, 88-90, 97, 99-102, 127, 131, 144, 151, 166-8, 180
folkloric movement 4, 5n, 13-4, 17-8, 20, 60, 64-7, 71-4, 76-80, 87, 90, 102-3, 126-8, 132, 138, 144-7, 157-8, 164-9, 172, 174
formaţie folclorică 68

Gagauz 2, 5, 8, 25, 33, 36-8, 42-6, 73, 94, 113-5, 122, 133, 144, 148n, 149, 152-61, 163
Gagauz Yeri 8, 26n, 39-40, 60, 65, 100, 102, 110, 160
gender 23, 95-6, 118, 165, 181
genre 12, 15, 19, 51, 56-7, 63-4, 67, 83, 85, 87, 96, 119, 126, 130, 140, 164, 173-4
German-Soviet Nonaggression Pact, *see* Molotov-Ribbentrop Pact
godparents 1-2, 6
government(s) 3, 5n, 9, 24, 26-7, 32-4, 37, 39-41, 45, 56, 58, 60-2, 67, 99n, 101, 133, 137, 142, 144, 149, 163, 169-70

handicrafts 56, 95; carpets 90, 95, 95n, 124, 172, 172n; ceramics 95; linens 95-6; textiles 90n, 95
holidays 59, 63n, 79n, 145, 154
horă 79n, 116, 137-9, 143-4, 152, 154, 162, 171
hospitality 77, 120, 183
House of Culture, *see* culture house(s)
households 91, 93, 96
Hram (patron saint's day) 59, 167

identity, and memory 133-5; salience 18, 106, 127, 134; situational 43, *see* boundary
identity personnel 52, 90, 166, 172, 184
ideology 7, 51, 68, 71, 102, 169; Communist 100; and ethnography 125, 175; nation of villages 164; national 18, 24, 68, 126; official

state (Moldova) 13, 19, 59, 169; Soviet 13, 17, 20, 54, 72-7, 99, 164, 183
inclusion 5n, 18, 20, 43, 106, 137-8, 145, 162, *see* exclusion
institutions 2, 15, 17, 19, 35, 39, 41, 51-3, 57, 60-1, 67, 69, 77, 79, 80, 95, 121, 132, 166, 168-9, 180, 184
intellectual(s) 15, 32, 34, 35, 37, 40, 48, 51, 52, 143; and postsocialist state 67-8, 99; under socialism 52-4
intelligentsia 47-8
international friendship 19, 66, 72, 74, 77
inter-war period 33, 48, 57n, 133
invention of tradition 14, 78, 139
irony (ironic readings) 77

Jews/Jewish 33, 42, 45-8, 133-4, 145-7, 151, 153, 158, 165
Joc, state ensemble of music and dance 57, 59, 110, 114, 147
județ(e) 62
jury(ies) 69, 71, 80-2, 92-3, 95, 127, 141, 146, 172, 174

klezmer 145-6

landownership and political rights 161
language; codification of the Romanian language 31-2; and ethnic identity 19, 23, 25-6, 30, 32-3, 43, 45-6, 148, 152-5; of education 32, 35, 45-6, 122; languages of prestige 35, 45-6; and minority rights 32-5, 37, 39, 41, 159-61, 168; Moldovan 30-6, 45-6; and the Moldovan/ Romanian question 25-6, 31, 34, 37, 99-100; politics 26, 36, 43, 159-61, 163; Russian language and social status 32, 35, 45-6, 133; state language 32, 39-40
Lazarelul 150
legislation and regulation of the arts 67-8
leisure 57, 60, 64
lifeworld 49, 168
local administration 48, 62, 82, 100, 140, 142

manuals for amateur ensembles 73-6
marriage; interethnic 8, 44-5, 121, 144; intervillage 105, 140, 165
Mărțişor 59
mazili 141, 143
memory 133-5, 165
migration 8, 23, 42-5, 126, 135n, 155, 167; rural-to-urban 18, 106, 132-4
Ministry of Culture 15, 56, 60-5, 73-4, 76, 129-32, 163, 169-70
Ministry of Education 15, 60-3
minority policy 39-42, 142-4, 157
Miorița 59, 74, 163
mişcarea folclorică 13, 72, *see* folkloric movement
model status 68, 149
Moldavia 26n
Moldova; History of 26-34, 169n
Moldovan Autonomous Soviet Socialist Republic (MASSR) 29, 33-5
Moldovan/Romanian question, *see* language
Moldovan Soviet Socialist Republic (MSSR) 26, 29, 34, 36, 56, 76, 91, 132
Moldovans 13, 19, 25-6, 31n, 32-5, 39-40, 43, 45-6, 48, 77n, 89-90, 99-100, 130-3, 139, 141, 151-3, 160-1, 164-5, 169n
Moldovița 99, 100, 156n
Molotov-Ribbentrop Pact 19, 27, 34

morality 12, 48, 95-6, 101-2, 125, 134, 142-3, 153, 165, 173-4, 177, 183
Moştenitorii 16, 83, 94, 99-102, 105, 110, 119
multiethnicity 3n, 4, 37, 39, 144, 165, 169, 170
multiculturalism 3, 8, 11, 19, 41, 58n, 166, 169, 171; and concept of "culture" 9; and cultural pluralism 9, 11-2; political philosophy 9
museum(s) 16, 19, 56, 61, 66, 124, 157n, 169, 180
music; classical 57, 130; and ethnic identity 133, 147, 149, 154; in the field 116, 121; professional 59, 60, 110, 129, 130; qualities of 66; schools 61, 110, 132, 147, 148; types of 64-5, 68, *see* choir(s), *fanfar*, *muzică de stradă*, *muzică populară*, *taraf*
muzică de stradă 163
muzică populară 59, 64, 66, 68, 73, 159

narodnyi ensemble(s) 63
naş/naşi, *see* godparents
nation; Soviet definition of 37; of villages 5, 49, 71, 102, 105, 137-8, 144, 164, 171
nation-state 2-3, 18, 21, 24-5, 37, 47, 51, 98, 125, 166, 184
nation-building 3, 11-2, 18-9, 25-6, 37, 40-2, 163; success and failure 9, 18, 35-6, 47-9
national; art forms 54, 57; cadre 54; identity (ethnic and civic) 3-5, 8, 20, 23, 69; identity (multiethnic and multicultural) 3-5, 8-9, 25, 37, 39, 42-3, 89, 144, 165, 169, 170, 183; ideology 68, 126; movement 34-7, 40-1, 60, 65n, 97
National Centre for Folk Arts 15-6, 19, 58, 62, 64-5, 67-8, 80, 99, 141, 149, 151
National Land Program 14
National Palace of Creativity for Children and Adolescents 15, 61, 131
nationalism 11, 14, 16-8, 23-4, 47, 51, 72, 98, 170, 183-4; civic 47; ethno-nationalism 12-4, 16, 47; Romanian 32; Romantic 3, 5, 13
nationalist 12-3, 16-7, 48, 51, 126, 135, 169n, 172, 182, *see also* identity personnel
nationality 34, 37, 43, 59, 126
nationalities policy 11, 35-7, 41
Noroc 59

oameni de cultură 52-3, 170-1
organization of culture 19, 54, 59-62, 78
organization of folkloric ensembles 18, 54, 80
Orthodox Christianity 8, 32, 153
Osoianu sisters 127-31, 167-9, 181
Ottoman Empire 23, 28-9, 31, 154, 156

patriotism 17n, 75, 89, 139
performance; content 98; context 99, 101; form 57; genre 51, 56, 67, 85, 119; meaning of 97-9, 102, 168
performing arts 35, 56, 60-1, 63, 64
pigs; free 142-3, 171
Pioneer Palace 15, 60-1, 78, 82, *see* National Palace of Creativity for Children and Adolescents
political; parties 31, 37, 41, 63, 101, *see also* Communist Party
popular ensemblc(s) 63, 65-8, 78, 90, 96-7, 103, 164
Popular Front 34, 37
population structure, *see* census data, migration
pro-Romanian 34, 36, 40, 126
professional ensembles 54, 59, 74
professionalism 57, 60, 79

raion(e) 61, 62, 80
răzeşi 141, 143
reflexivity 173-7
religion 10, 24, 153, 166, *see* Orthodox Christianity
repertoire creation 16, 114-5
representation 4-5, 8, 12, 18, 20, 34, 37, 41, 47-8, 52, 54, 61, 71, 88-90, 93, 96-7, 103, 107, 164-6, 169, 183; and consumption 97; textual dimensions 71; visual dimensions 72
revival; cultural 55, 122; folkloric 168
ritual 2, 5, 7-8, 13, 41, 59, 63, 66, 77, 83-4, 86, 96, 114, 121, 146, 150, 153, 164
Roma 25, 32, 39n, 42, 72n, 139, 145
Romania 19, 23-4, 27, 31, 33-4, 39-40, 53, 66, 79-81, 89, 111, 121, 126, 146, 150-3
Romanianism 39, *see* pro-Romanian
Romanians 25-6, 32-3, 35, 39, 43, 46, 48, 79, 89, 139, 151, 154-6, 162, 169
Russian Empire 28-9, 32, 133, 159
Russians 8, 25, 36, 39, 43-6, 130, 139-40, 142-3, 145, 148, 153, 165
Russification 32

salience, *see* identity
socialism 9, 52-3, 168, 183
socialization; of children 3; into ethnic and national identities 4; and ethnography 177, 179; through performance 74-6
Soviet; *see* amateur artistic activity, cultural policy, ideology, international friendship, nationality, nationalities policy
Soviet Union; organisation of republics 34, 37
state; and cultural production 53-4, see also cultural intimacy, government(s), local administration, organisation of culture, structural power
state-building 11, 14, 23-4
State Institute for the Arts 76, 128, 129, 146
Ştefan cel Mare 99, 125, 139, 141, 159-61
structural power 17-8, 184
stylization 66, 72
survivalism 125, 127, 157, 182

taraf 63, 68
Tălăncuţa 78, 127-9, 131, 147-8, 167
Tamazlâcaru, A. 64, 76-8, 114, 127-8, 131-2, 146, 169, 174, 181
Taraclia County 38-40, 65
teatru popular 63n
theatre 60, 63-4, 68, 76, 130, 163
toasts/toasting 164, 182
Transnistria 5n, 25-43 *passim*, 83
training and education 60-2, 71, 78, 95-6, 107, 113, 118, 123, 127, 132, 147, 149, 158n, 169, 173, 182

Ukrainians 8, 25, 33, 39, 44-6
University of the Arts 76n, 108, 110, 128, 145, 147, 170
urbanization 23, 107, 132-4, 147, 173

values 5-6, 12, 17-8, 41, 63, 74, 95-6, 99, 101, 103, 139, 141, 165, 172, 178, 182
villages; cultural activity in 56-7, 61, 66, 78, 80; historic types of 141; social stratum and relations 72-3, 92, 144
visual arts 76n

Wallachia 27-8, 31

wedding(s) 1-2, 5-8, 60, 84-6, 95-6, 105, 114n, 121, 131, 133, 140, 143-4, 147, 158, 171
wine 1, 42, 77, 91, 95, 154, 160, 167